THE TEACHER

THE TEACHER

by

E. B. CASTLE

*Emeritus Professor of Education
in the University of Hull*

Hence cometh all the need and fame of TEACHERS, men
of inborn nobility, call'd Prophets of God . . .
the sainted pioneers of civilization, unto whom
all wisdom won and all man's future hope is due.

Robert Bridges, *Testament of Beauty*, IV. 232-9

1970 OXFORD UNIVERSITY PRESS

Oxford University Press, Ely House, London W.1

GLASGOW NEW YORK TORONTO MELBOURNE WELLINGTON
CAPE TOWN SALISBURY IBADAN NAIROBI LUSAKA ADDIS ABABA
BOMBAY CALCUTTA MADRAS KARACHI LAHORE DACCA
KUALA LUMPUR SINGAPORE HONG KONG TOKYO

To
E. M. S.

PRINTED IN GREAT BRITAIN BY
NORTHUMBERLAND PRESS LTD., GATESHEAD

Preface

When Robert Bridges praised teachers as 'the sainted pioneers of civilization' he was not writing of schoolmasters so much as of prophets, poets, saints, rebels and philosophers whose teachings have formed the mind of the western world. But I like to think that he also had in mind the work of lesser men who contributed to the education of mankind in the narrower confines of the classroom. And so this book is an attempt to unite, in the single theme of The Teacher, the work of men who taught a whole civilization and the work of men and women who taught children in school. Sometimes, of course, these two roles unite in one person—in Quintilian and Vittorino certainly, in Thomas Arnold, perhaps—but this is rare. Nevertheless in the writings of the philosophers there appear images of the teacher in the classroom and of his evolving role in society. These images I have attempted to capture in the setting of the social conditions and mood of a particular period. In some respects the book is a brief history of educational ideals, not exhaustive by any means but deliberately selective, and seen more from the worms-eye view of the teacher than from the Olympian heights of philosophy.

It would have been desirable, maybe, to have referred to the great teachers of the orient in view of the increasing impact of the Asian civilizations on the western world. For two good reasons this has not been done: the subject is too vast for summary treatment and beyond my competence to treat adequately.

My ultimate aim has been to remind the teacher of today that the problems he now faces have a history, and that he is part of a long tradition whose roots lie buried in the past. For this reason the concluding chapters are confined to a discussion of the origins and growth of the teaching profession in Great Britain, to the modern teacher's professional status and the new problems confronting him in an era when the school is bound to play a more central role in the life of the community. For he now shares with his pupils the challenges of technological change in a civilization whose qualities, we hope, like those of Periclean Athens, will be judged not in terms of electronic gadgets but by the virtues that make good men . . .

E.B.C.

Corfe Castle
1969

Contents

PART V

THE BRITISH TEACHER TODAY

PART I

The ancient world

Judea, Greece and Rome were the nursing mothers of western civilization; from them we inherit the traditions of western education. During the two thousand and more years covered by this period the teacher appeared in several traditional roles—as poet, prophet, philosopher, as schoolmaster and university lecturer. Homer was the primary educator of the Greek world; the Hebrew prophets established the principles of Hebrew-Christian morality; Plato and Aristotle laid the foundations of western philosophy; and in the image of Socrates remains the model teacher for all time. In Greece appeared the first schoolmasters of western Europe; in Rome the first grammar schools. To Greece we owe ideals of human excellence that emerge in education as the culture of the whole personality. The conception of the community as teacher was born in the Athens of Pericles to remain with us in its modern version of the 'educative society'. But long before schoolmasters taught children in the classical world, the scribes of Egypt and Babylonia were teaching the art of writing, thereby establishing, maybe for ever, the enduring 'scribe culture' which continues in our schools and dominates the bureaucracies of the civilized world.

1 *The teacher as scribe*

In the Musée du Louvre there is a striking statue of a scribe of the Old Kingdom of Egypt. It is about 4,500 years old. He is carved in limestone and painted—hair black, flesh brown, eyes of alabaster, rock crystal and copper—an alert cross-legged figure, ready with his papyrus roll. To be so memorialized in stone the scribe must have played an important role in the eyes of his contemporaries. This was because he had mastered the major technique in civilized communication—he could write. On clay tablets, which were durable, or on papyrus from the marsh-lands of the Nile, which was less durable but more portable, he was the man who could register the temple and royal dues, the decisions of the courts of law, draw up marriage contracts, and record the financial transactions of commercial enterprise. He owed his prestige in society to his adeptness in accountancy and administration. Because he could write and cipher he could receive written instructions and eventually but inevitably became the man who could most easily execute them. Thus he became, whether high or low in the scale of royal servants, a member of an educated secretariat that directly or indirectly wielded the power behind the throne. In the deified kingships and theocracies of Egypt, Mesopotamia and Syria it was from the corps of scribes that the professional civil servant was recruited, and it was the educated scribe who made possible the elaborate adminis-tration necessary for the preservation of an empire.

Thus did the scribe become not only the first civil servant but the first literate teacher of civilized communities. We are told that the sign for the Egyptian character for 'scribe' (*sesh*) depicts the tools used in writing—a stylus, a water-pot and a pallete with two saucers, one for black ink, the other for red. Similarly in Hebrew the word for scribe is *sopher*, derived from *sapher*, meaning 'to write' or 'to count'.[1] Since it was in the temples and royal palaces that the scribe's duties originated it was in them that the scribe was trained. Here were the schools where he learned the difficult art of pictographic writing; here were the tools and materials, the dictionaries and syllabaries, the 'copy books' with the master's fair copy on one side for the pupil to copy on the other. Here also he learned arithmetic in which the basic numbers were six and ten; geometry for surveying; and astronomy for interpreting the solar calendar invented in Egypt 4,000 years before our era. When the young scribe had mastered these mysteries he ranked with a temple priest or a government official in the social hierarchy. He had entered a privileged class, but not without the toil and pain which then, as ever since, accompanied the schoolboy's progress: 'You brought me up when I was a boy,' wrote a grateful pupil to his master, 'you beat me on the back and your teaching penetrated my ears.'

This was written about a thousand years after our statue was carved, but the profession of scribe had still a long life before it and remained the lure of ambitious parents for many centuries. There is for example the anxious father beseeching his son to work hard in the School of Books through which alone he can avoid the toil of the lower orders where the artisan 'worketh beyond what his arms can do'. A thousand years later, under the New Empire, writes Arnold Toynbee, significantly in a chapter entitled 'The Nemesis of Creativity', 'the same spirit breathes through the copy-book exhortations and warnings to schoolboys which convey the bureaucracy's unfaltering good opinion of itself as it still bestrides the broken back of a plebs that, by this time, has collapsed under the burden. "Do not be a husband-man; do not be a soldier; do not be a charioteer; do not be a priest, or a baker. Be an official." These were the warnings with which the writing master, in those days, still drove home into his pupils' minds his exhortation to be diligent.'[2]

We have known similar dangerous exhortations in modern times where 'a scribe culture' tends to steer ambitious youth

[1] See H. I. Marrou, *A History of Education in Antiquity*, p. xv.
[2] *A Study of History*, Vol. IV. p. 419-20.

away from the land and workshop to the office—in India where we have seen its outcome in the 'failed B.A.', and now in Africa where efforts are being made to direct the newly educated away from the attractions of officialdom into the resources of the land and productive industry.[3] The 'developing countries' of today cannot afford the petrifying burden of a 'scribe' bureaucracy.

But there is another side to the coin. In an age that was essentially religious, in an empire whose pharaohs might be religious philosophers, in a land where the desert encouraged monotheism, it is not surprising that the more reflective minds in the scribe class were not entirely devoted to the management of the royal treasury or the government of a province. Over the centuries there developed a strong ethical element in literary education and out of the ancient profession of the scribe emerged the sage, the man of wisdom, whose life's purpose was not merely to teach a civil skill but to inform the responsibilities of high office with standards of integrity. Here is the birth of social conscience; and also the beginning of the intentionally didactic Wisdom Literature of Egypt, Mesopotamia and Palestine.

Best known among the Egyptian sages, and to judge by his writings a most benign person, was Amenemope whose Book of Wisdom is preserved on papyrus in the British Museum. The book was composed in the tenth century B.C. before a word of the Old Testament was written, and we know that this remarkable assembly of worldy wise admonitions, often enriched by a poetic monotheism, was translated into Hebrew and eventually found its way into the Old Testament, by paths too obscure to trace but indelibly evident in the Hebrew Wisdom Literature and especially in the Book of Proverbs. Amenemope is preparing his son for an official career in the Egyptian administration and in words that might well be found in the mouth of Shakespeare's Polonius warns him against the temptations of a corrupt officialdom: 'Remove not the landmark on the boundary of the fields. . . . Shift not corruptly the hand balance, nor falsify the weights.

---

[3] See E. B. Castle, *Growing Up in East Africa*.

. . . Better is poverty in the hands of God than riches in the storehouse.' But there are also the accents of prophecy and the poetic themes of the psalmist: compare, for instance, the First Psalm with this:

> The truly prudent man, who putteth himself aside,
> Is like a tree growing in a garden.
> He flourish and multiplieth his fruit,
> He abideth in the presence of his lord.[4]

Here then, in the teachings of the Egyptian sage, are the beginnings of our own moral tradition, which passes first through the refining and deeper spiritual levels of Hebrew prophecy, and later through the teaching of Hebrew scribes and the Wisdom Literature of Judea, into the Christian world. Thus the long story of the scribe in the ancient world which begins in the fourth millennium B.C., presents him as the trained person in a clerical skill, as a teacher of that skill and member of a privileged class in a 'scribe culture', and finally as a teacher of practical wisdom and seemly behaviour which developed into a high moral code touched with religious feeling. He appears again in the Old Testament. In the classical world he had no place until Rome's extended empire required his services; but we see him again in the clerical secretaries of medieval kings and episcopal princes. And perhaps we see him once more in the vast bureaucracies of the modern world, in Whitehall and Washington, guiding the steps of amateur statesmen obedient to Parkinson's Law.

[4] See J. H. Breasted, *The Dawn of Conscience*, 1935, ch. xvii.

2 *The teacher as prophet*

The history of the Jews in Palestine begins about 1400 B.C. when the Semitic tribes invading from the east 'burned Jericho with fire', as the historian of Joshua records, and proceeded to the conquest of Canaan. This fraction of fertile land between the great empires of the two rivers was the cockpit of the ancient world and, partly because of this, produced a civilization which for the western world has been far more significant than that of the empires which dominated its political history. With the history of Palestine we are not concerned, but only with the teachers it produced, as remarkable as any we shall find in the classical world of Greece and Rome. Priests and scribes, civil servants and wise men we have encountered in Egypt and Babylonia; but the Hebrews produced two types of teacher peculiar to themselves—the prophet and the parent-tutor.

THE HEBREW PROPHETS

If education is primarily concerned with what sort of persons people become we cannot exclude the Hebrew prophets from the community of teachers. Like the Greeks they educated a whole civilization, but with a deeper penetrating power than the poets and philosophers of Hellas. It was the Hebrew prophets who created a new dimension in religious values by insisting that worship unconcerned with human behaviour was not religious; that God demands of men not merely subservience and expiation expressed in ritual forms but obedience to his moral law demonstrated in human conduct. The prophets, then, were concerned with both individual and social behaviour, and these are the perennial concern of teachers. The relevance of their teaching, especially their social teaching, to the life of the twentieth century is far more evident than the parallel message we inherit from the classical world. The Hebrew prophets, far more emphatically than Christians at any time in the history of Christendom, firmly declared the unity of the religious and the social and, moreover, with a boldness and precision never since surpassed by religious men.

The Prophets conceived of history not as a purposeless succession of isolated events but as the dialectic between right and wrong in a universal moral order. They preached the inexorable association of human disaster with the personal and corporate sin that defies the law of righteousness upon which just societies are founded. Amos, the earliest of the writing prophets, gives us the signature tune to the prophetic message: 'Let judgement roll down as waters and righteousness as a mighty stream.' This is the Way and the Law. This theme of God at work in history distinguishes the prophets from all the saints of Christendom who have separated themselves from their fellows in the search for a mystic vision opening the way to a personal salvation outside historical time. Likewise, the prophets gave short shrift to the false notion that a man's material prosperity was a measure of his righteousness: the third Isaiah preached his great sermon to the rich and powerful to remove the yoke of oppression, and called upon his people to be 'the restorer of paths to dwell in' (Chapter 58). Theirs is a concept of justice that rendered of no account the relationship of individual virtue with the balance in the bank: 'Let the rich man glory in his riches. But let him that glorieth glory in this, that he understandeth and knoweth me, that I am the Lord which exercise loving kindness, judgement, and righteousness in the earth.'[1]

This theme of social justice, so vehement and so deeply poetical rather than philosophical, was not only a lesson the Jews had to learn. There was here no 'barbarian' outsider who was forever without the pale of Greekness; it was a message for all mankind. And, even more interesting and impressive, the rewards of the prophetic promise were not stored up in optimistic guesses about a mystical other-world beyond the storms of human

[1] Jeremiah 9 23-24.

conflict, but were firmly directed towards the creation on earth of the righteous man and the just society. It was in this world, where 'the crooked shall be made straight'. Thus the prophets 'rose above the boundaries of their own nation to a vision of a unified humanity and made the conception of mankind a content of religion'.[2] This concept is still with us. And if we in the western world owe it to Christendom that it has passed over into the realm of international politics, it is less to the Christian saints than to the Hebrew prophets that we are in debt. In this, and in the association of personal morality and social justice with religious profession, the prophets of Israel made far more lasting impact on the conscience of the common man than the philosophers of Greece and the lawmakers of Rome.

THE HEBREW SCRIBES

The age of great prophecy ended with the return of the Jews to Jerusalem following the conquest of Babylon by Cyrus in 538 B.C. Ezekiel the prophet-priest and the unknown Third Isaiah were the last voices in the line of Hebrew prophecy. How then was the prophetic message mediated to the common man for the revival of the Hebrew people? The answer is interesting because it illustrates how important the teacher may be in moulding the minds of a nation. First, we must note that the spearpoint of Jewish revival was the dynamism of Babylonian Jewry. A century after Zerubbabel led forth the 40,000 exiles from captivity we read that Ezra 'a ready scribe in the law of Moses', fresh from Babylon, 'had set his heart to seek the law of the Lord and to do it, and to teach in Israel statutes and judgements'[3]; and again, we read of the method to be used: 'So they read in the book in the law of God distinctly, and gave the sense, and caused them to understand the reading.'[4]

This was in effect a policy for nation-wide adult education. No longer was the Torah, God's Law, to be the monopoly of a priestly class who passed on a few divine crumbs deemed suitable for the people's understanding. Nor was it sufficient to read

[2] I. Epstein, *Judaism*, p. 59.   [3] Ezra 7 [10].   [4] Nehemiah 8 [8].

the Law on the sabbath in the synagogue. What was read had to be read 'distinctly' and explained so that every Jewish father took back to his family rules for worship and behaviour providing for every contingency in life. Slowly but surely, writes Isidore Epstein, 'the Torah became the final source of every Jewish norm and practice, rule and custom, in all departments of life—religious, moral, political, social, economic and domestic'.[5] Thus the work of these inspired men among the captive Jews of Babylon had tremendous consequences for the Jewish people and for Christian civilization.

The Torah, we must remember, was more than the Pentateuch, which was called the written Torah; and the Pentateuch, we must also note, contained, especially in the book of Deuteronomy, deep impressions of prophetic thought. The word Torah literally means 'instruction' and the term as applied to the Law included both the Pentateuch or *written* Law and also the Oral or unwritten Torah, 'the tradition of the elders' referred to by Jesus.[6] This was a body of oral tradition whose purpose was to preserve the written Torah as God's continuing revelation to his people, rendering it relevant and responsive to changes in time and circumstance, and thus to avoid the danger of the written Law becoming an obsolete and irrelevant curiosity.

THE WISE MEN

Like Ezra himself the earliest scribes were priests, but clearly his programme of popular education which was to enthrone the Torah in the hearts of his people, required a large body of lay teachers entirely devoted to this purpose. Thus, during the last four centuries of her existence as a nation, or rather as a theocratic state whose ruler was the Torah, the scribe class, the *sopherim*, emerged as teachers and leaders. In popular respect their status was high and the honorific titles of 'rabbi' or 'father' were accorded to them. They were the real teachers of the people; they held regular teaching sessions in the synagogues, explaining the Law, elucidating the messages of the

---

[5] Op. cit., p. 85.   [6] Matthew 15 [2].

prophets, and by the ancient means of legend and parable illustrated the meaning of religious ceremonies that even today punctuate the life of the devout Jew.

Thus the *sopherim* provided the structure of religious practice and also the teaching that gave meaning to the Law by which the Jews lived. Not for several centuries did their exist schools capable of giving the kind of religious instruction given by the scribes. But the prophets had their popularizers and interpreters in the *Hakimim*, the wise men, lesser men than the prophets, more circumspect, less inspired, but in much closer touch with the life and problems of the average man. The Hebrew sage had for centuries worked beside the prophets but at a more popular level. Jeremiah recognizes them as a definite group whose function it was to give 'counsel' to ordinary men.[7] Their task is defined in the opening verses of Proverbs:

> To know wisdom and instruction;
> To perceive the words of understanding;
> To receive the instruction of wisdom, justice, and judgement and equity;
> To give subtlety to the simple,
> to the young man knowledge and discretion.

The sages were moralists, interpreting the deeper values of prophecy in terms of social and moral behaviour, upholding the personal virtues of charity and fair dealing, condemning corruption in high places and the misuse of wealth, supporting the underdog in his struggle against adversity and oppression. All this with a down to earth application of a message otherwise too high for ordinary understanding.

The prophet, writes Isidore Epstein, 'is full of zeal and passion; the sage was dispassionate, calm and cool. The prophet is full of idealism; the sage is the realist who looks at life in a somewhat utilitarian way. The words of the prophet are those of the eloquent Preacher; the counsel of the sage that of the wise Teacher. . . . The prophet's task was to make known the know-

---

[7] Jeremiah 18 [18].

ledge of the Lord; the sage's to show how this knowledge was
to be applied in terms of daily life and conduct. . . . The sage
attacked the problem from below: his interest was in the man-
in-the-street, whom he recognized as the source of all ethical
development.'[8]

It is to these worldly-wise men that we owe the Wisdom
Literature of the Old Testament—the Books of Proverbs, Job,
Ecclesiastes, the Wisdom of Ben Sirach or Ecclesiasticus, the
Song of Songs, and the Wisdom of Solomon. With the exception
of Job all are on a lower spiritual plane than their great forerunners. The Book of Job stands apart as a sublime excursion,
not merely into the philosophical problem of good and evil in
a God-directed world, but also into the inscrutable mysteries
that are revealed when a man can say 'I heard of Thee by the
hearing of the ear, but now mine eye seeth Thee'.

To understand fully the impact of the sages on the Jewish
people we must be aware of two conditions that profoundly
affected Jewish life from the third century B.C. The first was the
fact of continuing misery in the Jewish experience which seemed
to belie all the prophetic promises of relief and redemption and
to render meaningless the teachings of their Torah. The second
was the steady penetration of a decadent Hellenism in the last
three centuries before the Christian era, so foreign and corrupt-
ing and yet so insidiously attractive to a younger generation
constrained by the rigidities of Hebrew training in the home.
Against the first the sages stood firmly on the side of the poor
and oppressed, preserving with a steady insistence their emphasis on a personal morality that would fortify men against tribulation. Among the sometimes shallow wisdom of Proverbs, in
phrases the simple man can understand, the waverer is reminded
that God rules over all, and that diligence and honesty have
their reward. Against the second the teachings of Ben Sirach
are especially significant, for he was himself much influenced
by the best in Greek culture. But in eloquent passages in
Ecclesiasticus, written about 200 B.C., he proclaims the superiority
of Hebrew wisdom over Greek philosophy and stirs his con-

Op. cit., p. 73.

temporaries to lay firm hold on the twofold truth that 'the word of God most high is the fountain of wisdom' and that if you 'keep the commandments the Lord shall give her unto thee'.[9] Thus wisdom becomes the practical task of obeying the Torah, a simple direction needing neither high intelligence nor saintly virtues to understand. Men like Ben Sirach fortified the Jewish home in its resistance to the blandishments of Hellenism, and the Book of Proverbs became required reading in the home and a text book in every Jewish school for centuries after the Jewish nation had ceased to exist.

Thus the prophetic teachings, in diluted form but still retaining their strongly moral emphasis, were mediated through the *sopherim* and *Hakimim* to the Jewish father and much later to the schoolmaster and his pupils.

FATHER AND SCHOOLMASTER

Strange to say the Jewish people, who through a thousand years produced one of the great literatures of all time, established no elementary school in Old Testament times. The teaching of the scribes and sages, we must realize, was adult education for fathers, centred in the life of the synagogue. The elementary school appeared only after the fall of Jerusalem in A.D. 135. Throughout the previous eight hundred years of superb achievement and miserable defeat it was the Jewish father who was the teacher of the Jewish boy, and the Jewish home with its daily ritual prayers that sustained the Jewish faith through the subsequent centuries of persecution and exile. His duties had been explicitly laid upon him in the noble verses of the *Shema* for over two thousand years the daily prayer of the devout Jew.[10]

'Hear O Israel: The Lord our God is one Lord: And thou shalt love the Lord thy God with all thine heart and with all thy soul and with all thy might. And these words which I command thee this day shall be upon thine heart: And thou shalt teach them diligently unto thy children, and shalt talk of them when thou

[9] Ecclesiasticus 1.   [10] Deuteronomy 6 [4-9].

sittest in thine house, when thou walkest by the way, and when thou liest down, and when thou risest up. And thou shalt bind them for a sign upon thine hand, and they shall be for frontlets between thine eyes. And thou shalt write them upon the posts of thy house, and upon thy gates.'

The Jewish attitude to children was different from that prevailing in the Graeco-Roman world where infanticide persisted into Christian times. Throughout the Bible there are many evidences of children being regarded as God's blessing on the parents: 'Give me children or I die', cries the childless Rachel; to the God-fearing man the psalmist promises the wife 'that shall be as a fruitful vine and children that shall adorn his table as olive trees.'[11] Moreover, dominant and even tyrannical as the Jewish father may have been, it was assumed that the child had rights, a rare view in the ancient world; and every child was able to feel that what in the way of conduct a stern father exacted from him a jealous God demanded of his father.

In the home, and in later times in the elementary school, the sole content of education, literary and moral, was the study of the *Torah* and practice in obedience to its teaching. All literary studies served this end. The sacred texts were learnt by heart, but it was the father's duty to explain their meaning in language suitable to his growing sons. The *Shema* was learned by heart at the age of three; the ritual feasts of the seasons and the holiness of the Sabbath were explained; and the Passover, rich in symbolical imagery of the birth and tribulation of the Jewish people, became the central ceremony for Jewish children, based on the educationally significant verse 'And thou shalt tell thy son'. But not 'thy daughter', for girls were not to enjoy the education given to boys, either in the home or in the school, for many generations after the Jewish nation had dispersed.

Schoolmasters appeared in the second century A.D. with the establishment of the elementary school for boys aged 7 to 13, meaningfully called *Beth-hasepher*, the House of the Book. Here study was entirely devoted to the Torah. Thus both in home and

---

[11] Psalm 128.

school the Jewish boy's education was intensely and entirely religious, and because it was Jewish it was also moral. For him school life was no primrose path. 'This is the way for the study of the Torah: bread and salt must thou eat, and water by measure must thou drink, upon the ground must thou sleep, and live a life of privation the while thou toilest at the Torah.'[12]

What this toil meant for both teacher and pupil may be surmised when we realize the orthographic and linguistic difficulties involved in the reading of the text of the sacred books. In the first place the spoken language of the Jews towards the end of Old Testament times was Aramaic not Hebrew, a language as little like Hebrew as modern English is like Anglo-Saxon. To the Jewish schoolboy Hebrew was a classical language entirely associated with the Torah. In the second place, until A.D. 500 at earliest, the Hebrew alphabet consisted of consonants only. Imagine an English boy faced with a string of unspaced consonants something like this: GDCRTDTHHVNNDTHRTH. Would he easily read the sentence as 'God created the heaven and the earth'? In cases of doubt how is he to decide upon the vowel sound necessary to complete the sense? Consider again a simple example—in English is PT to be rendered PAT, PET, PIT, POT or PUT? The obstacles multiply when, we are told, three of the Hebrew consonants may be read in eight different ways according to the vowels with which they are combined. Here is a nice problem in pedagogics. Some modern scholars suggest that it was the humble teacher of the *Beth-hasepher* who helped to solve it.

It has usually been assumed that the group of scholars called the Massoretes, who laboured from about A.D. 500 to 800 to unify the Old Testament texts, invented the vowel signs. But in a talk I had long ago with the late Dr. Nathan Morris he suggested that it was the practical teacher, faced with the task of teaching children to read a language without vowels, who out of sheer necessity initiated the use of vowel signs to render the task easier for the young learner. We can imagine a resourceful teacher contriving to place appropriate signs between the consonants to

---

[12] N. Morris, *The Jewish School*, p. 167.

indicate the sound required for the proper pronunciation of the word as an aid to more ready apprehension. Did the earlier Massoretes adopt the idea from the harassed schoolmaster, and construct the linguistic system that eventually gave us our Old Testament? It is a fascinating thought.

The elementary schoolmaster taught from sunrise to sunset, for which he was no better paid than the village craftsman. And unlike his Greek and Roman contemporaries, whom we shall consider later, he was expected to be a man of unblemished character, for the Talmud reads 'If the teacher can be compared to an angel of the Lord of Hosts the Torah may be sought at his mouth; if not the Torah may not be sought at his mouth'. It was no doubt because of the moral demands made upon him that, despite his penury, he was accorded the kind of respect given to English parsons whose stipends did not measure up to their devotion and learning. From the third century A.D. the curriculum he taught was widened to include the Psalms, sometimes the Prophets, and nearly always the Book of Proverbs, so that the older boys might be called upon to read from the scrolls in the synagogue. Thus it was the teacher's duty to ground the boy of thirteen in the religion of his fathers, in a course of study to which children of that age have seldom been subjected. Despite his lowly status, then, the Jewish elementary teacher was deemed to be a key worker in a community whose very existence depended on the effectiveness of a moral and religious education founded in the Law and a way of life.

About one-tenth of the boys aged thirteen to seventeen passed on to the *Beth-hamidrash*, the House of Study or Exposition, and here the teacher was a much more scholarly person than his humbler colleague in the *Beth-hasepher*, for the subject of study was the Oral Law which was codified at the end of the second century A.D. and was known as the *Mishna*. In this senior school classes were small and conducted on seminar lines. The teachers had the honoured title of 'rabbi', master. These were the scholars whom Jesus surprised with his penetrating questions at the age of twelve. In both elementary and secondary schools the teacher depended much on memorization, constant repetition, rhythmic chanting (the only music permitted in school!) and mnemonic devices, for scrolls were rare and costly. But it was his duty always to associate what was learnt with the personal conduct of his pupils. In all Jewish instruction, whether by the father or the schoolmaster, it was assumed that only when the boy was visibly practising the rules of conduct he had learned by heart had he really understood them: 'One must always be engaged in the study of the Torah,' writes a third-century scholar, 'and in the performance of the commandments, even if it is not for their own sake, for this will lead to an interest in them for their own sake.'[13]

For a guide to school and home management teachers and parents turned to that collection of rules for a disciplined life assembled between 300 to 100 B.C., not without borrowings from the Egyptian and Babylonian sages, known to us as the Books of Proverbs and attributed to Solomon. The injunction that 'He that spareth the rod hateth his son' was a real command to parents and a solace to harassed teachers of wayward schoolboys. The régime at home and school was severe, but it was a purposeful severity. A careful reading of Proverbs reveals no vengeful attitude against the child for his wilfulness or sins of omission. Chastisement is administered for his immediate correction, but always there is a reformative, forward-looking element in punishment, a sense of responsibility for a child's ultimate participation in the religious community. And the teacher's part in this intense moral conditioning ran parallel with discipline at home, both aiming to establish children firmly in the closely-knit family circle and in the wider life of the community. In each case severity and guidance were conditioned by a moral insight and a loftier aim than in any of the dominant civilizations in which the scattered Jewish communities lived out their separate existence. Certainly there has been no instance in the history of western education where parent and teacher have so fully co-operated. Parent and teacher share the honours with the Torah for preserving the cohesion of the Jewish people in a hostile world:

[13] Quoted by T. Woody: *Life and Education in Early Societies,* p. 44.

Dost thou wish to know the source
From which thy brethren oppressed . . .
Drew comfort from Above, patience and security . . .
Turn to the House of Study, old and worn. . . .[14]

[14] Translated from the modern Jewish poet Bialik by Joseph Bentwich, and quoted in *The Year Book of Education*, 1957, p. 370.

3 *The teachers of Greece*

When the ancestors of Pericles passed southwards into the Greek peninsula they encountered a land responsive only to physical toil and human ingenuity. Greece's rocky slopes yielded foothold and food only to the mountain goat; the thin soil of her valleys provided the olive and the grape but little corn. The sea alone, visible from every mountain summit, was the highway to the corn and merchandise of more favoured lands. Thus nature decided that every Greek should become a farmer, craftsman, soldier, sailor and trader as necessity demanded; and the Greek people over the centuries transformed the Mediterranean into a Greek lake, colonizing its shores from Asia Minor to Sicily and Marseilles with people of Greek stock. The response of these people to their physical environment displayed an amazing combination of sheer physical vitality, enterprise and vision, stimulated by danger and opportunity and by a poverty whose limitations they were determined to overcome. What C. M. Bowra has called 'The Greek Experience' still fascinates our own world: 'So potent,' says Bowra, 'has been the appeal of Greece, so passionate the devotion which it arouses, that there is almost no sphere of spiritual or intellectual activity which has not been touched by its living flame.' Who—or is it what—taught the people of whom this may be said?

THE POET AND THE CITY

It is not surprising in a people so responsive to the magic of words that initiative so challenged imposed on the Greeks an admiration for individual achievement which was expressed in a folklore devoted to the cult of the hero. It is in poetry, and supremely in Homer, that the three strands of Greek existence

—nature, man and the gods—were firmly interwoven. By portraying man the struggler and achiever in scenes of heroic strife Homer lays the foundation of Greek humanism. His heroes are god-sized but human in all that is most human. Every actor on his stage is an individual, different from all the others in character, superb in both strength and weakness but never small, all caught in the toils of fate, all subject to divine disapproval when pride usurps the prerogative of the gods, all obedient to the poet's knowledge of the human heart. Homer never preached; he never judged. In him the Greeks never ceased to find a deep well of human wisdom. His epics were both the Bible and the Shakespeare of the classical world. In Homer, I have said elsewhere 'the Homeric ideal played the part of the Greek conscience and became the mould of the Greek spirit. And, because of its origin in an aristocratic culture, Greek education never quite lost the initial stamp which the Homeric nobility had impressed upon it.[1]

It was Homer who first made articulate that elusive but lasting ideal of excellence summed up in the Greek word *areté*, the quality that makes a man, a poet, a soldier, or a statesman the best of their kind. In the changing expressions of the Greek genius throughout the centuries this is a theme that informs and purifies both purpose and achievement in the arts, in politics and philosophy. We see it first in Homer—'always be the best and keep ahead of the others' Peleus tells Achilles his son; Hector's *areté*, he explains to his sorrowing Andromache, was to 'win glory for my father and myself'. In its earliest manifestation in the epic *areté* is both personal and aristocratic, not for the common run of men. As time passed the ideal of valour achieved a refinement in the ideal of *Kalos Kagathos*, 'the man both beautiful and good', and still shines for us, writes Harold Nicolson, 'as a resplendent fiction, as the image of an individual combining personal beauty with great qualities of mind and soul, as something simultaneously nervous and serene'.[2]

The emergence of the city, the *polis*, gave birth to a new and

---

[1] *Ancient Education and Today*, p. 13.
[2] *Good Behaviour*, p. 40.

to a collective ideal; in Sparta, the static form of the totalitarian state, *areté* is to serve and die for the fatherland; in Periclean Athens a man's highest *areté* is the integrity and distinguished leadership of the good citizen. And finally, when Greece yielded her cities, but not her civilization, to the arms of Macedon, *areté* becomes the excellence of heart and mind that enables a man to make the most of his human nature. In the third century B.C. Plato and Isocrates called this consummation of a man's *areté* his *paedeia*, that which makes him truly a man. Touched, perhaps, with the escapism of Stoicism, confined to those few who can live outside the world's hurly burly, this typically Greek and typically aristocratic ideal of the cultivated man nevertheless remains the most sensitive appreciation of what it means to be civilized. When the Macedonian general Demetrius Poliorcetes offered compensation to the Stoic philosopher Stilop after the despoiling of his house at Megara, the philosopher was not interested: compensation for what? 'No one has taken away my *paideia*.' No one has taken away what makes me a man![3]

The Greek experience embraced not only her sunlit lands and seas but also the life of men in cities. Centuries of trial and error with kings and aristocratic rule, endemic inter-city strife accepted as a condition of communal existence, and class warfare between an ancient landed aristocracy on the one side and the middle class of merchants, farmers and craftsmen on the other, ended in the sixth century with the victory of the people. In this struggle Athens discovered she had invented democracy; and once again *areté* received deeper and richer interpretations, still with its origins in poetry but extended to the statesman and lawgiver. In Athens Solon was the creator of her democratic way of life, for he gave every free citizen a vote, devised just laws and organized the Assembly as the organ of government. He was also a poet whose *areté* was portrayed in seeking 'with force and justice working both in one' a fair balance between rich and poor.

We are not, then, surprised that three centuries later Plato wrote in *Protagoras*: 'When the boys knew their letters and were

[3] Jaeger, *Paideia*, Vol. II. p. 70.

beginning to understand what was written, the masters put beside them on the benches the works of good poets for them to read, and made them learn them by heart. They chose for this purpose poetry that contained many moral precepts, and narratives and praises of the heroes of old, in order that a boy might admire them and imitate them and desire to become such a man himself' (325E). And it should be noted, these boys were fed from the start, not with tales for children, but with the best literature available. Nor were they bothered with grammar, which came later, if at all. For it was the poet not the schoolmaster who was the first teacher of the Greeks: not only Homer, not only Solon whose elegies on civic morality and justice were as familiar to the educated youth of Athens as Homer's epics, but also, says Aristophanes in *The Frogs*, the words of her homelier poets:

> Next came old Hesiod, teaching us husbandry,
> Ploughing and sowing and rural affairs,
> Rural economy, rural astronomy,
> Homely morality, labour and thrift.

And so in Athens the poet and the city joined hands, at a time when it was Pericles' proud boast that 'our city as a whole is an education to Greece'. This was the 'educative society' as we now call the vision of a community whose worthiness to be the educator of youth still holds the imagination of teachers, for it is, as they well know, a far more potent teacher than the classroom. Here is Pericles' portrayal of the ideal teacher, in the words of Thucydides, still fresh for our edification in the translation of Alfred Zimmern:

'Our government is not copied from those of our neighbours. . . . Our constitution is named a democracy because it is in the hands of the many not of the few . . . our laws secure equal justice for all in their private disputes, and our public opinion welcomes and honours talent in every branch of achievement . . . we give free play to all in our public life . . . in our public acts we keep strictly within the control of law . . . we are obedient to whomsoever is set in authority, and to the laws . . . ours is no work-a-day city only. No other provides so many recreations for the

spirit . . . beauty in our public buildings to cheer the heart and
delight the eye. . . . We are lovers of beauty without extrava-
gance, and lovers of wisdom without unmanliness . . . our
citizens attend both to public and private duties, and do not allow
absorption in their own various affairs to interfere with their
knowledge of the city's. . . . We are noted for being at once adventurous in action and most reflective beforehand. . . . In a word
I claim that our city as a whole is an education to Greece, and
that her members yield to none, man by man, for independence
of spirit, many-sidedness of attainment, and complete self-reliance
in limbs and brain.'[4]

The city became also a means for the poet-teacher's didactic
purpose, above all providing the setting for a willing captive
audience to join in the soul-searching medium of the drama, the
crown of Greek poetry and a native product. Beneath the Parthenon, conceived, says Bonnard, 'according to the laws of a
geometry which is the geometry of life . . . a tree, as it were
heavy with fruit and growing out of the soil of the Acropolis,'[5]
amidst the timeless creations of Pheidias, Athenians young and
old saw unrolled the drama of their own lives as, very rarely, we
may see the truths of ours, revealed by subsidized Shakespeare
or on T.V. In the centuries that produced the Parthenon were
written the seven tragedies of Aeschylus, the seven of Sophocles,
the eighteen of Euripides and eleven comedies of Aristophanes—
all of them written by men who had received no more formal
literary education than that provided by our own primary schools.
But this was not all that the city could provide. The sons of the
citizen craftsmen were apprenticed to a craft, but the privileged
sons of the substantial citizens were introduced by their fathers
to the city's laws, heard the speeches of her orators, the arguments
of her politicians and merged with the teeming life of a maritime
power.

THE SCHOOLMASTER

We may well ask: with such teachers and with such richness

[4] *The Greek Commonwealth*, 1911, pp. 200-3.
[5] A. Bonnard, *Greek Civilization*, pp. 128-9.

to feed on, what use had the Greeks for schoolmasters? In Greece, as in all early civilized communities, the school teacher emerged as a professional when folk customs no longer sufficed to train the young in the simple skills of human communication. Schools appeared in the sixth and were well established in the fifth century as private enterprises. The priorities were physical education, music which included poetry; reading, writing and calculation—in that order. Physical education was necessary because every Greek citizen had to be fighting fit; if a boy was to know his poets he had to learn how to read them; to the Greek mind poetry was inseparable from music and both had an equal place in education. Moreover as a people of merchant sailors had to learn the rudiments of calculation and navigation, simple mathematics could not be neglected. To lay these foundations was the job of the primary teacher and on them the curriculum of the primary school was planned. The Greek boy had, then, three teachers each responsible for the three branches of instruction: the *paidotribes*, instructor in physical education, not to be confused with the *gymnastes* who trained young athletes in the public gymnasium; the *citharistes*, teacher of singing, the seven-stringed lyre and the *aulos*, best compared with our oboe; and the *grammatistes*, teacher of reading, writing and poetry. There was also a fourth string in juvenile education, the family pedagogue, *paidogogos*, not a teacher but a guardian of the boy's personal welfare and behaviour, usually a trusted family slave but held in higher esteem than the schoolmaster for he represented parental authority and attended his young charge throughout the school day. Thus the schoolmaster was a purveyor of elementary knowledge, too lowly a person to be entrusted even with the moral oversight delegated to a slave.

In that delightful book *Schools of Hellas*, K. J. Freeman gives us a picture of the Greek schoolmaster at his task—and we can also see him on Greek vases. The master sits on a stool, the boys on benches. On the walls hung writing tablets and baskets containing manuscript rolls; in the music school lyres and flutes and decorative vases. Writing was taught on wax tablets, the master writing a fair copy for the pupil to copy underneath. We have Plato's authority for this method: 'When a boy is not yet clever at writing the masters draw the lines and then give him the tablet and make him write as the lines direct.' Teaching boys to read required some ingenuity, for words were not spaced and sentences not punctuated, an odd practice for so intelligent a people as the Greeks, but shared we have seen with the Hebrews. So the teacher plodded on, with his wax tablets, fair copies, rhyming alphabet, learning by heart and recitation. This last was no dull affair for the Greeks were a nation of actors and they liked their poetry declaimed with dramatic meaning. The schoolmaster bothered little about grammar; what mattered was poetry and its feeling and meaning.

For these services schoolmasters were paid irregular pittances depending a good deal on the quality of their services. The teachers whose teaching material was the poetry of the ages were regarded with scorn by the parents, rich or poor, who employed them. The art of keeping school was one of the depressed voluntary social services. Excluded from social respect and therefore from the moral supervision of his pupils, badly paid, often incompetent with the book but always ready with the whip, the elementary teacher was an object of scorn and sometimes of pity to his employers. His profession was the last refuge of the unemployed. And here hangs a shadow over the shining Greek world—why should the most cultivated people of the ancient west have been content to employ these pathetic misfits to educate their sons? Was it a consciousness of the profounder didactic influences of their society which we have noted in earlier pages? Was it the fact that the Greek world was an adult world in which children were not regarded as of great importance, until Plato reminded them that 'the beginning, you know, is always the most important part' of education? Was it a mistaken and excessive reliance on the content of instruction, a neglect of the truth which the later philosophers emphasized, and which always confronts the planners of education, that if instruction is to become education its moral and aesthetic values have to be demonstrated by good men? Shoddy teaching even in noble themes rarely gets through to the pupil.

THE SOPHISTS

The old primary education failed. Good enough for the men of Athens' golden age—Pericles, Sophocles, Euripides, Pheidias were all born between 490 and 480 B.C.—it did not satisfy their grandchildren who were born into a different world where the prizes of wealth and power called to ambitious youth. There was no secondary or higher education until the end of the fifth century. And this was provided by the new brand of teachers called sophists who appeared in the Greek cities as both a response to and cause of new social and intellectual trends. The sophists were teachers of *sophia*, an omnibus expression that to the Greeks might mean anything from philosophy to practical 'know-how' and skill. It was described by Protagoras, a sophist respected by Plato, in true sophistical terms as 'the proper care of one's personal affairs and also of the state's affairs, so as to become a real power in the city, both as a speaker and a man of action'.[6] This was what the young Athenian most ardently desired and this was what the sophists purveyed, for a price. Socrates was concerned that men should pursue truth by first acknowledging their own ignorance. The sophists did not believe that universal truth existed, and regarded its philosophical pursuit as futile. Few of them were philosophers; they were professional teachers and remarkably good ones too. As Marrou says 'they never taught their pupils any truths about being or man, but merely how to be always, and in any kind of circumstances, right'.[7] They deserve our respect 'as the great forerunners, as the first teachers of advanced education, appearing at a time when Greece had known nothing but sports-trainers, foremen, and, in the academic field, humble schoolmasters . . . they were professional men for whom teaching was an occupation whose commercial success bore witness to its intrinsic value and its social utility'.[8]

The sophists, then, were the first sixth-form teachers and

[6] *Protagoras,* 319B.
[7] *A History of Education in Antiquity,* p. 51.
[8] Op. cit., p. 49.

university professors, as Socrates was the first university tutor. Unlike many of our professors they lectured supremely well; unlike Socrates they lectured for a fee; and like most of our university professors their aim was frankly vocational. Where we respond to a nation's demand for more technologists, nuclear physicists or teachers they supplied the demand for better trained politicians. In the hands of the greatest sophists, and in particular in the case of Isocrates, this was no ignoble occupation. Thus emerges a new and perhaps the most enduring image of the teacher; for the role of the teacher as vocational instructor has great survival value.

It is in Isocrates, the almost exact contemporary of Plato, that we see this concept in a nobler form. When in 338 B.C. he died at the great age of 98, he had spent fifty-five years striving towards an ideal that would infuse the study of rhetoric with moral purpose. For Isocrates rhetoric was not only a political weapon but a culture of the mind, the poetry of politics, and much more than a technique for winning in the power game. He was the true Hellene, a term he applies 'rather to those who share our culture, *paideia*, than to those who share a common blood'.[9] Although in intellectual stature not comparable with his great contemporary, his was no ignoble intention—to train young men for the political regeneration of Hellas; and it was he, not Plato, who educated fourth-century Greece and prepared Hellenism for its ultimate conquest of the Roman world. But he remained a true sophist, with his sights always directed to the achievable, always a little lower than the ideal. Perhaps this makes him a good teacher.

THE PHILOSOPHERS

Socrates conceded that Isocrates might have some philosophy in him, but in Socrates appeared a teacher as different from the sophists as could be. In method and purpose he was a radical innovator. He wrote nothing; he charged no fees. He established the seminar method in its purest and most ruthless form: by

[9] *Panegyricus*, 50.

asking the right questions at the right moment of the right pupil he aimed to convince his pupils that they already possessed the truth they were pursuing. He was the 'midwife', the bringer-forth of ideas that were waiting to be born. This method we see to perfection in Plato's dialogues, a way of teaching which seems even to ennoble the young disciple, since it deals with him 'as with an angel, asleep indeed, but nevertheless an angel'.[10] He opposed the sophists because they purveyed a package deal of 'know-how' which would deflect his young friends from seeking the truth by the travail of the mind, and damp down that intellectual curiosity which must always be the true *areté* of the student.

Socrates remains our perfect model of the teacher. He was at home in the philosophy, science and literature of his age; he was a man among men, for like all Greek citizens he had been a soldier and had fought bravely in many battles; he loved young people with a kind of anxious pity, even with a feeling of anguish, because in their immaturity they knew nothing about the soul. Plato would never have used his master as his mouthpiece if he had not revered the quality of his mind and the illuminating precision of his analysis of complex ideas. Nor could Plato's reverence for Socrates have been accorded to any but that person who had arrived at where he wanted his young friends to go. Socrates adapted himself to the capacity of each pupil; his good humour was unshakeable; his manners were gracious even with cynics and fools; and he wore his superiority with humility. Above all things this is the truly religious man, dedicated, even with the cup of hemlock in his hand, to the mission of leading youth towards the good life. He remains in his greatness the humble seeker after truth alongside those who know little but are capable of learning how to learn.

Some of his pupils became great men, Plato the greatest, but there were tragic failures too—Critias and Alcibiades. Were then his methods wrong? The question is put less bleakly in these words of Sir Charles Morris:

[10] J. Maritain, *Education at the Cross Roads*, p. 29.

'In Plato's writings Socrates wanted above all that the young men whom he taught should come to virtue, to the good life. He knew how he wanted them to live, what he wanted them to come to believe. He wanted them to set their affections on the things of pure reason and not the things of the body; to love the pure form of beauty; to do good even to their enemies; and so on. He had no doubt about these doctrines; he never changed his mind about them. Yet he did not feel entitled to set out to indoctrinate them in these things. In all his dealings with them he felt bound to his technique of 'midwifery'. He must help the young to elicit and clarify their own question and to follow the argument where it led. The individual must think for himself, and find truth for himself; if he seemed to be coming to error or delusion rather than to truth, he must simply be inspired to question more persistently and more profoundly. There was no other way by which a man could educate himself.'[11]

It was to solve this problem of the moral dangers that beset this pitiless necessity for intellectual curiosity if the ends of spiritual maturity are to be served, that Plato set his mind. He elaborated a metaphysical system, both rational and intuitive, that became the foundation of an equally elaborate system of education. How was pure reason to bring man to a knowledge of the good; how was this knowledge to lead men to a mastery of their instinctive appetites and to the performance of their moral duty? The beginning of his answer was this: knowledge comes from recollection rather than from teaching, from recollection of those purest 'forms' or 'ideas' of goodness and beauty that had held our vision in the heavenly realms which were our home before we became imprisoned in our earthly frame. Before men take on their frail humanity they have had a glimpse 'of the ideals and patterns which have a real existence independent of our minds'. Our life-long task, never fully achieved, is to recapture the vision our humanity has obscured. And it is the work of education to bring the forms of goodness and beauty, which are our ultimate truth, into sharper focus. This purely idealistic and rational process informs the three basic aims of

[11] A. V. Judges, Ed. *Education and the Philosophic Mind*, p. 33.

Plato's systems of education: first to lead men to their lost vision of the good which is the highest form; second to inform the life of the community with the quality of this vision; third, to make mature men and citizens, men who have achieved the self-mastery 'that leads you always to hate what you ought to hate, to love what you ought to love, from the beginning of life to the end'.[12]

Here, then, in the teaching of Socrates' great disciple, we encounter a development of the Socratic view that knowledge is in the learner. In his Academy, a school of political science as well as of philosophy, Plato aimed to train the political technician not to aspire to personal advancement but to seek the political and moral welfare of his own city. Within this great design he raises problems that are still with us; for instance, whether education should be a state concern not subject to the caprice of private enterprise; and the dilemma, still unresolved, of the balance between the arts and the sciences in general education; and still more tantalizing, the question of the education of an élite 'trained to despise existing honours as mean and worthless, caring only for the right and the honours to be gained from that, and above all for justice as the one thing indispensable'.[13]

But viewed from the seclusion of his academy the public life of Athens seemed less and less likely to display that 'justice' where each section of society was doing 'its own proper work'; and so, in the end, Plato turns in bitterness to the last refuge of the philosopher, to 'the city he bears within himself'.[14] Plato is the great exemplar of the teacher as philosopher. As a teacher he is unique, for he educated a whole civilization and with his pupil Aristotle laid the foundations of philosophy on which men have built for two thousand years.

Remote as high philosophy may be from the schoolroom Plato nevertheless leaves us with new concepts of the teacher's task, some profound, some wrong-headed. In the *Republic*, and

---

[12] *Laws*, 643.
[13] *Republic*, vii 540.
[14] *Republic*, ix 591.

in the *Laws*, the first written in his prime the second in his o[l]d age, several themes dominate his references to the rearing of children. First, there is the basic theme that education is *growth*. Despite his lofty intellectualism, says Jaeger, 'Plato's idea of education was that it is a slow vegetable growth', an idea almost entirely absent from the sophists.[15] It follows that the foundations of character are laid in childhood, even before birth in the emotional state of the pregnant mother—'the beginning, you know, is always the most important part, especially when you are dealing with anything young and tender'.[16] This must be regarded as a fundamental criticism of the prevailing indifference to childhood, and his must be the first reasoned presentation of the importance of play in the early years and of the inhibiting effect of fear on smooth emotional development. And nowhere in the history of education do we find a more persuasive and vivid demonstration of the influences of environment, whether of evil or of the 'inflowing power of beauty and goodness' over the growing mind. Plato also points a disapproving finger at the weakest element in the practice of education in his time—the fallacy that if the content of education is nobly conceived it matters little if ignoble teachers or incompetent scholars are in charge of it.

And yet it is at the point where Plato applies his principles that our doubts creep in. For in the *Laws*, where he deals with the schooling of ordinary children, education becomes a nurture in so strictly guarded an environment that we begin to discern the shades of the prison house. Children, bodies, minds and emotions, are to be moulded to a pattern approved by the state, to a point where the teacher's initiative is taken over by the director of education. The 'modes' of music are prescribed, the poets selected and if necessary bowdlerized; on pain of dismissal the teacher is required to educate in conformity with the city's laws, so that the young are moulded to a shape conformable to community views of the good citizen. Only the increasing degradation of Athenian youth, undoubtedly a matter of concern to the

[15] *Paideia*, Vol. I. p. 228.
[16] *Republic*, ii 377.

zens of Athens, can explain this restrictive ban
ty of teacher and taught. Nevertheless even in
's is a surprisingly authoritarian view of educa-
children to the arid experience of doing and
it they are told. Thus in his old age Plato denies
inity to choose and to learn by its own mistakes,
, ...y item in the progress towards the good life.

Nevertheless we are presented with several interesting concepts of the teacher, some more attractive than others. He is to
be a civil servant, a competent scholar, an interpreter of tradition,
a conditioner of environment, a preserver of community standards, a guardian of morals. But when we forget the drabness
and view the great Platonic theme in all its wholeness, we still
see shining through the bars of the prison house, the concept of
the teacher as one who lives the good life as far as a man can,
ceaselessly staying his gaze on the vision of the Good, occasionally
saying to his pupils—'do not look at me, look where I am
looking'.

Aristotle's metaphysics was founded on scientific observation
of man and society. For Plato man was an immortal soul tem-
porarily accommodated in a mortal body; Aristotle believed man
to be body and soul. He cannot accept his master's view that
men are born with a ready-made knowledge or that knowledge
is the path to virtue—'To know does little, even nothing, for
virtue.' For Aristotle education is not the art of re-discovering
the divine vision but the art of co-operating with nature; and
he is not sure that reason is always in control of the instinctive
appetites and certainly not in childhood; but he believed, nevertheless, that man's instinctive tendencies have a 'filial regard'
for the inner rational principle that activates learning through
sense experience, that the urges of our emotional life desire, so
to speak, to be 'obedient to our reason as a son to his father'.
But he asks us to observe also, what we all know now, that our
sensual inclinations too often defeat the rational principle that
shows us the right path to follow. That is why Aristotle emphasizes the need for forming good habits in childhood, and why
he presents us with the attractive doctrine of the 'mean', in which

men are advised to secure a balance in their lives between the defects of extremes which may lead to excessive indulgence or unnecessary austerity.

Many of us who are growing old, however imperfectly, will appreciate Aristotle's insistence that only the mature person can experience happiness in the good life. A survey of youth in the 1960's finally dissolves the speech-day myth that school days are the best time of our lives. They never were, of course, except in the memories of disappointed men. For there is much truth in the Aristotelian view that the true nature of a thing is not seen fully except in its maturity. He argues, then, that because the young are not 'complete' there is a natural difference between old and young in the sense that nature has fitted the old to govern and the young to be governed. No one, he says, 'takes offence at being governed when he is young'—words which have a hollow ring in university common rooms today! But youth has rights, and Aristotle concedes to youth the inalienable right to the highest skills of the teacher in the cultivation of the 'inner seeing power of the intelligence' which is as much a part of his natural endowment as is his body.

Here, then, Aristotle regards the mental activity of the learner and the intellectual guidance of the teacher to be the two dynamic elements in education. And of these two factors the most vital is the mental capacity of the child to be educated. The teacher thus becomes a secondary though indispensable agent in education, an opinion we shall meet on many occasions as we pass through the centuries with our eye on the relationships existing between the teacher and the learner. We shall encounter it for instance in Augustine and Aquinas and in modern times, but derived from different premises and having different implications.

Thus Aristotle enlarges our concept of the teacher by presenting him as the person who raises the pupil's sights towards a good higher than his own good. In the seventh book of the *Politics* Aristotle tells us that the whole of life is divided into two parts, 'business and leisure, war and peace, and all our actions are divided into such as are useful and such as are fine. . . . We ought to choose war for the sake of peace, and business for the

sake of leisure, and what is useful for the sake of what is fine.
. . . These are the aims we have to keep in view in the education
of children and people of every age who require education.'[17]
Aristotle's doctrine of the 'mean' conjures up an entrancing
picture of the teacher leading his pupil by the hand along the
narrow path between what is fine and what is useful as they
strive together towards the good life.

[17] *Politics*, vii 14.

4 *The teacher in Rome*

What societies expect from teachers and what kind of persons they think teachers should be, depends largely on the sort of communities they are. We have seen Greek education emerging from the cultural life of the city state and touched into life by the inspiration of her poets. The origins of Roman education were very different. The Romans were a community of farmers who could boast of no poets to illuminate their past, and Roman education in Rome's earliest days was a practical response to the needs of a farming people surrounded by predatory enemies. Theirs was a peasant culture, a little boorish perhaps, because rooted in the soil. Before his city had become the heart-beat of an empire the Roman citizen was a soldier-farmer who only on urgent civic occasions repaired to his city. In nostalgic bitterness, as the high tide of Greek ways swept over his father-land in the second century B.C., Cato declared 'when our fore-fathers would praise a worthy man, they praised him as a good husbandman and a good landlord; and they believed praise could go no further'.[1] There was here none of the Athenian's contempt for manual toil, for what to the practical Roman mind was useful was also to be respected.

In these early centuries before Greece 'took captive her bar-barian conqueror' the family was the focus of all religious and educational activity. Under the almost unique Roman custom embedded in *patria potestas*, the father had absolute rights of life and death over his wife and children; within the sphere of family life he was father, teacher, law-giver and priest. The one restraint on his absolute power was his own unyielding respect for the *mos maiorum*, the ancestral customs to which he yielded religious obedience and whose high priest he was. Vesta, the

[1] Cato, *De Re Rustica*, 1.

goddess of the city sanctuary and also the goddess of the domestic hearth, with the Lares and Penates, spirits of the farmlands and store cupboard, were reminders of the unity of the Roman family and the Roman state. In his private as in his public life the Roman citizen was thus impelled to remember that his welfare was dependent on the gods of Rome. Simple, definite even if superstitious, his religion was also a reminder that the approval of the gods demanded not only an unyielding patriotism but probity in personal affairs and obedience to the laws of Rome. There was in Roman religion a strongly ethical emphasis not so evident in the religious ritual of Greece.

Thus Roman children were born into a rigid custom of morality and law. Their fathers had little philosophical curiosity, little of the imaginative creativeness of the Greeks. The Romans were adaptable and imitative because practically minded, and the virtues singled out for praise were courage, obedience and resilience in the face of adversity not slickness of mind, the virtues that made patriots and men who could in emergency use the sword as manfully as the plough. The ancient virtues of *gravitas* and *pietas* were the Roman ideal. *Gravitas* was on its finer side the dignity and poise of the mature man; in its grimmer manifestation the harshness and ponderous solemnity that on occasion characterized the Roman in his private and public life. But the austerities of *gravitas* were softened by that most attractive of Roman ideals, *pietas*—reverence for the gods, loyalty to the fatherland and the stern gentleness that touched family life with the care that was truly familial, honest and good. *Pietas* is portrayed in its perfection by Plutarch in his description of Cato's loving concern for his little son at the wash-tub; how this last great Roman of the old school writes a history of Rome 'in large characters' for his son's easier reading, and condemns the man who raises his hand against a wife or child and reckoned a good husband as worthy of more praise than a good senator.[2] Rome shares with Judeea the highest concept in the ancient world of the teacher as father. There were schools in Rome in

[2] *Lives*, Vol. I. p. 534, Everyman edition.

fourth century B.C. but they played an insignificant part in a Roman boy's education.

With the spread of Greek civilization into all corners of the Mediterranean bringing with it the Greek language as its lingua franca, the situation wholly changed. By the first century B.C., the age of Caesar, Brutus and Cicero, the upper classes of Rome were receiving an education that was in essentials Greek, although it always bore the imprint of the utilitarian Roman mind, less interested in the pursuit of truth for its own sake than in the application of knowledge to government, politics and architecture. The Roman schools were on the Greek model, the Greek *paidogogos* became the Roman *paedagogus*, the *ludi magister* of the primary school had the same humble origin and was as incompetent and as badly paid as his Greek forerunner. He was placed by Juvenal in the same category as bath-attendants and tight-rope dancers who earned as much in a year as a charioteer earned in a day. His classes were riotous, his days laborious, and he not infrequently died in want.

The *grammaticus* of the secondary or grammar school was a far more important person, usually a good Greek and Latin scholar, badly paid but better paid than the *ludi magister*. His teaching was narrowly confined within a strictly linguistic and literary curriculum, no longer supplemented by the culture of the body or the liberating influence of music. During the years of the later Empire, imperial interest in education, stimulated by the pressing need for educated civil servants, considerably raised his prestige in the principal cities of the Roman provinces, and also improved his pay. In the ancient world respect for the secondary teacher was never higher than in the fourth century A.D. when the value of his services as the educator of potential administrators became evident. Thus once again the scribe was called in to bring order into an empire.

Another and surprising consequence of administrative need was the demand for secretaries skilled in the technique of writing shorthand. Here was an opportunity for teachers at the lower level of vocational instruction to improve their pay and status. The circumstances were almost identical with those prevailing in the first half of the twentieth century when Mr. Pitman and the stenographer came into their own. Poor teachers in the primary schools learned a not entirely new system of abbreviated words—shorthand; poor parents, unable to afford the fees of the *grammaticus*, saw opportunity, as they do today, in a training that promised 'a safe job with good prospects' for their sons. For in imperial Rome, as in our nineteenth century, there was always a chance of the office boy rising to the top. We are told that 'even in some remote spot in Upper Egypt a teacher had only to open a school and advertise that he could teach shorthand as well as literature and the people would come flocking to him'. Eventually the value of this new technique was more generally recognized. Even the Church patronized this useful skill: 'the reason why so many sermons composed by the Fathers of the Church in the fourth and fifth centuries have come down to us is that shorthand secretaries used to sit in the basilica at the feet of the bishop as he delivered his homily during the service'.[3] So a new vocational teacher appeared on the Roman educational scene. We cannot however assume that his classroom was markedly different from what it had always been. Throughout the centuries the flogging schoolmaster pursued his perennial way, immortalized in Horace's master Orbilius, a free man, learned but poor, whose reputation as *plagosus,* the flogger, has become the legendary prototype of the conventional schoolmaster throughout the ages.

But we have run far away from the *pietas* and *gravitas* of the old Roman society which portrayed for us the reverent upbringing, *disciplina,* of the boys of ancient Rome. We retrace our steps to consider the work of two men who attempted to elevate Roman education to a higher plane: Cicero the statesman and orator, and Quintilian the schoolmaster.

CICERO AND QUINTILIAN

In *De Republica* Cicero (106-43 B.C.) writes 'as a Roman citizen, who thanks to his father's care has had a liberal education

[3] See H. I. Marrou, *A History of Education in Antiquity*, pp. 312-13.

and who has loved study from boyhood, yet owed more to experience and to the lessons of home than to books'.[5] In 55 B.C. he made himself responsible for the education of his ten-year-old son Marcus and for his nephew Quintus, and wrote a catechism of rhetoric for the two boys. But Cicero's mind moved in a wider sphere than domestic instruction. He envisages his task in the Roman scene with the eyes of Isocrates: 'we must turn to our fellow countrymen for virtue and for our culture to the Greeks'.[5] This was the orator's call for a programme of educational reform, 'an appeal to the younger generation to imitate the example which he had set them and to aim at a wider and nobler culture than was usual in contemporary Roman society'.[6]

Cicero did for Rome what the great sophist had done for Hellas. But in Cicero's ideal the Isocratic notion of *paideia*, noble but with strong vocational undertones, is given a wider and a warmer meaning in the indefinable concept of *humanitas*. The truly cultivated man is not skilled only in rhetoric and learned in philosophy and the sciences, but has also to be 'a man in all that is most human and to be human in his relationship with other men'. Thus *humanitas*, the highest concept of culture in the Roman world, imparts to *gravitas*, with no impairment of its power and dignity, the gentler tones of courtesy, human kindliness, intellectual refinement and moral purpose.[7] Cicero, then, presents us with the concept of the teacher as philosopher-statesman, and we shall go far in the ancient and the modern world to find a better presentation.

Cicero was a great orator, a philosopher and a not very successful statesman. Quintilian was no philosopher but he was a very successful and highly paid schoolmaster, in Juvenal's view the most notable exception to the rule that schoolmasters are underpaid and over-worked. Unlike Cicero who met a violent and undeserved end, he retired from his twenty years tenure of the chair of rhetoric at Rome and wrote a long and detailed

---

[4] I. xxxii 36.
[5] *de Oratore* III. 137.
[6] A. Gwynn, *Roman Education from Cicero to Quintilian*, p. 80.
[7] See A. Gwynn, op. cit., p. 121.

treatise on the higher education of upper-class Roman boys—
the Etonians of late first century Rome. This was the *Institutio
Oratorio*, the *Institutes of Oratory*, published about A.D. 95.
Quintilian was a disciple of Cicero, and he revered Plato, and
yet we search in vain in the *Institutes* for any discussion of the
ultimate purposes of education. But we readily forgive him for
being a typical Roman. He is interesting because he was the first
writer on education in the ancient western world who was also a
first-rate teacher of adolescents, who had seen the whites of their
eyes in the classroom, felt the vital responses between teacher
and pupil, and being not over-burdened with a philosophic mind
was therefore, perhaps, gifted with an intuitive understanding
of youth. The *Institutes* is a characteristically able, practical,
wise and humane treatise on the education of the privileged boys
of his time. So good and durable was it that seventeen hundred
years later Dr. Keate was teaching Latin and Greek at Eton as
Quintilian said they should be taught, although, as we shall see,
he was running his school as Quintilian said it should not be
run (see p. 152).

Cicero would have the orator be a philosopher. Quintilian
thinks on a lower plane. My aim, he says, is to produce the
perfect orator:

'The first essential is that he should be a good man, and consequently we demand of him not merely the possession of excep-
tional gifts of speech, but of all the excellences of character as
well. For I will not admit that the principles of upright and
honourable living should, as some have held, be regarded as the
peculiar concern of philosophy. The man who can really play his
part as a citizen and is capable of meeting the demands both of
public and private business, the man who can guide a state by
his counsels, give it a firm basis by his legislation and purge its
vices by his decisions as a judge, is assuredly no other than the
orator.'[8]

Quintilian inherited from Cicero a germinal comment on the
teacher: 'The authority of those who teach often injures those

[8] *Institutio Oratoria*, I. 9-10.

who wish to learn.'[9] Is it too much to assume, as I like to, that this Ciceronian wisdom inspired Quintilian to be 'the first serious student of the pupil's reaction to teaching'?[10] For that is what he was—the first professional in Greek or Roman education to emphasize not only the importance of method and the critical examination of its results, but the importance of understanding children and of working upon the positive impulses of temperament in the exercise of school discipline, a wisdom that led him in a flogging world to condemn corporal punishment.

The immediate impression one receives from the earlier books of the *Institutes* is Quintilian's emphasis on the *growing* nature of children. As Plato is his greatest love in Greek literature this is not surprising. He would not, he declares, set himself against the will of nature; we must treat young children like the mother bird who urges fledglings from the nest and gives them 'the freedom of the open sky, left to trust in themselves'; the pruning hook is 'not to be applied when the leaves are young'; the teacher must consider 'how much a child's mind is capable of receiving, for things beyond his grasp will not enter his mind'. Both teaching methods and the content of instruction should be tempered to a boy's abilities and aptitudes; the dangers of cramming are pressed home in the well-worn figure of 'vessels with narrow mouths'; and we are warned that a child who is 'not old enough to love his studies' may come to hate them if he is punished for his failures but unpraised for his achievements, for 'study depends on the good will of the student, a quality that cannot be secured by compulsion'. Thus the wise teacher works on the positive impulses of temperament, guiding and restraining but always using what capacities his pupil possesses. This is good psychology and good pedagogics.

For his description of the good schoolmaster's virtues and class relationships it is worth quoting the master at greater length:

'Let him therefore adopt a parental attitude to his pupils, and

[9] *De Natura Deorum*, I. 5. 10.
[10] W. J. McCallister, *The Growth of Freedom in Education*, p. 68.

regard himself as the representative of those who have committed their children to his charge. Let him be free from vice himself and refuse to tolerate it in others. Let him be strict but not austere, genial but not too familiar: for austerity will make him unpopular, while familiarity breeds contempt. Let his discourse continually turn on what is good and honourable; the more he admonishes, the less he will have to punish. He must control his temper without however shutting his eyes to faults requiring correction; his instruction must be free from affectation, his industry great, his demands on his class continuous, but not extravagant. He must be ready to answer questions and to put them unasked to those who sit silent. In praising the recitations of his pupils he must be neither grudging nor over-generous: the former quality will give them a distaste for work, while the latter will produce a complacent self-satisfaction. In correcting faults he must avoid sarcasm and above all abuse: for teachers whose rebukes seem to imply positive dislike discourage industry.'[11]

Quintilian's well known condemnation of corporal punishment is consistent with all his schoolroom attitudes, but it is nevertheless remarkable in an age when flogging prevailed in almost every Greek and Roman school throughout the empire. As the *Institutes* became a textbook of method for five centuries after his death and was resurrected into fashion after its discovery by the Renaissance scholar Andrea Poggio in 1416, it is not unfair to add that the neglect of his reflections on corporal punishment became one more monument to the disinclination of schoolmasters to scrutinize their practices in the light of a new idea. This is what Quintilian says:

'I disapprove of flogging, although it is the regular custom and meets with the approval of Chrysippus, because in the first place it is a disgraceful form of punishment and fit only for slaves, and is in any case an insult, as you will realize, if you imagine its infliction at a later age. Secondly, if a boy is so insensible to instruction that reproof is useless, he will, like the worst type of slave, merely become hardened to blows. Finally, there will be

[11] II. ii 5-8.

absolutely no need of such punishment if the master is a thorough disciplinarian. As it is, we try to make amends for the boy's *paedagogus,* not by forcing him to do what is right, but by punishing him for not doing what is right. And though you may compel a child with blows, what are you to do with him when he is a young man no longer amenable to such threats and confronted with tasks of far greater difficulty? Moreover when children are beaten, pain or fear frequently have results of which it is not pleasant to speak and which are likely subsequently to be a source of shame, a shame which unnerves and depresses the mind and leads the child to shun and loathe the light. Further if inadequate care is taken in the choices of respectable governors and instructors, I blush to mention the shameful abuse which scoundrels sometimes make of their right to administer corporal punishment or the opportunity not infrequently offered to others by the fear thus caused in the victims. I will not linger on this subject; it is more than enough if I have made my meaning clear. I will content myself with saying that children are helpless and easily victimized, and that therefore no one should be given unlimited power over them.'[12]

But we must not read too much into Quintilian's liberal attitude towards his pupils. This is no 'child-centred' education immersed in the study of motive and emotional development at the cost of learning. It is no more than a good schoolmaster's attitude towards his pupils, derived from acute observation of their reaction to teaching and based on a clear view of the means to be employed to secure a clearly envisaged end—to make the good orator, not the man both beautiful and good, but the good man skilled in speech. We discern, then, in Quintilian the conservative reformer, the innovator in method rather than of purpose. He would have made a splendid Victorian headmaster, not an Arnold of Rugby, not quite a Thring of Uppingham, more likely a Butler of Shrewsbury. But if we reckon with his voluminous writings on pedagogy he might be regarded as the first professor of education.

Unfortunately it was not Quintilian's liberal views on the

<hr>

[12] I. iii 14-17.

education of boys that held the minds of teachers in the schools of the empire. As the years passed the Roman teacher lapsed into a sterile linguistic pedantry, an admirable candidate for Seneca's condemnation that they taught 'for the classroom not for life'—*non vitae sed scholae discimus.* But however far they failed to attain the heights of Quintilian, let us not forget that it was the Roman schoolmasters who carried the torch of learning into the early Middle Ages.

PART II

The growth of the European tradition

Western Christendom drew its inspiration from the Graeco-Roman and the Biblical-Hebrew worlds. Although the Christian Fathers were educated in the pagan schools of Rome their minds were formed by the Hebrew and Christian scriptures. Pre-eminent among them was St. Augustine of Hippo, a teacher on the grand scale, who directed the thinking of Christendom for a thousand years. His works were the seed plot of the scholastic controversies which dominated the intellectual life of the middle ages and produced their most typical and outstanding teachers—Peter Abelard in the twelfth and Thomas Aquinas in the thirteenth centuries. Abelard shocked his contemporaries by his ruthless logical analysis of accepted doctrine; Aquinas built Christian doctrine into a structure of reason. Today his teachings on the nature of man have more significance for education than they had in his own day. But even in this era when pure logic claimed to be the only way to truth new means to knowledge were breaking through, stimulated by the more scientific thinking of Arabic scholarship. While Aquinas was labouring with his monumental *Summa Theologica* Roger Bacon and Ramon Lull were already engaged in speculations into the nature of the physical universe slowly to turn men's minds away from scholastic debate to the world of observable facts. These were the dim beginnings of a scientific mode of thinking which was eventually to transform the teacher's outlook and his role in society. In this period also the schoolmaster's image became more firmly outlined in the medieval grammar schools, which can claim their remote parentage in the schools of Rome.

5 The teachers of the early Church

G. C. Coulton has written that the collapse of the Roman empire was 'the worst catastrophe recorded in the whole history of the western world'. He also said that the Middle Ages 'can be rightly understood only as a period of convalescence'.[1] Two influences made this convalescence possible: the first was the amazing capacity of the Roman Church not only to preserve but to strengthen its institutions in a period of universal tumult and destruction; the second was the work of the Christian Fathers in defining and propagating a faith that proclaimed the indestructibility of the human spirit. The defences of physical existence were down and despair had become the normal response to the human condition; but the Fathers, combining the roles of priest, prophet and scribe promised glory in the life to come as more than compensation for the failure of the rulers of this world. It is among these tenacious, contentious, often intolerant but single-minded scholars, that we find the significant teachers of this dark age. Above them all towers Augustine whose stature on any standard places him, like Plato and Aristotle, among those who shape a civilization. Although all were engaged in the controversies over doctrine that beset the Church in the early centuries, they were also concerned for religious education in the family and in the adult congregations in the villages and townships of the dissolving empire.

When we bring to mind the conditions of their lives, the traditions both pagan and Christian they inherited, and the distant horizons of their hopes, we shall not be surprised to find a strange medley of motives and ideas in the early Christian communities of the Mediterranean world. These isolated groups

[1] *Medieval Panorama*, Ch. I.

struggling to preserve their identity in what was to them a spiritually alien civilization, were heirs to both the ancient Hebrew and the new Christian teaching. Their schools were the Roman schools for they had none of their own, and the faith they lived by was a product of the uneasy companionship of Judea and Hellas.

This was the setting in which they sought to establish a way of life in this world that would find approval in the next. Each of these little communities regarded itself as a spiritual enterprise in the service of its Master, in which the responsibility of individuals for the moral welfare of all, and the governance of children through the teaching and example of their parents, were part of the Christian's corporate duty. This was not the educative society on the grand scale, but the small educative community whose bonds were those of the family and of a new morality which, as the great apostle required, must be as binding on the parents as on the children. In a very real sense it is true to say that with the first few generations of Christians their teacher was the risen Christ, whose imminent return was their great expectation. These early hopes were dimmed as the years passed, but not the Christian's ultimate expectation of the life to come. It was in preparation for the life beyond that education in the home and in the schools for converts was conducted.

Unfortunately by the end of the second century the pressures for ecclesiastical uniformity had changed the order of Christian priorities. The sacred offices of the church became the mediators of salvation, and the family ceased to be the centre of Christian education. Moreover, when celibacy, for men as well as for women, became the young Church's expression of the highest personal good, it was not to be expected that a view of marriage as a lesser good than perpetual virginity would strengthen the family tie and preserve the home as the primary school in the art of Christian living.

ATHLETES FOR CHRIST

Thus in the early centuries of the Church there was one over-riding educational purpose but many conflicting ideas as to how it was to be achieved. There were so many strands of tradition to be disentangled. Was the divine approval, for instance, given equally to the injunctions of Solomon, Jesus and Paul? Were the gentler tones of their Lord and his apostle to replace, at least to mitigate if not to destroy, the traditional austerities of the Roman schools? This was one dilemma. But the purpose of the early Christians was clear, expressed with simple clarity by St. Basil of Caesarea (330-379): 'We place our hopes on the things that are beyond and in preparation for the life eternal do we all things that we do.'[2] Much earlier Clement of Alexandria (160-215) had declared that 'the true Teacher is the Logos, the Holy spirit, whose desire it is to train up his children to the virtuous not to the intellectual life'. Here is the Hebrew emphasis dominating the Greek. No self-respecting Hellene could so separate virtue from intelligence.

The softer tones of gospel charity are heard once more in the touching letters of St. Jerome (331-420), written from his retreat in Bethlehem, concerning the education of the little daughters of his friends Laeta and Gaudentius. Here Jerome describes the carefully guarded education necessary for these young children whose parents had already dedicated them to Christ—gentle but austere, no silks or gems, no frivolous associations, but astonishingly large doses of the Old and New Testaments, always with a particular reverence for Solomon, and always returning to the persistent refrain, which seems to be inevitably characteristic of religious education, that the present must always be the servant of the future.

It is in the most comprehensive treatise on Christian education in this period, *On Vainglory and the Right Way for Parents to Bring up Their Children*, written by St. Jerome's contemporary St. Chrysostom (334-404) that the dilemma of the Christian teacher is revealed.[3] How is he to express the gospel of love with Solomon's rod in his hand? This is, of course, the dilemma

---

[2] 'Address to Young Men', W. K. L. Clarke, *The Ascetic Works of St. Basil.*
[3] See M. L. W. Laistner, *Christianity and Pagan Culture*, Appendix.

so firmly and clearly resolved by Augustine, and as it remains so important an issue even today, these far off predicaments of Chrysostom are worth a moment's study. His single-minded aim was to train up each child as an 'athlete for Christ', Paul's interesting simile taken from the Roman arena. Chrysostom's fearsome régime is full of inconsistencies. Children are to be ruled by fear, but not by the rod; they are to be *threatened* with chastisement which they are never to receive; for it is a fear to be deeply engrained in the growing mind by horrific accounts of God's will with the evil-doer. Bedtime, for instance, is deemed a most suitable time to impress children with the punishments meted out to Cain and Esau, and the rewards to Joseph, by the all-seeing eye of divine justice 'so that this fear that comes from God, this complete fear, has possessed the boy and shakes his soul'. Only at fifteen will he be introduced to the New Testament where he will hear 'deeds of grace and of hell'. From this age softer counsels prevail as Chrysostom conducts the boy through his painful training as an athlete for Christ. Like so many sincere Christians since his day, Chrysostom had not fully appreciated the nature of the challenge with which the New Testament confronts the Old. He could not shake off the inhibitions created by his experience in the Roman schools in which most Christian leaders were educated. Hence he continued to hover in perplexity between the austerities of Proverbs and the implications for education of the redeeming love of Jesus and Paul.

AUGUSTINE

It was the humanity of Augustine (354-430) that resolved their bewilderment. Even his doctrine of original sin, an Augustinian invention, becomes a reason for the tender regard the teacher must have for his pupils. Augustine was that rare person who remembers childhood vividly but unsentimentally, even though, as he tells us in his *Confessions*, his earliest prayers were his 'childish inducements to God' to relieve his daily fears of the schoolmaster's rod. Far beyond any of his contemporaries Augustine is free from the illusion that chastisement in early youth is the way to learning. Rejecting Solomon he turns to the method of his Master who made himself 'weak to the weak that he might gain the weak'. In his writings *On Christian Doctrine* and *On Catechising the Uninstructed* he asks teachers to appeal to the pupil's curiosity, to stir his intelligence by simplicity of exposition, by kindliness and reasonableness, and suggests that when we fail 'we rather ought to address ourselves to God for him than address much to him concerning God'.

Thus does Augustine present us with the wholesome view of the teacher-pupil relationship as 'a dwelling in each other', a two-way movement of sympathy that affects the pupil while the teacher speaks and the teacher while the pupil learns.[4] The essential disciplines of study are no longer the crude products of oppression but the expression of reciprocal service and affection. Nevertheless, as Augustine takes pains to impress on his natural son Adeodatus, the inner power of the pupil to apprehend truth is not Aristotle's 'rational principle within us', but the Holy Spirit, the Master Himself 'who dwells within and gives me counsel about words spoken externally in the ear'.[5] By thus confronting the teacher with the Pauline concept of the pupil's body as the temple of the Holy Spirit, Augustine elevates the teacher's vocation immeasurably; and in thus establishing the inherent dignity of the human person he joins with Plato and Aristotle to demonstrate that in the practice of education the person that matters most is the person to be educated.

Augustine was a teacher on the universal scale; like Isocrates, Plato and Aristotle, he laid the foundations of a new civilization. He was both the founder of western Christianity and the bridge between the classical and the Christian worlds. In him we see the unification of the Graeco-Roman and Hebrew traditions: his writings are the primary source of Christian theology. In the monumental vision of his *De Civitate Dei*, the *City of God*, he portrays earthly kingdoms in an international order of neighbourly concord and in this gives birth to a Christian theory of the

[4] W. J. McCallister, *The Growth of Freedom in Education*, p. 96.
[5] 'The Teacher', in J. H. S. Burleigh, *Augustine. Early Writings*, VI. p. 101.

state. Through his monastic foundations at Tagaste and Hippo, and through the monastic life he himself followed as bishop of Hippo, he became the father of western monasticism. Friedrich Heer says of him: 'The staggering breadth of Augustine's experience is the explanation of his enormous influence on orthodox and nonconformist thinking during the ensuing fifteen hundred years. He became an inexhaustible source of ideas for every direction and grouping in later Christianity largely because virtually everything could be found somewhere in his work: the defence of reason and of authority, of free will and predestination in its harshest form . . . he was the father of western enlightenment and of every intellectual rebellion in our history.'[6] Amidst his greater labours he found time to write tenderly about the education of children. On all counts he was the greatest teacher of his age.

[6] F. Heer, *The Intellectual History of Europe*, p. 21.

6 *The Middle Ages*

THE SCHOOLMASTERS

Our knowledge of schools and schoolmasters in the Middle Ages is very limited, and what we know serves to emphasize the truth of Coulton's judgement that this was a period of convalescence, no less in education than in secular society. In feudal England, which we may safely regard as not untypical of the European social condition, the total population never exceeded that of twentieth century south Lancashire. Plague, malnutrition and poverty shortened the expectation of life and restrained population increase; the feudal structure of society tied the thinly distributed rural population to the land. It was not only poverty but attitudes deeply embedded in feudal society that held back social and educational advance. As late as 1391 the Commons petitioned Richard II 'to ordain that no serfe or villein henceforward put his children to school'; and it was not until the Statute of Apprentices in 1406 that the disapproval of the feudal landowner was legally ignored in the interests of a Church that required clerks for its own purposes. On the continent the separation of the soldier-landowner, the clergy and the peasant was even more definite; but Coulton observes that even the democratic author of *Piers Plowman* regarded it as a topsy-turvy world where 'bondsmen's bairns be made bishops', although this was an extremely rare happening and for Langland probably 'a manner of speaking'. Coulton reminds us that 'That jealousy of primary education which remains one of the vividest political pictures in the minds of those who remember the struggle of 1870 and the following years, must be multiplied fourfold when we think ourselves back to the Middle Ages'.[1]

[1] *The Medieval Village*, p. 254.

Throughout Europe education was entirely controlled by the Church; and although the condition of medieval society did not encourage the growth of schools, there would have been no schools at all but for the Church's concern for a continuing supply of literate clergy. The monasteries confined instruction mainly to their own oblates and novices and contributed little to the education of the laity.[2] Nevertheless it was in the monastic schools, and especially through the monks of Celtic Ireland in the seventh century, that learning was preserved. From the twelfth century the secular schools of the cathedral chapters, although immediately concerned to educate boys for the priesthood, began to instruct local pupils in Latin, the rudiments of Christian belief, the Bible and probably singing. In his scholarly little book[3] J. Lawson thus summarizes the general situation in medieval England: 'Schools with a permanent existence were few and mostly in the towns; elsewhere they tended to be sporadic and intermittent. London with a relatively large and wealthy population of 50,000 had five established schools in 1446. A moderately-sized town of 2,000 inhabitants might contain no more than 20 or 30 boys whose parents could afford book-learning. An isolated village with 10 or 20 families would not muster enough children to warrant a school, even if poverty had not excluded one. . . . The schools we know most about are grammar schools and of these we know little enough.'

Thus any picture of the teacher in these remote times must be based on scanty knowledge, inference and surmise. We can imagine the master of novices teaching the oblates the rules of his Order, the forms of the liturgy and prayers and selected passages from the Bible; and the village priest, Chaucer's devoted Poore Persoun of a Towne, or the parish clerk, imparting the elements of the faith and of the Bible to a group of his most promising youngsters in a corner of the church; or the much more important *magister scholarum* or *scholasticus* of the cathedral school, the prototype of the grammar school master, teach-

[2] See G. G. Coulton, 'Monastic Schools of the Middle Ages', in *Medieval Studies*, No. 10, 1913.

[3] *Medieval Education and the Reformation*, 1967, pp. 4-5.

ing Latin to boys preparing for the Church's service, and also to boys in the neighbourhood whose merchant fathers could pay the fees. In Chaucer's day the complaint of the early fourteenth century monastic chronicler Higden that the schoolmaster compelled his scholars to construe Latin into French, a relic of Norman England, no longer held good; but we have it on Chaucer's authority that the *clergeoun's felawe* in *the Prioresses Tale* sang the hymn to the Virgin with little understanding—'I learne song, I can but small grammere'—which suggests that the teaching left something to be desired. The school of the 'little clergeon' would be the song school which prepared boys for the grammar master in the cathedral school, hence this criticism may not be warranted, for the song school was the elementary school of the time whose main object was to train choir-boys not Latinists. Bishop Grandison of Exeter has severe things to say on this count, when he gives instructions to the schoolmasters of his diocese: 'We ourselves do strictly command and enjoin and warn that they should not, as hitherto, teach the boys whom they receive as grammar pupils only to read and learn by heart, but rather that they should make them construe and understand the Lord's Prayer, the Ave Maria, the Creed, the Matins and Hours of the Blessed Virgin and decline and parse the words therein, before permitting them to pass on to other books.' Indeed, the bishop declares that he will not confer clerical orders on boys so taught.[4]

In the later Middle Ages, when expanding commerce demanded literate clerks to deal with a town's trade we have a clearer picture of the town grammar master serving the interests of local patrons by teaching Latin, reading, writing and calculation to the sons of the burgesses. His was a monopoly employment, licensed by the bishop or town ordinance, which guaranteed him a stipend from fees by forbidding the encroachments of all other competitors in the grammar school field: 'The right to keep a school was then a privilege as exclusive, and sometimes as lucrative, as the landlord's right to keep a mill' writes Coulton.[5]

[4] See G. G. Coulton, *Medieval Panorama*, pp. 15-16.
[5] See J. Lawson, op. cit., pp. 12-16.

Throughout these twilight years of schooling we occasionally catch glimpses of teachers of whom, by reason of their eminence or piety, some records remain. It was written of Egbert, friend of the Venerable Bede and founder of the cathedral school at York, that no pupil went to his rest before the master's hand was laid in blessing on his head. In his panegyric on Egbert's successor Albert, Alcuin refers to his beloved master as 'a good man and just, broad, pious and kind, who moistened thirsty hearts with divers streams of teaching and the various dews of learning'.[6] He refers to the 'stream' of the fifth century *trivium* and *quadrivium*—grammar, rhetoric and logic, the elementary and basic subjects for beginners; music, arithmetic, geometry and astronomy, for the early equivalent of our sixth formers. But when called to be Charlemagne's Minister of Education Alcuin was less concerned to preserve these relics of pagan schooling than to imbue his pupils with the seven gifts of the Holy Spirit, the seven pillars of the Christian life—Wisdom, Understanding, Counsel, Fortitude, Knowledge, Righteousness and Godly Fear. Alcuin was a true disciple of Augustine. He was also a prolific producer of school books, on grammar, orthography, general knowledge, even arithmetical puzzles of considerable ingenuity—*Problems for Sharpening the Wits of Youth*—all devised to ease the path of learning for his aristocratic pupils in Charlemagne's Palace School.

Around 1000 A.D. we find Aelfric, Abbot of Eynsham a renowned teacher, writing of his master Aethelwold 'it was ever sweet to him to teach youths and little ones, to explain their Latin books to them in English . . . and to allure them by cheerful words to study improvement'.[7] Aelfric himself wrote a book for children, a simplified version of the standard grammars of the fifth century, Donatus and Priscian, which dominated the teaching of grammar for a thousand years. He writes in English 'so that you may be able to instil both languages, Latin and English, into your youthful minds'. He was clearly a teacher of resource for he brought the Direct Method to the teaching of

[6] A. F. Leach, *Educational Charters*, p. 13.
[7] A. T. Drane, *Christian Schools and Scholars*, p. 219.

Latin in *The Colloquy*, which aimed at bringing some reality and fun into the classroom by dialogues dealing with the everyday life of his pupils, e.g.

Master: Were you flogged today?
Boy: I was not because I was very careful.
Master: How about the others?
Boy: I daren't tell you our secrets.

Over a century later we find Archbishop Anselm, when Abbot of Bec, chiding a fellow Abbot for beating his novices in the monastery school: 'You beat them, you tell me. But is a beautiful statue of gold or silver formed only by blows? The weak must be treated with gentleness and won by love; you must invite a soul to virtue with cheerfulness and charitably bear with its defects.' And again, jumping the centuries, we find another great teacher in John Gerson (1363-1429), famous chancellor of the University of Paris, who said 'If I want to be useful to children then it is necessary to adapt my habits to theirs; and that I step down in order to lift them up'. A teacher, he writes in his treatise *On Leading Children to Christ*, 'will never penetrate the shyness of children unless he smiles kindly at the laughing ones, encourages those who play, praises their progress in learning and when remonstrating, avoids all that is bitter and insulting'.[8]

These were the great ones of whom we know something. Of their humbler colleagues in these times we know nothing, except what they taught. We know that teachers, whether monk, priest or layman, were usually unsparing of the rod, as Solomon advised, and that the discipline they exerted had changed little since the days of Orbilius Plagosus. Indeed, Ratherius, Bishop of Verona who lived in the tenth century, wrote a little book with the humane title Spare-the-Back (*Spara-dorsum*) hoping that its helpful advice might spare schoolboys from the birch. In these brief glimpses of greater men we see that most appealing of all

[8] Translated by R. Ulich in *Three Thousand Years of Educational Wisdom*, pp. 181-90.

concepts of the teacher—the teacher as father of his flock, the man holding together a community of young people. We shall meet him again.

THE SCHOOLMEN

We turn now to the most representative teachers of the later Middle Ages, the schoolmen who moulded the intellectual revolution which dominated European learning from the twelfth to fourteenth centuries. The schoolmen attempted to construct a logical system of knowledge by the fusion of philosophy and theology, a process which resulted in all secular and philosophical problems becoming theological. In the ancient schools of the cathedral chapters scholars had developed a method of instruction similar to that of Socrates—question and answer, catechism and dialectic—but with this difference: whereas Socrates was willing to take the argument withersoever it might lead, the schoolmen usually knew the answers before the argument began. They were not therefore very good philosophers. But we must remember that they were faced with two obstacles: in the first place the limits of the search for truth were set by the Church and restricted to the Word of Scripture, the teachings of the Fathers and to the imperfect works of Aristotle then available. With notable exceptions—Grosseteste, Roger Bacon and Ramon Lull who will be mentioned later—the schoolmen indulged in little investigation of the concrete facts of physical existence. The Church forbade the study of medicine or anatomy and suppressed all ideas of the cosmos that were not biblical or Aristotelian.

Moreover until the middle of the twelfth century, the works of Aristotle were known only in the fragmentary Latin translation of Boethius who lived in the sixth century. Not until the second half of the twelfth century did Aristotle's major philosophical works appear via Arabic translations of Syriac versions imperfectly turned into Latin by Christian scholars in Spain. Improved Latin versions appeared in 1267 translated directly from the Greek by William of Moerboeke, Dominican Archbishop of Corinth and friend of Aquinas. Thus Thomas Aquinas had available the first competent version of Aristotle's works, which enabled him to engage upon his task of building Aristotelian philosophy into the Church's structure of belief. Aristotle, says Haskins, 'through his compact, clear cut and systematic style of presentation, appealed to an age which loved manuals and text-books and found these under Aristotle's name in almost every field of philosophy and science'.[9]

From this world of the schoolmen emerged the two pre-eminent teachers of the Middle Ages—Peter Abelard and Thomas Aquinas. To understand the controversies in which these two men were involved we must return to Anselm of Bec, later Archbishop of Canterbury (1033-1109), who began the great debate of the Middle Ages when he restated Augustine's famous declaration *credo ut intelligam*, 'I believe in order that I may understand'. In thus reaffirming faith to be the growing point for a full comprehension of God, an undisturbed faith that nevertheless seeks to understand, Anselm established a delicate balance between faith as the 'inward spaciousness' in which alone reason can work, and reason itself. Not to put faith first, he said, is presumption; not to appeal to reason is negligence; for to understand one's faith is to draw nearer to the sight of God. First, then we believe the mysteries as given to us in the revelation of the Scriptures; then we seek to understand what we believe.[10]

PETER ABELARD

Here was substance enough to set the stage for the dramatic controversies of the twelfth century. For men took sides: was the believing heart or the doubting mind the pathway to truth? The debate is still with us, but not conducted with the incredible acrimony that dominated the bitter conflict of two great figures: the Cistercian Bernard of Clairvaux (1091-1153) who fought for the primacy of the heart; and the Breton scholar Peter Abelard

[9] *The Renaissance of the Twelfth Century*, p. 342.
[10] See Etienne Gilson, *The History of Christian Philosophy in the Middle Ages*, p. 129.

(1079-1142) for the primacy of mind. Abelard secures our attention not only for his daring logical incursions into the very citadel of Christian belief, but also because as a superb teacher he gained such ascendancy over the minds of European youth.

First we must take a brief glimpse at the age in which his life was set. The twelfth century was remarkable not only for the intensity of its intellectual activity, but also for the astonishing physical mobility of its people in all classes. Crusaders, pilgrims, merchants and craftsmen, monks, wandering teachers and scholars, passed without hindrance across a Europe without frontiers. New manners, customs, knowledge and ideas were exchanged between east and west in the restless coming and going. It was an open century, audacious and enterprising in its adventure as it was uninhibited in its thinking. And it was a century, in this respect like our own, when 'youth made its first appearance on the European stage'. This was a theologically minded youth, asking questions and demanding answers more satisfying than those proffered in the older unadventurous theology that had dominated Europe since the days of Augustine. For the most part these young men were the unbeneficed clerks of the cathedral schools. Pre-eminent among them was the School of Chartres whose reputation for higher learning was soon to yield pride of place to the School of Notre Dame in Paris. Until the early years of the century Chartres had been the centre of unrestrained intellectual inquiry, the *intellectibilitas* that sought 'a perception of God, the Cosmos, nature and man through the exercise of the understanding'. Her scholars established relations with the Arabic and Jewish scholars of Spain and the translation of Arabic works became a major scholarly industry. Even the Koran was included for the information of the West.[11]

In the early twelfth century Paris took over the intellectual leadership of Chartres and of France—and France of Europe. The schools multiplied. Not much equipment was required to establish a school of theology and philosophy. Just a hall, a lectern and a lecturer. For all knowledge was in books, handwritten on parchment, and therefore costly and scarce. This fact

[11] See F. Heer: *The Intellectual History of Europe*, p. 109.

determined the manner of teaching, thus described by Johan Huizinga in his essay on Abelard:

For a proper understanding of the twelfth century one must imagine a society in which books are rare, those who can read them are also rare, and those who can explain them are even rarer. Hugh of St. Victor explains the use of the word *lego* in the language of the school: *lego librum*—I read the book myself; *lego librum illi*—I explain it to someone else, I give a course on it; *lego librum ab illo*—I hear him explain it, I follow his lecture. The rarity of books and the art of reading gave an extraordinary effect to the word of the master. For us, flooded as we are by the stream of words in print and on the air, the word is losing more and more of what is basically still a magic effect. In a more primeval society the word falls on a virgin soil thirsting after fecundity, it convinces and commands, it banishes and binds, in short, it effectuates. The authority of the few masters who have a command of it is extraordinarily great. Every master is more or less of a wonder. He knows, he has secrets that he will reveal to us if we propitiate him.[12]

We have a first-hand description of a young scholar's life at this time in the autobiography of John of Salisbury (1120?-1180), illustrious churchman, friend of Thomas à Becket and witness of his martyrdom. The extract refers to the years 1136-1147:

'When I was a lad I first went into Gaul for the cause of study. I addressed myself to the Peripatetic of Palais (Abelard) who then presided upon the Mount Saint Genovefa, an illustrious teacher and admired of all men. There at his feet I acquired the first rudiments of the dialectical art, and snatched according to the scant measure of my wits whatever passed his lips with entire greediness of mind. . . . I applied myself for the full space of two years to practice in the commonplaces and rules and other rudimentary elements, which are instilled into the minds of boys and wherein the aforesaid doctors were most able and ready; so that methought I knew all these things as well as my nails and fingers. This at least I had learned in the lightness

---

[12] Johan Huizinga, *Men and Ideas*, p. 188.

of youth to account my knowledge of more worth than it was.'[13]

It was this Peter Abelard, most renowned among the freelance teachers of the century, who in 1113 had set up his school on the Mont Saint Geneviève overlooking the rival school of Notre Dame. Students came from all Europe to hear this master of dialectic submit the obscurities of the Church's Fathers to logical analysis. But this was not his only appeal to the expectant youth of western Europe. They saw him as a new phenomenon among scholars; not an aloof theologian defending the faith from the seclusion of the cloister, but a fearless critic alive to the corruptions of the church and to the unexamined superstitions of monkish teachers, and also a poet whose love songs were sung in the streets of Paris. Even the dark scandal of his misadventure with Héloïse, although widening the circle of his enemies, did not obscure the philosopher and the man. In Abelard, it has been said, 'there was not only a deeply serious theologian and a great philosopher, but also a knight, an artist, a schoolmaster and a journalist'.[14]

Abelard's dialectical method became the model for the scholastics of the next two centuries. The method of inquiry is best seen in his work entitled *Sic et Non*, Yea or Nay, written to exemplify and explain his principle that 'constant questioning is the first key to wisdom. For through doubt we are led to inquiry, and by inquiry we discern the truth.' In *Sic et Non* he selects 158 contradictory statements of the Christian Fathers and submits them to logical analysis. For example—'Should human faith be based on reason or no?'—the issue we remember raised and answered by Anselm. Again, 'Is God a substance or no? Is God the author of evil or no? That works of mercy do not profit those without faith, or no?' To none of these questions does Abelard give an answer. His intention was to demonstrate a method essential to the discovery of right answers. It was a textbook of classroom method, not a statement of belief. But in

[13] R. L. Poole, *Illustrations of the History of Medieval Thought and Learning*, 1920, p. 177.
[14] Huizinga, op., cit., p. 188.

effect it was also an exercise in scepticism that profoundly
shocked his orthodox contemporaries. Abelard's method is an
admirable means of teaching and learning so long as the material
to be examined embraces a comprehensive range of knowledge.
This condition, as we have seen, did not exist in his time. Hence
this skilled use of dialectic was deployed in too narrow a field to
provide any scientific system of knowledge. For the schoolmen
any argument was conclusive if it was founded in formal logic.[15]

To understand the impact of Abelard on the minds of his
young followers we must picture to ourselves the publicity of
the learning situation in his time. The twelfth century was a
Homeric age in which personal prowess was up for proof and
challenge in personal contest: the knight in armour fought in
the tournament, the scholar in the hall of disputation. In this
game Abelard was supreme. But it was not his professional skill
and elegance of exposition, not even his intellectual arrogance,
that evoked the condemnation of Bernard and his traditionalist
followers, all faithful to their Augustinian allegiance; it was
Abelard's ruthless subjection of hallowed doctrine to the scalpel
of reason. This man, thundered Bernard, 'is content to see nothing
through a glass darkly, but must behold all face to face; his
shameless curiosity attempts to penetrate even into the untouch-
able heart of God'. Even the central mystery of the Trinity, and
the ancient teachings of the Church's Fathers on redemption and
damnation, are not exempt from his probing intelligence.

Bearing in mind that this was the twelfth and not the twentieth
century one can sympathize if not agree with Bernard's anxieties.
The extent of Abelard's heretical modernity may be judged
from his arguments in *Theologia Christiana* (1124). The question
is: are the unbelievers who had no chance of knowing Christ
irrevocably damned? Let an authority explain:

'The principle that unbelief excludes unbelievers from the
kingdom of God remains intact, but who are the unbelievers?
What about the pagan philosophers, for example; do they deserve

[15] See C. H. Haskins, *The Renaissance of the Twelfth Century*,
pp. 353-5.

this name? Reaching back across the centuries to join the most liberal theses of Saint Justin, Abelard makes sure that those of them who led a more chastened life received from God a certain light of truth. They knew that there was only one God; some of them, as is apparent from reading Saint Augustine, had a presentiment of the dogma of the Trinity, or even the mysteries of the Incarnation and Redemption. Since God revealed the essential of the saving truths to the Jews by the Prophets, and to the pagans by the philosophers, they are not to be excused if they did not listen to the teaching of their masters; on the contrary, those of them who did listen were certainly saved. Abelard considers that many pagans and some Jews were saved, and among the pagans, the Greeks first, then the Latins who followed their doctrine. . . . Abelard concludes: "We find that their lives, as well as their doctrine, express to the greatest degree evangelical and apostolic perfection, that they deviate but little or not at all from the Christian religion, and that they are united with us not only by their ways of life, but even in name. For we call ourselves Christians because the true wisdom, that is, the wisdom of God the Father, is Christ; we therefore truly deserve the name of philosophers if we truly love Christ."[16]

So Socrates and the Hebrew prophets are saved! Even in our day there are still people who doubt it.

Bernard condemned Abelard as a heretic and a corrupter of youth. We remember another great teacher who was condemned for urging young men to ask questions—in the fourth century B.C. Nevertheless Bernard's position does explain what the conflict was about. In essence this was a contest for the minds of Europe's youth. Bernard saw in Abelard the architect of betrayal, the conspirator bent on destroying ancient wisdom and piety by intellectualizing, and therefore de-Christianizing, theology. But Abelard was not the monster his enemies portrayed him to be. His astringent intellect concealed a sensitive spirit seeking only to see truth in its nakedness and power. He too was deeply involved in the education of youth and with an agonizing concern for their spiritual welfare. 'He aimed,' says Heer, 'at pure

[16] Etienne Gilson, *History of Christian Philosophy in the Middle Ages*, 1955, p. 162.

knowledge and a purified faith; he could not see God as the Lord of Dread, *Rex Tremendae Majestatis*, menacing mankind with slavery; for him God was pure spirit, burning with the refining fire of the Holy Ghost. God as spirit gave himself to mankind in two precious gifts, reason and love.'[17]

The last twenty years of Abelard's life were lived in misery and persecution. In 1140 the final blow came when Bernard contrived his condemnation as a heretic. He was banished to a monastery; his books were burned; Innocent II assisted at the burning at St. Peter's. He died in 1142 at the abbey of Cluny whose Abbot Peter treated him with love and honour. Friends conveyed his remains to Héloïse, now abbess of the convent of the Paraclete founded by her Abelard, and in 1164 she was interred in the same grave. After strange vicissitudes their bones found a final resting place in Père-la-Chaise cemetery in Paris.

But the spirit of Abelard was not consumed in the papal bonfire. His influence was enduring. As a thinker he rationalized theology and defined the course which scholasticism was to take. He bequeathed to scholarship, says Gilson, 'an ideal of technical strictness and exhaustive justification . . . and imposed an intellectual standard which no one henceforth cared to lower'.[18] As a teacher he had no equal in his day. The sad course of his relations with Héloïse bears the mark of Greek and Shakespearian tragedy and serves to emphasize his humanity. He was, wrote G. G. Coulton, 'the John the Baptist of the university movement, the last of those of whom it can be said that, wherever they were, a sort of university gathered round them . . . greatest among those who by teaching at Paris raised that cathedral school so high above the rest that it became naturally the first French university'. When after grievous persecutions and disgrace he sought rest in the wilderness near Troyes, pupils still scented him out. Their faithfulness Abelard thus describes in *Historia Calamitatum* 'Here, instead of spacious houses, they built themselves little tabernacles; for delicate food they ate nought but herbs of the field and rough country bread; for soft

---

[17] *The Medieval World*, p. 83.
[18] Op. cit., p. 162.

couches they gathered straw and stubble; nor had they any tables save clods of earth.'[19]

ST. THOMAS AQUINAS

No churchman since Augustine has had so enduring an influence on education as St. Thomas Aquinas (1225-1274) whose works, produced during a lifetime of tremendous literary activity, form the basis of Roman Catholic religious philosophy. Because his massive logical system in the *Summa Theologica* sets forth a complete philosophy of man, it becomes a work of great educational significance and is still one of the foundations of Catholic thinking on education as represented, for instance, in the neo-Thomist writings of Jacques Maritain and others of that school. Indeed, St. Thomas's influence is greater today than it was in the Middle Ages.

What chiefly concerns us here is the argument proceeding from the Thomist view of man as God's highest creation—created in the image of God, the only part of the creation endowed with the unique gifts of intelligence and will. The argument proceeds something like this: Because man is intelligent he is also a responsible being, self-determining (*dominium sui*), in charge of himself, even committed to making himself. Just as man is the highest part of creation so are intellect and will the highest powers of personality; to the degree that the powers of the intellect and will are perfected so is human personality perfected. And only through the co-operation of will with intelligence can truth and goodness and love, the supreme moral values of the Christian faith, be established in the human person.

The raw material of education, then, is the imperfect individual human person. The goal of education is the perfection of human personality. The method of education is to train the pupil's mental powers, as yet but in the germ; to start him along the path towards self-mastery and self-formation by informing his reason, by forming his conscience and by enlarging his under-

[19] G. G. Coulton, *Medieval Panorama*, Vol. II. 1938, cheap edition 1961, pp. 17-18.

standing. The immediate or practical objective of education is to establish good habits, which St. Thomas calls virtues. The virtues are both intellectual and moral: through good intellectual habits the intellect is strengthened and progressively enables the pupil to see the truth; through habituation to good moral habits the appetites are trained to enable the pupil to do what is right. The last and greatest virtue is wisdom, which is 'the habit by which we are able to know the first causes of things . . . the kind of knowledge whereby many conclusions are brought together in terms of relatively few general principles'.[20] Without equal development of both mental and moral habits education is not possible.

How then does this high philosophy penetrate to the lowly schoolroom? What human relationships are involved in pupil-teacher relationships? Where is the emphasis placed in the processes of learning and teaching? To begin with, because each child is unique and by definition no two uniques are alike, children are not equal, but nevertheless equally deserve the teacher's respect for what Maritain calls their 'mysterious identity'. Again, because the child is 'self-forming' he is the primary agent in his education; but because he is not complete but rather in a state of becoming, he is free only to do what he ought to do.

Similarly, the relationship of teacher and pupil must be founded on love, but because children are born 'not free but freeable; not perfect but perfectible' the teacher's part is to co-operate with the pupil's autonomy (an important word in the Thomist vocabulary).[21] Submission, then, is the child's path to freedom, but the Thomist teacher's task is always to stimulate a child's self-determining capacity. It is interesting to relate this Thomist view to the modern issues of discipline and self-discipline referred to in Chapter 17 below. The danger of all authoritarian doctrines is that when practised they tend to forget

[20] R. P. Joly, *The Human Personality in a Philosophy of Education*, 1965, p. 134.
[21] See W. Lawson, 'Neo-Thomism', in *Education and the Philosophical Mind*, ed. A. V. Judges, 1959.

the desired end which the exercise of authority is expected to achieve. Jacques Maritain, whose Neo-Thomist views on education hold many attractions, does not see the teacher as an authoritarian figure but as a 'ministerial agent' who 'comforts the mind of the pupil by putting before him the logical connections of ideas which the pupil's mind may not be strong enough to establish by itself'.[22] But, of course, the teacher is more than this: he is the representative, the exemplar, of Christian culture, of its faith and order of values, without which the pupil is deprived of the ultimate truth on which his progress towards personal completion inevitably depends.

It is not surprising that the Thomist view of education has not only informed the practices of the Catholic teaching Orders and the teachers in our own Catholic schools, but, modified and sometimes obscured in Protestant guises, has been the acknowledged antagonist of all subsequent naturalistic and pragmatic views of education of modern times. The theme of the autonomy of the child has in practice taken many forms; it seems to be as easily adaptable to the theory and practice of Dewey and A. S. Neill as to those of the Jesuit schools, and strange to say, appealed to as readily by the authoritarians as by all libertarians since Rousseau. Our views obviously depend on what we mean by autonomy, self-development and freedom!

The characteristic feature of scholasticism, said Professor John Adams, 'is an excessive development of form at the expense of matter'. This defect had an inhibiting influence on the progress of education for several centuries, for it conditioned a conservative profession with habits that took long to eradicate. In the grammar schools of the later Middle Ages the study of grammar, for instance, was treated in the formal manner in which it appealed to the mature mind. Vives criticized the schools of the later Middle Ages for perpetuating this error, for continuing 'the old trick of the schools', of throwing all knowledge into dilemmas for the sake of disputation. Boys left school, he said, conceited, argumentative, loud and self-assertive, proud

[22] *Education at the Crossroads*, p. 31.

to be smart and ingenious rather than well informed.[23] Thus the object of study became less important than the manner of studying it, and the teacher was concerned less for his own and his pupil's knowledge of language than for his logical exposition of its grammar. This may have been excusable in the era of the schoolmen for the amount of knowledge to be learned was, as we have seen, woefully limited.

NEW WAYS OF THINKING

Nevertheless there was new light breaking through even during the golden age of scholasticism when Aquinas was completing his monument to reason. Were the first gleams seen in the Christian pantheism of St. Francis, whose stigma witnessed to his suffering for Christ, for whom the earth was sister and mother, the fire his brother, and who sang his canticle to the sun? If the lastingness of a teacher's lessons are a measure of his greatness then Francis was the greatest teacher of the Middle Ages. We see an echo of his reading of the book of nature in the words of his scholarly disciple Bonaventura (1221-1274) who declared that 'the created world is like unto a sort of book in which the Trinity that made it is read'. Here is the new theme: can there be full understanding of the divine image without knowledge of the world God had made?

The answer was given by the group of Franciscan scholars at Oxford, who were stirred to scientific inquiry by the study of Arab and Jewish texts and almost certainly by the presence of a Jewish community at Oxford itself. The scientific tradition was founded at Oxford by Robert Grosseteste, later bishop of Lincoln, whose studies in the properties of light, included experiment and inductive inquiry based on mathematical principles. His pupil Roger Bacon, (1214-1294) also a Franciscan, sold his birthright to engage in pseudo-scientific studies which evoked the ridicule of teachers and students and landed him in prison. His was a very medieval type of science, inherited from

[23] W. H. Woodward, *Studies in Education during the Age of the Renaissance*, 1906, p. 202.

the twelfth century, an odd mixture of chemistry, alchemy, astrology and honest mathematics used to plumb the mysteries of the natural world. Like Leonardo he had visions of a technical world of the future—self-propelled ships, submarines, aeroplanes—and desired that boys should be taught how to experiment in school.

We must not regard this early probing into the nature of the physical world as the birth of modern science, although it may have some claim to be that. The object of these medieval investigators was wholly religious: to liberate theology from the shackles of formal logic, to purify learning, and to arm Christendom against Islam with a more persuasive weapon than the swords of illiterate crusading gentlemen.[24]

In the fourteenth century these aspirations were gathered together in the work of the Catalan Ramon Lull (1232-1316) whose life is one of the epics of the Middle Ages. We find him in the courts of princes and papacy, in the lecture halls of Paris, in the streets of African cities and in the end tortured and dying for his faith on his last missionary voyage in his eighty-third year. In intervals of almost ceaseless travel and adventure he engaged in prodigious intellectual and literary activity and two hundred works, including a novel, are attributed to his name.

The aim of this remarkable man was the same as that of Roger Bacon. On Mount Randa near his birthplace in Majorca there came to him a vision of a system of universal knowledge whereby theology and science were united: 'It seems as though a light had been given me with which to discern the divine perfections, as to some of the properties and their mutual relationships.' In his *Ars Magna*, which followed this illumination, he attempted by an intricate process of co-ordinating elements in ethics, theology, philosophy and natural science, to discover a unifying theme between their 'mutual relationships'. One result was an amazing machine: 'It consists essentially in circles in which are inscribed the fundamental concepts, in such a way that by combining the various possible positions of these circles with regard to one another, one can automatically obtain all the relations of concepts corresponding to the essential verities of religion.'[25] This

[24] See F. Heer: *The Medieval World*, pp. 240-5.

must have been the first exercise in what today we call computer construction. He had in fact attempted to combine in a single system of knowledge all the secrets of nature which the human intellect can comprehend. Lull was profoundly concerned with education. He founded schools believing that they should not only teach morality and science but that the world of Jews and Muslims should be revealed to children as part of the enlightenment that was to bring to birth an era of universal peace.

The last of the schoolmen, William of Ockham (d. 1349?) still further disturbed orthodox thought when, during a life of controversy, he insisted that the dogmas of the Church cannot be proved by logic but only accepted by faith, whereas philosophical problems must be examined by reason. This view enabled scientific enquiry to be carried on without any restraining theological presuppositions. Even more interesting is his speculation that 'there is nothing in the understanding that was not previously in the senses', for in these words he foreshadows the philosophy and psychology that prompted men to seek knowledge outside the confines of logic in the natural world and in human behaviour.

The speculations of Roger Bacon, Ramon Lull and William of Ockham, so far removed from the classroom, may seem to be irrelevant to the work of the teacher. But they belong here because they were among the influences that marked the final breakthrough from the medieval to the modern world. These three men were among those forerunners in the study of the natural world who not only revealed new things to know but also new methods of coming to know them. Over the next two centuries their confused beginnings culminated in the more precise formulations of Francis Bacon and Descartes. Thus Ockham takes us along the line of educational thought through Erasmus and Vives to Locke and beyond.

[25] See Etienne Gilson, pp. 351-2.

PART III

The broadening of the teacher's role

In the European Renaissance of the fifteenth and sixteenth centuries it became the task of Christian humanist scholars to reconcile classical modes of thought with the Christian faith. The harmony thus achieved produced teachers of genius, both schoolmasters and educational reformers. Pre-eminent among the former were the Italian Vittorino da Feltre and the Englishman Richard Mulcaster, who first among schoolmasters brought new dimensions into the schooling of boys and the broader purposes of education. Vittorino appeals as the true father of his flock; Mulcaster presents us with the humane austerity of the reforming headmaster. Among the reformers Erasmus and Vives remain supreme. The finest scholar of his age, the humanist prophet of Christian reason and enlightenment, the critic of obscurantism in the Church and of pedantry in school, Erasmus strove to bring humanity and sanity into the conduct of education. His friend Vives was the first teacher-philosopher since Plato and Aristotle to 'psychologize' education, to relate teaching to the teacher's understanding of his pupils, to establish learning on the pupil's experience of his own familiar world, and to envisage the schoolmaster as a professional practitioner. Typical also of the best in Renaissance humanism was the Frenchman Montaigne who exposed the pedantry of schoolmaster grammarians and revived the ancient theme of education for 'wholeness' with wisdom, humanity and wit. Finally in the sixteenth and seventeenth centuries teachers are called upon to play special roles in periods of religious and social stress: as defenders of the faith and as custodians of the morals of the young. These are no more than isolated examples of distinctive roles teachers are called upon to play in the changed circumstances of today.

7 *The teacher as humanist*

When we turn from 'the exhausted themes of the unseen, super-sensible universe' of the schoolmen to the Renaissance in Italy and northern Europe we seem to enter a recognizable world, a way of feeling and thinking more like our own. Pico della Mirandola (1463-1494) touches a sympathetic chord in our minds as he did in his contemporaries when he portrayed man as little lower than the angels and master of his own destiny: 'I created thee a being, says the Creator to Adam, neither heavenly nor earthly, neither mortal nor immortal only, that thou mightest be free to shape and overcome thyself.' Slowly during the fourteenth and fifteenth centuries men were thus becoming conscious of themselves as individuals and also of the visible and audible world around them. Of Alberti it is said that at the sight of noble trees and waving corn he shed tears; of Leonardo (1452-1519) that he bought caged birds for the joy of setting them free. From a scholastic theology men were turning to the exploration of observable facts, and to the literatures of the ancient world where men lived not as souls to be saved but as beings endowed with gifts for limitless exploitation. In Italy the ancient theme of *areté* was reborn in *l'uomo universale*, the man of many gifts— the soldier, the courtier, the scholar, the lover of the arts. There was little in this new world that had no roots in the Middle Ages. It was a flowering of earlier perceptions, less a revival of antiquity than a recognition of its unity with the temper of the Italian people.

Thus this gradual awakening of men to a new view of man was not merely a product of scholarship which revealed earlier and greater civilizations and a more congenial way of life to men bored by medieval inhibitions. In Italy it was to a high degree a spontaneous and native growth, slower in its ripening than the outburst of genius in fifth century Athens, but similar in character. Men like Giotto, Leonardo and Michelangelo had no need to copy the Greeks. Nevertheless the humanist scholars were indeed exploring the classical languages and learning from the ancient masters, acknowledging both their profounder humanism and also their more scientifically structured modes of thought. But the classical literatures were pagan, and devout Christian scholars saw in this enthusiasm for a non-Christian way of life a disturbing menace to Christian morality. There was indeed in the riotous life of the Italian cities sufficient proof that this inflation of human personality portended a weakening in moral standards, which had never been very high. It thus became one of the accepted tasks of the Christian humanist scholars of the fifteenth and sixteenth centuries to harmonize classical studies with Christian piety, a task, of course, that had been undertaken by pious men since the days of Augustine, but they were dealing with a more boorish people than the elegant sons of fifteenth century courtiers.

Fortunately, the sincere interest of the more cultivated parents of the Italian Renaissance in the education of their children came to their aid. Pre-eminent among these men was the gifted Florentine Leo Battista Alberti (1404-1472) a fine example of *l'uomo universale*—athlete, musician, writer, architect, mathematician, but above all a man who with sympathetic intensity entered into the whole of life around him. He was deeply concerned with education in the home and, in his *Trattato della Curia della Famiglia*, models the parent-teacher on the elder Cato who trained his son not only in letters but in self-control, frugality and physical fitness. His is in some ways a more rounded conception of educating for 'the whole man' than any conceived in Greece: Plato's 'care of the body for the sake of the soul' we see reflected in Alberti's insistence that 'no end may be preferred to that of physical soundness; . . . and letters stand in harmony with gentle manners; they dignify the mind and add grace and might to personality'.[1]

[1] W. H. Woodward, *Studies in Education During the Renaissance*, pp. 60-1.

There were then, in an age continuously receptive to new ideas, a group of men who made enduring contributions to the theory and practice of education. They were not always original in their thinking, the influence of Plutarch and Quintilian is plainly evident in their writing, but old ideas were easily adapted with imagination and humanity to what they deemed to be the needs of their time. Even earlier than Alberti, Vergerio (1349-1428), teacher of logic at the university of Padua, and Vittorino's most beloved master, had outlined the first humanist adaptation of the Greek education for 'wholeness' in his declaration on liberal studies:

'we call those studies *liberal* which are worthy of a free man; those studies by which we attain and practise virtue and wisdom; that education which calls forth, trains and develops those highest gifts of body and mind which ennoble men, and which are rightly judged to rank next in dignity to virtue only. For to a vulgar temper gain and pleasure are the one aim of existence, to a lofty nature, moral worth and fame. It is, then, of the highest importance that even from infancy this aim, this effort, should constantly be kept alive in growing minds. For I may affirm with fullest conviction that we shall not have attained wisdom in our later years unless in our earliest we have sincerely entered on its search.'[2]

But these men were not schoolmasters. Who was to translate these liberal ideas into the fabric of a real school? Fortunately the man was at hand in the great teacher who was Vergerio's pupil. We turn, then, to Vittorino and to the picture of a good man and a scholar nurturing youth in the intimate setting of a school which was also a home. This to my mind is the most appealing, the most effective because the most humane, form of schooling to be found in the annals of education; and in Vittorino is the perfect image of the schoolmaster as father of his flock.

[2] W. H. Woodward, *Vittorino da Feltre and Other Humanist Educators*, p. 102.

THE FIRST MODERN SCHOOLMASTER

Vittorino (1378-1446) was born in the hill town of Feltre on the northern fringe of the Venetian plain. In 1423, after twenty years at Padua and Venice as student and teacher he received an invitation from the Marquis Gonzaga, Lord of Mantua, to undertake the education of his family. 'I accept the post,' said Vittorino, 'on this understanding only, that you require from me nothing which shall be in any way unworthy of either of us; and I will continue to serve you so long as your own life shall command my respect.' These were the circumstances in which Vittorino began the last and longest period of his life as scholar and schoolmaster. Housed in Gonzaga's villa *La Gioiosa*, the *Pleasure House*, ingeniously renamed *La Giocosa*, the *Pleasant House*, Vittorino collected his pupils from the family of Gonzaga, and other patrician families, from his own friends and from among the gifted sons of the poor of Mantua, insisting that the rich should pay their fees. He stripped the house of lavish furnishings without despoiling it of its beautiful proportions and established a remarkable community of masters and boys in which the privileges of rank had no place.

At the age of forty-six Vittorino was already one of the most distinguished teachers of the New Learning. But above all things it was his desire to inform classical learning with the Christian spirit. Between the best of classical humanism and Christian teaching he saw no contradiction. He and his pupils attended Mass daily at the cathedral; alongside this pious observance he held before them the stoical philosophy and Cicero's *humanitas* as ideals worthy of their regard. In this Christian setting his pupils studied classical literature, history and philosophy, in which Vittorino was careful to match the literary excellence of the text with its ethical value. To these studies were added arithmetic and geometry applied to mensuration and surveying, natural history and carefully supervised instruction in music and choral singing. The humanist educators shared with Plato the suspicion that music can both debase and purify the passions of the young. In the hands of Vittorino and his assistants this was no mean or narrow curriculum, except, perhaps, that all teaching was in Latin at a time when the Italian vernacular was becoming a popular means of communication.

The education of the body was also Vittorino's concern, not only as an aid to study but because the Greek ideal of bodily perfection fitted well into the humanist view of courtly education of which he approved. His régime was neither spartan nor indulgent. He supervised the boys' diet with care. An interesting instance is recorded: two of his pupils were the sons of his patron Gonzaga; Ludovico was lazy and fat, Carlo full of nervous activity but physically delicate. Therefore he induced Carlo to eat more and Ludovico to eat much less, with successful results in each case. He encouraged all manner of games and athletics and took his pupils on strenuous three-day tramps in the mountains. In one respect he departed from Greek attitudes to physical training for he was less interested in individual athletic prowess than in toughening young bodies to endure hardship.

But Vittorino had higher aims than the production of scholars and courtiers. To live with him in *La Giocosa* was a moral experience that touched every part of a young man's physical, mental and religious life. His English biographer thus portrays the sort of school it was:

'His school entirely absorbed him. He watched the youngest with affection and hope, the elders with pride and confidence. Himself moving always amid the larger things of life, the power that went forth from him insensibly raised the tone of thought and motive in those around him. His singleness of purpose was quickly felt, and a word or even a glance of disapproval was, with the keenly sensitive Italian youth, often sufficient to bring tears of shame and repentance to the eyes of a culprit. Living a common life with his scholars in meals, in games, in excursions, always sharing their interests and pleasures, his control over the sixty or seventy boys under his charge was such that harsh punishments were not needed. Naturally quick-tempered, he had schooled himself to a self-control which never gave way except in face of irreverence or looseness. Corporal punishment was very seldom resorted to, and then only after deliberation, and as the alternative to expulsion. For ill-prepared work the penalty imposed was the compulsory re-learning of the task after school hours. But it was part of Vittorino's purpose to attract rather than to drive, and to respect the dignity and the freedom of his boys. So he refused, after fair trial made, to force learning upon an unwilling scholar, holding that nature had not endowed all with taste or capacity for study. . . . If any fell ill his care was unremitting. Indeed the tie of personal affection which united him with his pupils was manifest in all relations. His keen desire for their progress, and his pride in it; his peculiar insight into individual character; the absence of all considerations of self, so affected the methods of discipline that in the truest *La Giocosa* was an ideal school, and, so far as a school ever may be, an ideal home.'[3]

Thus in Vittorino seemed to be assembled most of the attitudes of a great teacher. He was a scholar and in touch with the rife ideas of his age; he gathered from ancient wisdoms what was relevant to his schoolmaster's task but without slavish imitation. Slight in stature, modest but vital in manner, his penetrating and musical voice added to his great personal charm. He was that rare headmaster who evoked the confidence of parents and the affection and respect of his pupils. He knew them well, because he taught them seven hours a day and because he loved them. Although greatly learned he was a humble man, and nothing he exacted from his staff and pupils in the way of personal disciplines did he fail first to demand of himself. He ruled neither by precept nor by the birch but by example, and in so doing Vittorino redeems the schoolmaster from the contempt with which his profession has been burdened for centuries before and since his day. And so we can say with confidence that *La Giocosa* was the finest school of the Renaissance; and it is difficult to discover a better school in the centuries that follow, if we are to judge a school on the quality of its scholarship and the humanity of its disciplines.

On the broader stage of European education we must also discern in Vittorino's work the rejection of that peculiarly medieval conception of moral training that stressed the fateful

[3] W. H. Woodward, *Vittorino da Feltre*, 1905, pp. 34-36.

disharmony of body and spirit. An ascetic himself, he never-theless had little sympathy with the medieval ascetic ideal; at heart a monk, by nature an aristocrat, and living in a profligate age in which fame was the spur, he was yet able to demonstrate that Renaissance education need not involve self-conceit and irreligion, and that not every humanist was obsessed with the lust for personal fame. Perhaps that is one reason why he wrote nothing; or why nothing he wrote has survived.[4]

ERASMUS AND VIVES

Even in Vittorino's day there were signs that the Renaissance schools were forsaking the humane study of the ancient literatures for the narrower disciplines of grammar and style. To compose Latin in Ciceronian perfection was more important than to discover the meaning of *humanitas*. This we have seen, and still may see, is one of the fates of great literatures and great causes when entrusted to a profession too often resistant to the impact of a new idea. And so it was with the Renaissance schoolmaster, who relapsed into the ultimate sin against literary culture by treating literature merely as language, and teaching like Seneca's false schoolmasters 'for the classroom not for life'. It was to stem this retreat from Vittorino's example that two humanist scholars, Erasmus the Dutchman and Vives the Spaniard, attemp-ted to raise the teacher's gaze towards a nobler view of his duties. In the eyes of these men the revival of humane letters, the reform of teaching in the schools and universities and the pre-paration of a more skilled generation of teachers, were instru-ments for restoring health to an ailing Church.

Erasmus was born in 1466 at Rotterdam, son of a priest and a physician's daughter. He died at Basel in 1536. In his address *In Commemoration of Erasmus* (1936) Johan Huizinga asks why the world cannot forget this man, so much of whose work is now outdated. It is true that to some significant aspects of his time Erasmus seems to have been indifferent : to the great aesthetic movement that in the minds of most of us is the true

[4] See *Cambridge Medieval History*, Vol. VIII. pp. 705-10.

mark of this age, he made no contribution; of the first strivings of science he was hardly aware and foresaw none of their consequences; he was less interested in Columbus than in the Argonauts. His admirers can only answer that genius is not only expressed in the arts and sciences. St. Paul, for instance, was probably lacking in aesthetic sensibility. In some respects Erasmus was not unlike Paul, with the difference that his intellectual roots were in the classical not the Hebrew world. Nevertheless, Erasmus possessed the prophetic quality of interpreting some if not all of the signs of his times. He was acutely aware of his age as a climacteric period in European experience in which new knowledge and a new culture might release men from war, political division and famine, and from what he regarded as the vulgar philistinism of the wealthy middle classes of northern Europe. Above all he saw the Church freed from falsehood and obscurantism by a renewal of spiritual power founded on reason and humanity. This is the sphere in which Erasmus was at home: 'We cannot forget him because he stood for a rare quality of mind, an attitude of the intellect, that in the realms of religion and culture constituted the very essence of Renaissance Europe: the noble proportion, the clarity, the simple dignity, the high seriousness, the deep longing for an eternal unity in all things.'[5]

Erasmus was educated under the distinguished scholar and schoolmaster Hegius in a school of the Brethren of the Common Life at Deventer, and although critical of his schooling, especially of its harshness, he admits that here he found his enduring interest in classical studies. At the age of thirty-three he visited England and began his life-long friendship with the Oxford humanists Sir Thomas More and John Colet, founder of St. Paul's School. For some years he was Lady Margaret Professor of Divinity at Cambridge. Among his English humanist friends Erasmus found congenial spirits striving like himself to rid primitive Christianity of the ecclesiastical accretions that had obscured the witness of its early years. Their object was to reveal the origins of the Faith by a disciplined historical and

[5] J. Huizinga, op. cit., p. 324.

philosophical study of the Greek and Hebrew texts of the Bible. In effect these men were seeking answers to simple but profoundly disturbing questions that are still with us: What is the true Christian life as revealed in the Gospels? What did Christ and Paul teach to the people of their time?

The first twenty years of a century that was to be a period of religious conflict and war were for Erasmus years that held a golden promise of light to the dark places of Christendom. These were the years before the forces of reform had split into the forces of Protestant Revolution and Counter-Reformation. Before Luther had nailed his challenge on the church door at Wittenburg in 1517, Erasmus had written three works which set the direction of his life as a teacher, not in the schoolroom for he never taught children, but as the teacher of an age. In 1509 appeared his *Praise of Folly*, a satirical broadside in praise of the ruling power of stupidity in high places. Princes, bishops, popes, scholastics and grammarians, rich and poor, all are shown to be in bondage to Folly. No rank or vocation is spared. In 1511 his keen interest in John Colet's project at St. Paul's prompted him to write, in addition to several textbooks, a treatise on *The Right Method of Learning (De Ratione Studii)*. In 1516 from Froben's famous press at Basel came his edition of the Greek Testament, 'doing more to the liberation of the human mind, from the thraldom of the clergy,' writes one biographer, 'than all the uproar and rage of Luther's pamphlets'. This and his edition of Jerome's Vulgate was the first piece of biblical scholarship to reveal the inaccuracies of St. Jerome's version, then as now the Bible of the Roman Church. Thus in these brief years of comparative calm the course of Erasmus is set: to fight ignorance and superstition with the weapons of ridicule, commonsense and sound learning; to supplant the narrow education purveyed by the grammarians with a literary culture founded on the noblest achievements of the classical authors.

Viewed through the rose-tinted spectacles of the humanist the ancient world was indeed the New World, the world he wanted his own world to become. Any doubts concerning the incompatibility of pagan and Christian cultures were allayed for Erasmus and his friends by the conviction that there could be no antagonism between Christianity and intelligence. Erasmus was always the 'man of letters' before he was a scholar; scholarship was to be an instrument in the service of God, in the cultivation of personality, in the enlightenment both of the rulers and the communities they ruled.

But there were enemies to be suppressed. First the upholders of a dying scholasticism 'who think they support the Catholic Church with propositions and syllogisms no less than Atlas is feigned by the poets to sustain on his shoulders a tottering universe . . . with discoveries that had never come to light if they had not struck the fire of subtlety out of the flint of obscurity'. Second, were the 'Ciceronians', second-rate thinkers who forbade the use of any vocabulary, phrase or style not found in the works of their master. This fettering of the flexible Latin tongue to a purely imitative language not only kept the mind in bondage but was dangerous on the deeper level of actually paganizing Christian teaching. Complete subjection to Cicero was for Erasmus a betrayal of Christ, for nowhere in pagan writings does the Christian God or Christian doctrine hold a place. Against these enemies he wrote the dialogue on *The Ciceronians*, a bitter satire in which he pillories them with a *reductio ad absurdum* when, for lack of a better way, they substituted the deities of the pagan pantheon for the most sacred names of the Faith: God the Father became Jupiter; Christ became Apollo; for the Virgin we must read Diana. How ridiculous can we get? The creed would run as follows: 'The interpreter and son of Jupiter Optimus Maximus, our Saviour and our sovereign, according to the responses of the oracles (Holy Ghost?) came down to earth from Olympus, and having assumed human shape, of his own free will sacrificed himself for the safety of the republic. . . .' This was part of the war Erasmus waged against the humourless stupidities of the intellectuals who mistook language for life.

It is not then surprising that Erasmus, like his friend John Colet, should call upon schools and schoolmasters to serve in the cultural and religious revolution for which he longed. His purpose was not only to produce scholars but men conditioned to live responsibly in a civilized community. True, we must sow the seeds of piety, he says; and so engage our pupils that they may love and learn the liberal studies; but we must also prepare them for Christian citizenship. Your children, he writes to parents, 'are not begotten to yourself alone, but to your country; not to your country alone, but to God'.[6] Here is a new image of the teacher—a person of importance in the growth of a civilized society: 'which brings me', he continues, 'to claim it as a duty incumbent in Statesmen and Churchmen alike to provide that there be a due supply of men qualified to educate the youth of a nation. It is a public obligation in no way inferior to the ordering of an army.' This is one of the first declarations in modern times of the social role of the schoolmaster.

In the classical literatures, as we have seen, Erasmus found a record of human experience to which young people would eagerly respond, but like the Italian humanists whose homes he knew well, he placed the refining influences of a cultured home and parental example highest among the formative influences of education. He is repelled by customary methods of school discipline—'teaching by beating is not a liberal education'—and he rejects Solomon's rod for the greater wisdom of Quintilian and Vittorino. He has no patience with 'the stupidity of the average teacher who wastes precious years hammering rules into children's heads'; there are only three rules: 'understand, arrange, repeat'—as succinct a prescription for successful mental exercise as we are ever likely to get.

Erasmus distinguished three factors in the education of children: *nature*, or the innate capacity for being taught; *training*, the skilled management of instruction and guidance; and *practice*, the free exercise on the pupil's part of the energies he is born with. Let all three work in harness. We are not to hurry; we are to avoid difficulties which can be safely by-passed; free school tasks from toilsomeness, and give to learning the joy that comes from achievement. Here Erasmus is not commending a gentler

[6] *De Pueris Instituendis:* W. H. Woodward, *Erasmus Concerning Education*, p. 187.

and more rational pedagogy on merely humane grounds, he is insisting that teaching will be more *effective* if teachers make use of their pupils' inclination to respond to demands on their intelligence and self-respect. He is appealing for a new type of schoolmaster who respects learning so much that he is willing to share it with those he teaches. And on the grander scale of values his image comes to us down the years as a man of intellect whose clarity of mind in ethical and rational judgements might bring some light to a world in greater danger than his own.

But Erasmus' thinking on education although invariably humane and sensible was defective on two counts. He failed to realize that the culture of the ancient world was unlikely to appeal to the expanding middle classes of Western Europe whose 'barbarism' he was so concerned to enlighten. Even more fundamental was his neglect of the vernacular languages as the proper teaching medium for the new age. Latin remained the language of international scholarship for another century; but the tongues of Machiavelli and Shakespeare, Cervantes, Montaigne and Luther, and the new vernacular Bibles of Protestant Europe, were already deciding that Latin, no matter how elegant and persuasive, was not to be the language of the future.

In 1519 Sir Thomas More wrote to Erasmus in praise of a young scholar named Vives, who was twenty-seven at that time: 'You will scarcely find one anywhere at so green an age,' he wrote, 'who has mastered so completely the whole round of knowledge.' Erasmus replied that Vives 'is one of the number of those who will overshadow the name of Erasmus'. This remark was more generous than true, but not perhaps in the history of education. Juan Luis Vives (1492-1540) was a Spaniard trained in the medieval scholastic philosophy at Valencia and Paris universities, and was at one time Fellow of Corpus Christi College, Oxford. At Paris he had forsaken the old scholasticism for the Christian humanism of Erasmus.

Vives brought an unusually imaginative and constructive mind to the problems of teaching. It was not enough for him to break away from the formalism of the grammarians or to join with Erasmus in humanizing instruction and discipline. He broke

new ground by turning to a study of the learning mind as the
first step to effective instruction, and for this revolutionary and
original advance we have good reason to regard him as the first
educational psychologist of modern times. He was the first to
examine empirically the areas of mental activity outside the
sphere of pure reasoning—sensation, and the separate senses,
memory, imagination, emotion and the association of ideas—
and, moreover, he conducted his inquiries in real classroom
situations by observation of mental processes as he saw them
functioning in his pupils. His claim to distinction rests, not on
his solution of problems that still vex us, but on the fact that he
was the first to recognize their existence. Teachers will respect
Vives all the more because his brilliant but tentative contributions to the psychology of learning were a product of his careful
observation and sympathetic understanding of boys.

Vives' foundation work on education, *De Tradendis Discip-
linis* (*The Transmission of Knowledge*), was published in 1531.
We are indebted to Foster Watson for an English version.[7] The
psychological bases of his educational theory were elaborated in
a later work *De Anima et Vita* (*On the Soul and Life*), published
in 1538. This was the first modern work on psychology: in it
Vives insists that psychological inquiry should concentrate not
on the *nature* of mind but on how it works. This strikingly
modern attitude establishes Vives as the forerunner of modern
empirical psychology and anticipates by three centuries modern
theories on the association of ideas: 'The course of learning,' he
writes, 'is from the senses to the imagination, and from that to the
mind of which it is the life and nature, and so progress is made
from individual facts to groups of facts, from individual facts
to the universal. This is to be noted in boys.'[8]

This first suggestion of the inductive method of learning, even
now but partially practised although an accepted principle of
modern pedagogy, came nearly a century before Bacon more

---

[7] *Vives: On Education*, 1913, which includes a translation of the *De
Tradendis*.
[8] *De Anima*, ii 8. Quoted by W. Boyd, *The History of Western
Education*, p. 180.

precisely defined the new way of thinking. In a remarkable passage Vives outlines with exciting exactitude the foundations of a science of education:

'In teaching the arts, we shall collect many experiments and observe the experience of many teachers, so that from them general rules may be formed. If some of the experiments do not agree with the rule, then the reason why this happens must be noted. If the reason is not apparent, and there are some deviations, they must be noted down. If there are more deviations than agreements or an equal number a dogma must not be established from that fact, but the facts must be transmitted to the astonishment of posterity, so that from astonishment—as has been the case in the past—philosophy may grow. All the arts connected with doing, or making things, are best acquired from observing the actions and work of those who have been best instructed in them by nature, study, and habit. From such inventors, as we have shown, the arts were born.'[9]

For one who has thus departed from the conventional way of teaching it is but a short step to turn to the world of facts upon which the pupil's mind may be exercised: the pupil 'should now begin to consider more closely human life and to take an interest in the arts and inventions of men: in those arts which pertain to eating, clothing, dwelling. In these subjects he will be assisted by writers on husbandry. Then he should pass on to those subjects which treat of the nature and strength of herbs, and of living animals. . . . He should not be ashamed to enter into shops and factories and to ask questions from craftsmen and get to know about the details of their work. Formerly learned men disdained to enquire into these things. . . . Thus ignorance grew . . . so that we know far more of the age of Cicero or Pliny than of that of our grandfathers.'[10]

It was bound to follow from this emphasis on the facts of contemporary living that Vives should regard the vernacular as an essential medium of learning. He was proud of his own

[9] Foster Watson, *Vives: On Education*, p. 87.
[10] Foster Watson, pp. 208-9.

Castilian and realized that only through their native tongue could the schoolmaster penetrate the understanding of his boys. Like other Christian humanists Erasmus had not dreamed of using any other language than Latin in the schools. Vives taught Latin to young children through the vernacular. He preferred good English, French or Spanish to bad Latin: 'Let the teacher know the mother tongue of the boys exactly, so that by means of their vernacular he may make his instruction easier and more pleasant for them.'[1]

In several ways, then, Vives revolutionized the contemporary image of the teacher. By 'psychologizing' education, he had drawn the attention of the schoolmaster away from subjects to be learnt to the individual boy who had to learn them; and he sought to turn the eyes of the grammar ridden schoolboy to the realities of his own countryside and of the home and community in which he lived. The schoolmaster emerges as a *professional* whose sights are raised beyond the grammar book to a study of the human material with which he has to contend; and to a recognition that there is a world of facts that are moulding his pupils' lives. In a practical but prophetic way Vives had prepared the ground for the realistic approach to education that increasingly caught the imagination of educators in the following century and far beyond. Even his remark on teachers' pay has its relevance: 'as much as a good man will desire but a wicked man disdain'.[12]

A GREAT ENGLISH HEADMASTER

We began this section on humanist teachers with an account of a great Italian schoolmaster. We conclude it with praise for a great English headmaster, a contemporary of Shakespeare, the first of a long line of men whom Englishmen regard as a peculiarly native product. Some would claim that Richard Mulcaster (1531-1611) is not a typical representative of humanist education, but in his work and writings there is sufficient evidence of influences

[11] Foster Watson, p. 103.
[12] Foster Watson, p. 57.

from Erasmus, Vives and his contemporary Montaigne to suggest that he educated boys in the true humanist tradition. Perhaps the doubt is due to the gap that often separates those who write about education and those who practise in schools. Mulcaster was headmaster of two of England's best known schools: for twenty-five years at Merchant Taylors' and from the age of sixty-four to seventy-five of St. Paul's.

Mulcaster lived at a time when cultivated men held very poor opinion of schoolmasters. In Europe Luther was not alone in describing them as 'tyrants and jailers who made schools nothing but dungeons and hells'.[13] Roger Ascham reveals royal Eton in no better case. Sir William Cecil reports that 'divers scholars of Eaton be runne from Schole for fear of beatinge'; and Ascham himself says 'Many schole-masters . . . be of so crooked a nature as, when they meet with a hard-witted scholar, they rather breake him than bowe him, rather marre than mend him'.[14] Similar views on the general run of teachers continue into the seventeenth century: 'the worst and unworthiest of men' says Sir William Petty in the middle of the century, incompetent and so badly paid especially at the primary level, that their meagre pittance had to be supplemented by other work. The abundance of books, many written by schoolmasters in this period—the most lurid as regards title being Thomas Grantham's *The Brainbreaker's Breaker* (1644)—refer both to senseless harshness and incompetent teaching. An astonishing demonstration of these censures appeared in 1661 when a group of Members presented *The Children's Petition* to Parliament, 'a modest remonstrance of that intolerable grievance our youth lie under in the accustomed severities of the school discipline of the Nation'. Dr. Busby of Westminster School, John Locke's headmaster, comes under especial condemnation. But the flogging schoolmaster could always appeal to Holy Writ for approval of his faithfulness to Solomon's advice. There were notable exceptions of more humane reforming headmasters during these years, among whom John Brinsley from 1600 to 1618 master of the grammar school

[13] F. Eby, *Early Protestant Educators*, p. 32.
[14] Aldis Wright, *English Works of Roger Ascham*, pp. 175-9.

at Ashby-de-la-Zouche, and Charles Hoole of Rotherham (1610-1667) were the most remarkable for their efforts to soften the prevailing harshness.[15]

It was towards the end of his headship at Merchant Taylors' that Mulcaster wrote his two long essays on the education of boys: *The Positions wherein those Primitive Curcumstances be examined, which are necessarie for the Training Up of Children, either for skill in their Books, or Health in their bodie* (1581) and *The First Part of the Elementarie* (1582). Mulcaster was one of that rare company of schoolmasters who was capable not only of recognizing a good principle of education even if it were a new one, but of adapting it to the practice of the classroom. It is his prophetic insight and his genius for seeing his job in the round that are so impressive: 'it is not a mind, it is not a body that we have to educate but a man, and we cannot divide him'. Here he echoes Montaigne. And two centuries before Rousseau loosed his *Emile* on Western Europe Mulcaster was reminding schoolmasters that 'ripeness in children does not come at the same time for all', that some are quick and some are slow, that teachers should 'wait on Nature' and by their professional skill 'help Nature to perfection'. His warning that 'hastie pressing onward is the great enemie' we have met before in Erasmus. There is a splendid sanity in his requirement that the best teachers, and moreover the best paid teachers, should teach the youngest pupils. His recognition of the need for professional skill in the teacher prompts him to make a reasoned plea for a training college. Even more astonishing when we recollect the enduring conservatism of the universities, and three hundred years before it came to pass, he suggests that they should establish teaching as a profession along with the professions of church, law and medicine. In the *Positions* Mulcaster gives reasons for his advocacy of the professional education of teachers that have never been bettered:

'Is the framing of young minds and the training of their bodies

[15] See E. B. Castle, *Moral Education in Christian Times*, 1958, pp. 90-102.

so meane a point of cunning? . . . He that will not allow of
this careful provision for such a seminarie of maisters, is most
unworthy either to have had a good maister him selfe, or here-
after to have a good one for his children. Why should not
teachers be well provided for, to continue their whole life in the
schoole, as Divines, Lawyers, Physicians do in their several
professions?'

This insistence on the proper preparation of the schoolmaster
for his job is one aspect of Mulcaster's conviction that not only
the quality of the teacher but the impact of an orderly school
community, must be part of the child's experience of education.
We may with reason suspect that this great headmaster of two
famous schools was no practitioner of a soft pedagogy and that
authority was established with no hesitant soul-searching. Mulcaster believed in *order*, in conformity to rules without sharp
edges; in uniformity of teaching method with suitable adaptations to 'age and aptitude'; in the seemly ordering of school life
so that his pupils knew just where they stood and where he was
determined to stand. And yet so comprehensive were his views
on the whole body of influences that help boys to grow up, that
he brought parents into conference with his staff, that they might
co-operate with the school, support its objects and introduce
into their homes the same ordered life—regularity in meal and
bed times, in prayer and church attendance.

Mulcaster's views on physical education were distinctly
'modern'. Centuries before we rid our schools of the drill sergeant
he declared that the man responsible for the cultivation of a
schoolboy's mind should also be responsible for the training of
his body: 'for how can that man judge wel of the soule whose
travell consisteth in the bodie alone?' He even brought order
into the frantic affrays that went under the name of football. He
invented the referee, a person 'who can judge of the play, and is
judge of the parties, and hath authoritie to commaunde'.

As we have said, this progressive conservative was no disciple
of the permissive school of discipline. He confessed to having
discovered no better weapon than the birch for the grosser school

sins. Agreeing that there are occasions for courtesy and gentleness in the intercourse of school life, like our own teachers associations and ministers of education he preferred the schoolmaster's discretion in the use of the rod to any decree against it: 'if that sceptre be thought too fearful for boyes . . . I will not strive with any man for it, so he leave us some means which in a multitude may worke obedience'. But sixteenth-century Mulcaster held one firm conviction that may still be a guiding line for some schoolmasters today: 'to beate him for learning which is willing enough to learne, when his witte will not serve, were more than frantike'.

Nevertheless, neither by temperament, training nor experience could Mulcaster deny that nature, child nature, was the foundation on which the good schoolmaster must strive to make the good man—'we cannot divide him'. 'Good nature', he says, is 'the maister's delite'; it is also 'the maister's *encouragement*, the childe's *ease*, the parent's *contentment*, the bannishment of *bondage*, the triumph over *torture*, and an *allurement* to many good attempts in all kinde of schooles'. But while recognizing this encouraging provision of nature he does not trust children 'to trot on before' as Montaigne would. Nor can we believe that the compulsive attraction of Vittorino was an attribute sweetly evident in the Englishman. Mulcaster's concern, equally great, was less gently manifested. His trust reposed less in his pupils' capacities than in the teacher's professional competence; his devotion to their welfare was expressed more in his own humane severity than in Montaigne's 'sweet severe mildness'. But he was a great schoolmaster; one of England's greatest.

8 *Education for life*

The vitality of the early Renaissance and the liberating ideas of Erasmus did not penetrate far into the mind of the average schoolmaster; nor did the Protestant call to individual piety bring any new dimension into the teacher's world. Characteristically unresponsive to new ideas, schoolmasters carried on the old routine of instruction and discipline in ways not markedly different from those of their medieval forerunners. There were also other influences encouraging the conservative attitude of schoolmasters. The progress of the Protestant Revolution from its first phase of struggle for freedom from papal control to the formulation of new creeds founded on scriptural authority, and the corresponding determination of the Catholic Church to combat heresy, resulted in education entering the arena on each side of the conflict. Later we shall see these influences operating in the schools of the Jesuits and in the educational plans of Luther, Calvin and Knox. In each case Christian faith was deemed to be founded on a knowledge of the languages of the Scriptures—Greek, Latin and Hebrew—which required many years of study to acquire even moderate competence, all the longer and more strenuous because of the archaic methods used by all but the most able schoolmasters. It was this narrow linguistic furrow that the schoolmaster was expected and was usually content to plough.

There were, then, reasons other than his own conservatism that restrained the schoolmaster from indulging in new ideas. In the first place the schools suffered from the characteristic tendency of all reforming movements to consolidate their initial success by clamping down on further advance. This usually ends in emphasizing means above ends; in the case of the schools it resulted in a concentration on linguistic study at the expense of a wider curriculum. In the second place, when education becomes a weapon in religious warfare the teacher with unconventional views on the content and method of instruction may easily be suspected of more sinful heresies. Thus by the end of the sixteenth century both Catholic and Protestant schools had forsaken the 'lettered piety' of Erasmus and Vives; and were settling down into a very solid and very narrow scheme of classical study.

EDUCATING GENTLEMEN

It was in protest against this linguistic strait jacket that a group of worldly wise men livened educational theory in the sixteenth century. None of them was a schoolmaster; all of them recaptured something of the humanist attitudes of the early Renaissance; all of them called for education, whether in home or school, more relevant to the specific needs of their day; all of them ridiculed the schoolmaster who beat grammar into sullen heads; all deplored the absence of good schools; all of them wrote in their own vernacular. Their plea was for a broader education that fused the literary aims of Erasmus and the more advanced methods of Vives with antique wisdom and social usefulness.

From the cultivated life of the Italian princely court came first *The Book of the Courtier* of Baldassare Castiglione (1478-1529), described by the Emperor Charles V as the 'finest gentleman of our time'. In this vivid portrayal of the ideal man Castiglione revives and enriches the image of Vittorino's scholar gentleman. It is far more than the conventional courtier that Castiglione portrays, for the court in the sixteenth century in England as well as in Italy and France stood 'for the central impulse and acknowledged standard of every higher activity of the community'.[1] The courtier is the gentleman and statesman, a man of action, at home in the literatures of the ancient world and of his own, a man in whom moral integrity, intelligence and statecraft are harmonized in gracious manners. *The Courtier*'s fame

[1] W. H. Woodward, *Education in the Age of the Renaissance*, p. 252.

in Europe was immediate and lasting. It was written in Italian in 1516, printed in 1528; rendered into French in 1538; into Spanish in 1540, into English in 1561, and Sir Philip Sidney carried it in his pocket as a social guide.

Three years after the publication of *The Courtier* Sir Thomas Elyot (1490-1546), not a university man but a pupil of the fine Greek scholar Linacre, Clerk to the Privy Council, published *The Boke Called the Governour* (1531). This was the first book on education to be written in English. Elyot brings to the Tudor court and to the rising middle class who were to assume increasing administrative responsibilities in the coming years, the concept of a liberalizing education that would prepare them for service to the state. His definition of the 'governour' was wide enough to include the highest officers of the crown, judges, ambassadors, sheriffs and the humbler J.P. It was a vocational education he commended, but only in the sense that it was to be a training in 'sapience' and 'prudentia', in courtesy, worldly wisdom and literary scholarship fitting for the cultivated man of affairs. He leans heavily on Quintilian and Erasmus for his programme but there are conspicuous deviations. He follows Vives in requiring that the mother tongue be used in the learning of Latin; from the ideals of Greek education he derives his enthusiasm for the cult of the body but gives all physical exercises an English flavour—shooting with the long bow, sword exercise, swimming and hunting; he diversifies the hard grind of learning languages with the introduction of drawing and music. But for the education deemed necessary to train his governors Elyot had no place for schoolmasters. Their contemporary performance did not secure his confidence: 'Lord God, how many good and clean wits of children be nowadays perished by ignorant schoolmasters.' And so, he prescribes the tutor 'of sober and virtuous disposition'.

The sad condition of the schoolmaster was a reflection, as it always is, of the social values of the society to which he belongs but also of the schoolmaster's own estimation of his duties. In the sixteenth century neither were commendable, and both had come under the condemnation of Erasmus and Elyot. The propertied classes, especially the country gentry, were remarkable for their boorishness and for their indifference to any excellence in a tutor or schoolmaster except his cheapness. And there were few schoolmasters at this time who could possibly have carried out Elyot's humane educational programme. They were either too ignorant or if learned they were pedants; and in any case not morally of the calibre to pass on to a future statesman either the humane wisdom of the ancients or the attributes of a gentleman. Moreover these blemishes in the average schoolmaster were not reduced by the religious revolution of the sixteenth century, whose leaders did little to arrest the pedantic treatment of the literary wealth of antiquity, being less concerned to release learning from its chains than to use it in support of the new doctrines.

THE SUFFICIENT MAN

The trend of education away from the strait-jacket of ancient authority and the schoolmaster's pedantry was accelerated by three Frenchmen—Rabelais, Ramus and Montaigne. The fantastic satires *Pantagruel* and *Gargantua* of Rabelais (1494-1553) were in fact a serious plea that the growth of a student's natural gifts should not be restrained by the formalities of his schooling, and that much neglected knowledge can be gathered from the facts of daily experience: 'Let there be no sea, river or pool of which you do not know the fishes. Learn about all the fowls of the air, all the shrubs and trees in forest and orchard, all the herbs and flowers of the ground, all the metals hid in the bowels of the earth.' Here is the voice of Vives speaking.

A greater man was Peter Ramus (Pierre de la Ramée, 1515-1572), generally recognized as the greatest scholar of the University of Paris, whose course was set when at twenty-one he chose the startling theme for his master's degree 'Everything that Aristotle said is false'. He was not then disapproving of Aristotle; he was in arms against the prevailing university attitude that was willing to accept opinion on authority. The human mind must be unfettered in its search for truth; he adopts the attitude and method of Socrates in pursuit of it, and in this is the forerunner of Descartes and Bacon. But equally important was the development from this position of his views on method. His object was to assure that all knowledge resulted in practice; grammar for instance in correct speech; logic in the proper development of argument; and instead of studying science in the books of Aristotle he requires the student to examine natural phenomena and draw conclusions from his observation. So one more contribution was made towards the movement away from an education founded on the uncritical appeal to authority. Ramus died a Protestant in the massacre of St. Bartholomew— the most original French scholar and the bravest defender of his principles in the sixteenth century.[2]

It was Michel de Montaigne (1532-1592) who most fervently criticized the teachers of the sixteenth century. He was able to measure their standards by his own felicitous education, rare in those times. Brought up in a family 'geared by his father to the production of a model child', where he learnt to speak Latin from infancy 'sans art, sans livre, sans grammair ou précept, sans fuet et sans larmes', he proceeded to the Collège de Guyenne at Bordeaux, a school remarkable alike for its scholarship and the personal distinction of its teachers. But Montaigne was always far more grateful for his father's upbringing than for the instruction he received at school. In his famous *Essays* he reflects critically on the meagre interpretation of the humanist tradition in contemporary schools, on the narrow classical curriculum, on the restrictive discipline and flogging and the bookishness of the school programme: 'Only the man who pictures to himself our mother nature in all her majesty and beholds the eternal variety of her face, who regards not only himself but even a whole kingdom as but the merest point, esteems things at their real worth. In fine, I would have the world my scholar's choise book.'

Montaigne is an enemy of the second-hand; 'the pupil must harbour nothing in his head by mere authority' for it is no sign of learning that a man 'yield up his meat even as he swallowed the same'. Knowledge is useless unless it becomes an enrichment

[2] See Barnard, H. C., *The French Tradition in Education*, 1922.

of the whole personality to produce 'a sufficient man rather than a bare learned man! . . . for it is not a mind, it is not a body that we erect, but it is a man, and we must not make two parts of him'.[3] Hence it is the teacher's view of what he wants his pupils to become that will determine what he teaches and how he teaches. Do we want a pedant or a wise man, who knows 'what it is to know and not to know; what valour, what temperance, what justice is?' It is the pedantic schoolmaster tied to his bookish routine who deprives the young of their right to become wise men: 'Does he know Greek and Latin? . . . what we really want to know is whether he is growing wiser.' We may say Cicero says this or Aristotle that, 'but what do we say of our own selves? What do we judge, what do we do? . . . Would I arm myself against the terror of death? I do it at Seneca's expense. Do I crave consolation for myself or a friend? I borrow it from Cicero.'

This distinction between knowing the text book and being wise dominates Montaigne's views on the method of instruction. He insists first that every lesson should be regarded as an opportunity not for memorizing the words of wise men but for exercising the pupil's reason and judgement; and secondly that knowledge that cannot 'be compassed by reason' cannot be attained by force and constraint. In a passage from the essay *On the Institution and Education of Children* Montaigne delightfully summarizes his theme of 'a sweet severe mildnesse' in the rearing of children, and incidentally expresses his low opinion of the average schoolmaster in the 'Colleges' of his time:

'As for other matters, this institution ought to be directed by a sweet-severe mildnesse; Not as some do, who in lieu of gently-bidding children to the banquet of letters, present them with nothing by horror and crueltie. Let me have this violence and compulsion removed, there is nothing that, in my seeming, doth more bastardise and dizzie a wel-borne and gentle nature: If you would have him stand in awe of shame and punishment, doe not so much enure him to it: accustome him patiently to endure

[3] *Essays* I. 25.

sweat and cold, the sharpnesse of the wind, the heat of the sunne, and how to despise all hazards. Remove from him all nicenesse and quaintenesse in clothing, in lying, in eating, and in drinking: fashion him to all things; that he prove not a faire and wanton-puling boy, but a lustie and vigorous boy: When I was a child, being a man, and now am old, I have ever judged and believed the same. But amongst other things, I could never away with this kind of discipline used in most of our Colleges. It had peradventure been lesse hurtfull, if they had somewhat inclinde to mildnesse, or gentle intreatie. It is a verie prison of captivated youth, and proves dissolute, in punishing before it be so. Come upon them when they going to their lesson, and you heare nothing but whipping and brawling, both of children tormented, and masters besotted with anger and chafing. How wise are they, which go about to allure a child's mind to go to his booke, being yet but tender and fearefull, with a sterne-frowning countenance, and with handsfull of rods?'[4]

Montaigne, then, prefers the pupil to 'trot on before' but the teacher to keep good hold on the reins.

[4] *Essays* I. 25.

9 *Defenders of the faith*

Despite the heresies that so frequently beset it the medieval Church had little need to defend its faith, only to explain it, for there was rarely a powerful religious competitor within or without the Church to dispute its divine authority. The universal Church was there, as much a part of men's lives as the changing seasons; the only enemy within the fold was man's sinfulness, with which the priesthood were properly equipped to deal; the only opposition came from princes who disputed the Church's worldly power but not its right to teach eternal truth and to decide man's ultimate destiny. But in the fifteenth and sixteenth centuries there appeared heresies that seriously threatened the ancient institutions of Christendom. These dangers were the fruit of the northern Renaissance which in the starker lands beyond the Alps had assumed a more sober vein than its fore-runner in Italy. The assault on papal authority called the Reformation, more accurately described as the Protestant Revolt, was a challenge to the Roman Church's claim to be either universal or the sole source of Christian truth.

Thus there emerged a situation of conflict in which the Church was called upon to defend its faith against heresy, and the heretics were challenged to defend their newly found religious freedom. In each camp education was used as a weapon of defence and the teacher was called in to play his part. In this way a new concept of the teacher was born: he was to be, with pastor, priest and soldier, a defender of the faith accepted by the community he served. In the plans of Luther, Calvin and John Knox on the one side, and in the schools of the Society of Jesus on the other, we can see the new concept at work.

THE PROTESTANT TEACHER

The Lutheran revolt had replaced the authority of a universal Church with the authority of a Book, and Luther at first believed that if the common people of Germany could read the Bible in their native tongue the Protestant religion would continue on firm foundations. In 1520 he had declared the Scriptures to be a sufficient vehicle of salvation, but after the Peasants' Revolt of 1525, which he ruthlessly opposed, he doubted the wisdom of putting such social dynamite into the minds of the ignorant poor and in 1530 decided that his revised catechism was a less explosive medium for imparting such Christian doctrine as was necessary to salvation. His attitude to the central requirement of Christian education is summed up in his own interpretation of Paul's reference to 'the nurture and admonition of the Lord': for 'nurture' Luther prescribed an education in Christian doctrine as presented in his catechism; by 'admonition' he refers to the terrors of divine judgement on the sinner. His catechism was to be used in preference even to the Gospels for religious education in both home and school.

Through all his writings there runs the theme that only by a thorough moral and religious education can the new Church and the Reforming states of Germany hope to generate a new type of citizen. It is to his credit that he declared the vocation of teaching only second to that of preaching, although he was unable to do much to raise the lowly status of the teacher. With the help of his scholarly contemporary and friend Melancthon he planned a system of Protestant schools throughout Germany, based on three principles: the first, that the study of the classical languages was basic to the understanding of the Scriptures; the second that in some measure education should be open to any social class; the third that it was the duty of the secular authorities to provide schools.

This programme was not strikingly successful for two not very admirable reasons. First, Melancthon's insistence that 'the truths of religion and moral duty cannot be rightly perceived except by minds soundly prepared by a training based on the practice of past ages', resulted in a narrow linguistic training in his new secondary schools which made no appeal to the burghers of the German cities and ended in producing a generation of teachers chiefly concerned to teach Latin grammar.[1] The second cause was Luther's increasing subservience to the secular arm on which he depended for the political success of his religious revolution. He had tied himself to the chariot wheels of the princes. When he died his church had become little more than a department of state in which both pastors and teachers were civil servants. It can hardly be claimed, then, that he met much success in this attempt to organize the teacher into a lay priest in defence of the faith. Planning with a keener cutting edge was required and this was supplied for the protestant cause by Calvin, and for the Roman Church by Ignatius Loyola.

The formidable logic of Calvin's blend of Protestantism, elaborated in precise detail in his *Institutes of the Christian Religion* (1534), written when he was twenty-six and already renowned in theological polemics, became a far more potent adversary in the religious contest. At Geneva Calvin reversed Luther's solution to the problem of relationship between church and state by creating a theocracy in which the elders of his Reformed Church ruled through the civic power in all matters pertaining to religion and conduct. From 1541 until his death in 1569 Calvin maintained a ruthless supervision of private morals involving penalties for moral backsliding unparalleled for their severity in any form of puritanical tyranny. His rules for the conduct of schools were much more humane but involved strict supervision, unbreakable routine, complete suppression of individuality, although free from deliberate harshness. Teachers were in effect the lay officers of the Church, as much subject to its discipline as its pastors. Thus the whole purpose of the city's government and schools was concentrated on a single aim: 'to sustain the Church unharmed'.

From Geneva the principles of Church and school government

[1] See W. H. Woodward, *Education in the Age of the Renaissance*, Ch. XI.

spread to other countries where Calvin's doctrines claimed
adherents—to the Reformed Churches of France and Holland,
to the Puritans of England but particularly, under the influence
of John Knox (1505-1572) to the Presbyterians of Scotland. Knox
in exile at Geneva had been a close co-operator with Calvin
for several years and on returning to his native soil was determined to establish education as the willing servant of a god-
fearing state. In the *First Book of Discipline* he planned a
system of schools under Church control, which, says Dr. William
Boyd, 'for its breadth and comprehensiveness has no peer among
the educational proposals of this period'. The scheme advocated
'the assumption of direct responsibility for the schools by the
Church, the equal care of all children irrespective of sex or
social class, the attempt to direct education to social ends by
making it culminate in a training for the service of church and
state'.[2] The *Book of Discipline* was not accepted by the Church
or the Scottish Parliament, but its influence penetrated deep and
played no small part in confirming the reverence for learning
among the Scottish people. No one can say that Calvin's doctrines have not had strong survival value north of the Border.
Thus throughout Europe it was not Lutheranism but Calvinism
that became the spearpoint of the Reformation, and its tenacity
was due not only to the gloomy doctrine of 'the elect' but to the
recognition that teachers in schools and universities, when conditioned by disciplined instruction, had their part to play in
propagating and defending the faith. This truth was recognized
with even more single-minded conviction by the priestly soldiers
of the Counter Reformation, who were preparing their campaign
to defend the Roman Church while Calvin was establishing his
grim theocracy at Geneva.

THE JESUIT TEACHER

On the Feast of the Assumption 1534, in the crypt of the
Church of the Blessed Virgin in Paris, Ignatius Loyola (1491-
1556) and five student companions of the University of Paris,

[2] W. Boyd, *The History of Western Education*, p. 201.

among whom was the saintly Francis Xavier, pledged themselves to absolute obedience to Christ. At this meeting was
planned the foundation of the Society of Jesus, to be recognized
by the Pope in 1540. The Society proved to be one of the most
potent instruments in restraining the tide of reforming Pro-
testanism. The story of Ignatius, the Spanish soldier, is moving
and remarkable. During the period of recovery from a severe
wound received at the battle of Pampeluna he underwent a deep
religious experience that impelled him to forsake a soldier's
life and to enter upon eleven years of patient study in preparation for service to the Church. At forty-three his real life's work
began.

Although it was originally far from his intention that his
newly formed Society should wage the war against Protestant
heresy, he had eventually come to realize that the formidable
intellectual power and religious fervour which directed the Protestant Revolt could only be combated by equal scholarly competence and devotion. Under this conviction he entered upon
a crusade in which higher education and absolute religious
obedience were to be the means to victory. In this aim the Jesuits
were supported by the reforming elements within the Church,
and at the Founder's death in 1556 the Society of Jesus had
organized over a hundred schools and colleges in Western
Europe. By the end of the century this number had doubled and
in the eighteenth century there were over 700 schools and semi-
naries, spreading from the Atlantic coast to the borders of Russia
and into the outposts of the New World.

This extension of the Jesuit schools and the maintenance of
their standards over so long a period is one of the epics of
educational history. The success of the movement is largely
attributable to the genius of its founder, to his limitless idealism,
to his remarkable ability to choose co-workers as able and dedicated as himself, and to the exacting devotional and intellectual
disciplines the rules of the Order imposed. In 1599, over thirty
years after his death and following fifteen years of critically
observed experience, the Society issued the *Ratio Studiorum*
(Plan of Studies) which was a set of regulations establishing in

the smallest detail a uniform system of education in all Jesuit schools throughout the world. Every duty of the teacher, every aspect of school management and discipline, the curriculum and teaching methods, the system of rewards and punishments, even the approved manner of marking exercises, were prescribed in detail.

All Jesuit teachers were trained for their profession: 'It would be most profitable for the schools,' reported the committee which had been appointed by Aquaviva, the General of the Order, to draw up the Plan of Study, 'if those who are to be Preceptors were privately taken in hand by someone of great skill and for two months or more were trained by him in the method of reading, teaching, writing, correcting and managing a class. If teachers have not learned these things beforehand, they are forced to learn them afterwards at the expense of their scholars.'[3] The Jesuits were the first organized educational body to realize that teaching is a skilled craft demanding professional training. Teachers were chosen with great care and worldly wisdom; Ignatius himself once said that 'a comely presence for the edification of those with whom we have to deal' had its value in the classroom. In spite of the strictness of the school régime the relationship between teachers and boys was usually friendly and touched with respect and affection.

When even the enemies of the Jesuit Order praised its schools, as Voltaire did 'for the care spent on us', we may conclude that the teacher as a defender of the faith need not necessarily be a joyless pedagogue concerned only with indoctrination. But it is difficult to believe that the teacher who plays this role can ever be free, or enable his pupils to be free, to loose the bonds that inhibit the free exercise of individual mental initiative. There remains the nagging question: should it ever be the function of the teacher to defend and propagate a particular faith, whether it be religious, political or social? If we believe that this is a worthy role, then we shall go far before we see it better portrayed than in the schools of the Jesuits, in which we see the first instance in educational history of a body of men, unpaid, highly com-

[3] Quoted by W. Boyd, op. cit., p. 206.

petent and entirely dedicated to the education of boys within the limits imposed by a strictly regulated system. They succeeded where Luther failed; but John Knox was a close competitor in the Protestant field.

10   *The custodian of morals*

Throughout educational history, and especially in the history of religious institutions, there have always been systems of education whose aim has been to protect children from the errors of false belief or from the temptations of the world. This theme we have seen in Plato's guarded education, in the efforts of the Christian Fathers to preserve Christian children from pagan ways of life in a non-Christian world, in the monastic and cathedral schools of the Middle Ages, in the fatherly oversight of Vittorino and in the Calvinist and Jesuit schools. Other versions of it appear in the education of Rousseau's *Emile*, in the denominational education in England during several centuries, and in the ideological emphasis of communistic education in our own century. Even in the freedom-loving schools of the 'new education' the aim is to protect children from influences in society that prevent their becoming 'free' personalities. Children, of course, in their formative years have to be guarded against something. What they are to be protected against depends on the views of the educator or of the community in which the children grow up. In all these situations the teacher's role is primarily that of a custodian of a particular way of life, of a morality that the school exists to preserve. To illustrate this role of the teacher I select one clearly defined example from the seventeenth century, the Little Schools of Port Royal.

THE PORT-ROYALISTS

The Little Schools of Port Royal, established in Paris in 1646 by the devout followers of De Hauranne, Abbé of Saint Cyran and usually known by the name of his abbey, were the product of two oddly assorted influences: the one a theology, the other

a philosophy. The theology was that propagated by the Dutchman Cornelius Jansen; the philosophy was that of the Frenchman
Descartes (1596-1650). Jansen in association with Saint-Cyran
had revived what they regarded as the neglected teaching of St.
Augustine on grace and original sin founded on the Pauline
definition: 'By grace are ye saved through faith; and that not of
yourselves; it is the gift of God, not of works, lest any man
should boast.'[1] And further, the Jansenists held, that although
the sacrament of baptism restores the child born into original
sin to a state of innocence, he is nevertheless always prone to
relapse into his unredeemed state. This gloomy doctrine seems
to bear little promise of producing an enlightened form of education. But in Saint-Cyran's hands this is just what it did. Because
an innocent child might so easily lapse into sinful ways he con-
cluded that only by a closely supervised education could this
unhappy end be averted. It was to preserve children from the
consequences of Adam's Fall that Saint-Cyran established classes
for boys at the Convent of Port Royal in Paris. But he died in
1643 after five years' rigorous imprisonment under Richelieu
and bitter opposition from the Jesuits, who with the Church
hierarchy, regarded Jansenism as near heresy. The Little Schools
of Port Royal were established by his followers three years
later—'*petites écoles*' to avoid trouble with the '*grandes écoles*'
of the Jesuits—and included a girls' school whose headmistress
was a sister of Pascal, himself a Jansenist.

The followers of Saint-Cyran were also influenced by the
teaching of the Frenchman Descartes, the founder of modern
philosophy. His well-known premise—*Cogito ergo sum*, 'I think,
therefore I am'—and the new way of thinking developed from
this logical beginning, elevated human reason above all other
means of distinguishing truth from error. A systematic philosophy
which required men to think in a mathematically logical
sequence, from what is simple, distinctly clear and known, to
whatever truth that lies at the end of thinking, could lead to
dangerous heresy. For this reason it was rejected by orthodox
theology and strenuously opposed by the Jesuits. But the Port-

[1] *2 Ephesians*, 2 [8].

Royalists discovered in Cartesian method a ready and relevant instrument in their educational work. As they interpreted Descartes, education, in the words of Nicole, a devoted disciple of Saint-Cyran, became a process in which reason sought moral ends:

'To educate is to form the judgement—that is, to give the mind a taste for the good and the power to recognize it; to make the mind keen to recognize false reasoning when it is somewhat obscured; to teach it not to be dazzled by a show of vain talk with no sense in it, or satisfied with mere words or vague principles, and never to be content until one has penetrated to the very bottom of a thing. It is to make the mind quick to seize the point at issue in an involved matter and to recognize what is irrelevant. It is to find the truth of all matters and especially of those where the truth is most needed.'[2]

We must remember that education at Port Royal was primarily a moral education whose object was 'to preserve their pupils in the innocence of their baptism'. Such an aim might suggest not only a rigorously guarded life but also a severely coercive practice in the schools. But, as with Augustine whose teaching they followed, such a conclusion was always far from their way of thinking. On the contrary, apart from what today we should regard as an over-secluded way of life, it produced the sweetest and most humane schooling in that or any other age. Port-Royal education had one weakness and two rare virtues: its weakness is seen in the over-protection of its pupils from even the mildest of worldly influences, which is not necessarily the same thing, or as desirable an end, as developing their resistance to temptation; and its two virtues were the intelligently humane discipline and the insistence of the teachers that their pupils should learn by thinking.

As custodians of morals the Little Schools were excessively restrictive. Contact with the outside world virtually ceased on the admission of a pupil; the children were under constant supervision day and night; visits to the theatre and the reading of

[2] H. C. Barnard, *The Port-Royalists on Education*, 1918, p. 71.

fiction were forbidden and classical texts carefully edited. But allowing for such close custody of children in a licentious age, the children gained much by living and learning in a cultured community where a loving relationship of a rare quality prevailed between teacher and pupil. Of these relationships the words of the Port-Royalists will speak better than mine. The following quotations from their writings will provide useful bedtime reading for teachers today, whether they serve in the A or D streams of our public or private schools.[3]

1. There is this consolation in work which one undertakes for God, that He demands of us the work and not its success.
2. Saint-Cyran usually summed up our duty in respect to children in these three maxims: Speak little; endure much; pray still more.
3. At the hour of death one of the greatest consolations we could feel was to have contributed to the good education of some child.
4. The aim of instruction is to carry the mind to the highest point that it is capable of reaching. It does not impart memory or imagination or intelligence, but it cultivates all these faculties by strengthening one of them by means of the others.
5. We ought to show special love and pity for those who appear most defective and backward—those, that is to say whom original sin has most deeply wounded. He could not bear us in dealing with them to use too stern a look or too domineering a manner . . . on the contrary he wished us to treat them with genial familiarity which would win them over by studied kindness and by a truly paternal affection. . . . For we can do nothing so long as they have no confidence in us.
6. There will always be enough difficulties—whether they arise from our pupils' intellects or from their inclinations and natural dislike for study—without our adding extra ones of our own by the incompetent manner in which we set about our teaching.

Thus the Port-Royalists were teachers who believed that it is

[3] The quotations are from translations by H. C. Barnard in his *The Port-Royalists on Education*, pp. 62-115.

system and method, the master's intellectual equipment, his skill in inciting the unwilling to effort, his breeding and example, his capacity to turn growing minds to what is pre-eminently worthwhile, that count most in the training of children. Whatever be our views on the limitations of the role of the teacher as a guardian of morals we shall find no instance before or since where this role was more faithfully and creatively performed. In 1660, only fourteen years after their formation, the Little Schools of Port Royal were closed under the pressure of Jesuit opposition.

PART IV

The foundations of modern teaching

In the Baconian, Cartesian, Newtonian world of the seventeenth century the modern teacher will find himself on familiar ground. Comenius, the 'father of modern pedagogy', established the importance of classroom method. Locke framed the terms of the unending debate on discipline and the educability of children. Rousseau's rebellious creed, modified in practice by the deeper experience of Pestalozzi and Froebel, placed the child in the forefront of the teacher's attention and laid the foundations of child study and modern progressive education. These three were the rebels who emancipated teachers from the 'dark formalistic arts' of the classroom. The philosophers of the eighteenth and early nineteenth centuries—Kant, Hegel and Herbart—present the teacher with the concept of education as a moral culture. Pedagogy is 'the art of making man moral' says Hegel, but his philosophic idealism ends in reducing the teacher's role to that of a servant of the state. For Herbart the field of a teacher's activity is the student's mind, and for this reason he became for a century the teacher's philosopher and his guide to method in the classroom. In the writings of all these teachers of teachers are formulated the tensions still existing between the conflicting claims of authority and freedom in school. In the concluding pages of Chapter 12 the nature of these opposing claims are examined.

Finally, a more recent development in educational history has been the emergence of the school community itself as teacher, a concept particularly characteristic of the English-speaking world. Among its modern origins are the paternalistic schools of von Fellenberg, the ill-fated experiment of the Hills at Hazelwood and the English public schools. New interpretations of the community ideal appeared in the 'New School' movement at the turn of the century. It remained for the American John Dewey to develop a new version of the educative school community and to provide it with a reasoned philosophy. All these developments implied new roles for the teacher, new approaches to human relationships in school and new methods of teaching which remain part of modern school practice.

11 The father of modern pedagogy

In the realms of religion and politics the seventeenth century was a period of adjustment to the Reformation and Counter-Reformation. The Pope had not quelled Luther; Luther had not dethroned the Pope; religious wars violently disturbed the peace in Europe and Calvin's stern followers were resisting the divine right of kings in Britain. More important for education, the reasonable voice of Erasmus had yielded place to the Baconian theme that 'human science and human power do really meet in one' and to the mathematical logic of Descartes. Before the foundation of the Royal Society in 1662, the Copernican revolution had been accomplished, William Gilbert had founded the sciences of magnetism and electricity, Galileo had dropped his stone from the tower of Pisa and improved the telescope, Kepler had confirmed the motion of the planets, William Harvey had discovered the circulation of the blood. In 1687 Newton's *Principia* laid the foundations of modern science.

No wonder that Bacon confidently declared to his contemporaries that it would eventually be within the scope of man's powers to organize and unify knowledge, not 'on the frivolous disputations, confutations and verbosities' of the schoolmen, not on the 'old' *Organon* of Aristotle, but through the employment of the *Novum Organum*, the 'New Instrument' of inductive thinking, experiment and the controlled observation of the physical world. This was one of those rare moments in history when men, standing on the brink of new discoveries, saw themselves subduing their physical environment to their own use. From the New Method would come a new system of knowledge, even a universal wisdom—*pansophia*—by which man would control his destiny. With twentieth century hindsight we now know that the knowledge and power came without the wisdom; which was a disaster few even of the finer spirits of that age foresaw. It was nevertheless implicit in the whole life's work of Comenius, with whom we are now concerned, that this disaster should not happen.

It was not only Baconian ideas that determined the direction of educational thought at this time. The enlightened Puritanism that affected both Catholic and Protestant attitudes in the seventeenth century was represented in Central Europe by Comenius and in England by Milton and his circle. As in the schools of Port Royal, far from submerging educational enterprise under a pious acquiescence in man's fallen estate, the revived emphasis on original sin inspired the Protestant educational reformers 'to repair the ruins of our first Parents' by a tender regard for children and improved educational practice. It was Comenius who brought together the Baconian and religious strands in current thought by breaking new ground in the purposes and methods of schooling. The general educational issue ceased to be a question of the proper teaching of grammar and became a much broader issue: if knowledge is to be sought through observation and experiment how is the physical world to be brought within the scope of the pupil's experience, and by what means can the observed facts of the world of nature be brought within the range of the pupil's understanding?

Some part of the answer was provided by John Amos Komensky (1592-1670), usually known as Comenius, a bishop of the Moravian Brethren who spent most of his life in exile from his native Bohemia, partly in England among the group of Puritan reformers in the circle of John Milton. Between 1628 and 1632 he wrote *The Great Didactic*, first in his native Czech, in 1657 to be published in Latin. In this work there are few educational ideas that cannot be found in Plato and Aristotle, Plutarch and Quintilian, Augustine, Vives and Erasmus, and his debt to Bacon is considerable. His gifts lay not in the creativity of an original mind but in his sensitive appreciation and imaginative treatment of what had already been written, in his capacity to integrate and to apply his own teaching experience to what his forerunners had said and what his contemporaries were saying. This gift for integration of relevant knowledge was an expression of a deeply pious spirit convinced of his unity with an evolving and purposeful universe and with his fellow men.

The reformers associated with Comenius had several aims in common: all believed with a deep seriousness in the Christian purpose of education; all were led to advocate a closely protective schooling; all placed great emphasis on the method of instruction and on a wider curriculum including studies relevant to the practical affairs of life; all were responsive to Bacon's insistence on the value of factual experience in learning; all refused to regard the classical tongues as the main concern of the educator; all were distinguished products of the liberal culture that had produced some of the finest spirits of the century, including Milton himself who most wonderfully enriched it. One further characteristic of very great social significance for the future was their interest in the extension of education to the under-privileged classes. This vision of universal education actually appears in the sub-title of *The Great Didactic*, which reads: 'not the children of the rich or of the powerful only but all alike, boys and girls, both noble and ignoble, rich and poor, in all cities and towns, villages and hamlets, should be sent to school'.

Comenius, then, foresaw with Bacon 'the general direction which progress in knowledge was destined to take' and he also shared with Bacon 'a well-nigh superstitious confidence in the power of method'.[1] In education the most obvious trend was the passing of the age of narrowly erudite schooling based on study of the classical languages. To this linguistic erudition Comenius opposed his 'pansophic' ideal which was in essence a school course founded on common human experience rather than on authority and tradition. The teacher was to engage in what we now call 'modern studies' and the vernacular was to be established throughout primary and secondary schooling as a worthy

[1] J. W. Adamson, *Pioneers of Modern Education*, p. 78.

and effective medium for teaching and learning. Reduced to its elements his method requires that children should first study *things*; that it is not the logic of the subject matter—e.g. grammar —but the way a child thinks that should determine the method of instruction; and that no learning takes place unless the pupil understands what he is being taught—all obvious principles to the modern teacher but in those days almost totally neglected. Hence the 'psychologizing' of education we have seen tentatively introduced by Vives is here brought more emphatically into the detailed method of the classroom. Throughout *The Great Didactic* are scattered in profusion many practical suggestions that make of it a very 'modern' treatise on teaching method.

More than most of his contemporaries Comenius saw the need to establish a new image of the teacher, for he had small hope of success with his pansophic plans unless good teachers were readily available. His demands were high, rather higher than our modest and more realistic demands today, for example, 'men without blemish in the eyes of man', an élite 'endowed with no less wisdom and practical ability than the shepherds of the churches and the superiors of communities'. The pay of such paragons is to be such as to free them from financial strain and at least sufficient 'to prevent a man of excellent gifts having reason to desert his appointment'. Apart from the status which adequate salary confers a teacher must rely for social approval on his own personal qualities and classroom competence.[2]

At first glance Comenius seems to present his ideal teacher as a lone figure on a dais dispensing knowledge to willing ears: 'the teacher should never step up to any one scholar or allow any of them to come to him separately, but should remain in his seat where he can be seen by all, just as the sun sends his rays over all things'—an instance of Comenius' weakness for analogy which often led him astray. Even more depressing, 'the mouth of the teacher is a spring from which streams of knowledge issue and flow over [the pupils] and whenever they see the spring open, they should place their attention like a cistern beneath

[2] See J. E. Sadler, *J. A. Comenius and the Concept of Universal Education*, pp. 242-6.

it'. Nevertheless, despite these odd images of the teacher's role, not even Pestalozzi relies more than Comenius on sense-perception as the growing point of learning. The activity of the pupil's mind receives far more attention than in the past and although the teacher remains on the platform, classroom problems are seen very much the worm's eye view of the pupil. The teacher regards his class with professional respect, providing scope for spontaneous effort, utilizing as one 'mind, tongue and hand' in practical activities, seeking to establish a concrete relationship between what is to be learned and the pupil's interests and personal experience. This is the 'modern' element in Comenius' works and why he is rightly regarded as 'the father of modern pedagogy'.

We also see these principles at work in the opinions and practice of the group of Puritan reformers with whom Comenius associated in England. The very title of Hezekiah Woodward's book, *A Childe's Patrimony laid out upon the Culture or tilling over of His Whole Man* (1640), is itself a charming portrayal of the teacher's role: Let the teacher walk alongside the learner, 'so that he does not pull at a dead thing'; let the schoolmaster 'put some life into it that the child may see it stir'; let him 'quicken the child's fancy to see itself joyned as a party in the work'. And inspiring this movement towards a more realistic, relevant and humane schooling was the liberating culture of the Puritan poet of England for whom 'reason is but choosing' and the end of education 'to repair the ruins of our first Parents by regaining to know God aright'.

Thus at the end of a century remarkable for the liveliness of its educational strivings we are presented with a conception of the teacher more exacting as regards his professional competence and as demanding on his moral capacity as any we have so far encountered. Unfortunately *The Great Didactic*, the major work of Comenius, passed into oblivion with his death to be rediscovered by Froebel over a century later. His minor works, the *Janua Linguarum Reserata* or *Gateway of Language Unlocked* (1631) and the *Orbis Sensualium Pictus* (1658) remained available and were the most used school books throughout

England and Western Europe well on into the nineteenth century. The former was an aid to Latin teaching, the latter was famous as the first junior illustrated encyclopaedia—three hundred pictures on every subject under the sun.

12 Authority, freedom and activity

JOHN LOCKE

The theory and practice of education throughout the eighteenth century were dominated by two men markedly different in temperament and philosophical outlook, but whose ideas on the training of children were in several ways complementary. The first was John Locke (1631-1702), the second Jean-Jacques Rousseau (1712-1778).

The commonsensical mind of Locke seems to have performed the office of a sieve through which ancient and modern educational themes passed for further scrutiny. It is indeed difficult to find any principle engaging the minds of educational reformers in the next two centuries that is not found somewhere in his two works *Some Thoughts concerning Education* (1693) and the more reasoned essay *Of the Conduct of the Understanding* (1697). Locke says little about education that had not been said before —in Quintilian, Erasmus, Vives, Castiglione, Montaigne, Mulcaster and the Puritan reformers, in Descartes and Comenius— from all of whom we find an echo in his writings. It was not his originality but his genius for asking the right questions that brought into clearer focus the issues involved in rearing children.

Locke's influence can be discerned not only in the writings of historical figures like Rousseau, Condillac and Helvetius in France or of Kant and Basedow in Germany, but also in practising schoolmasters in England throughout the eighteenth century. We find references to Locke's opinions for example in the Writings of Isaac Watts and John Wesley, Lord Kames and Dr. Samuel Johnson, and in those of schoolmasters like John Clark of Hull, Vicesimus Knox of Tonbridge School, Dr. Talbot in his handbook for charity school teachers, David Manson of Belfast, and David Williams of Chelsea.[1]

Locke asked a fundamental question: What is the primary condition of a child's mind at birth? It is, he says, a sheet of white paper 'void of all characters', or, as he expresses the same idea in *Some Thoughts*, 'wax to be moulded and fashioned as one pleases'. There are no innate ideas, 'no characters as it were stamped upon the mind of man which the soul receives in its very first being and brings into the world with it'. Whence then, he asks, comes 'that vast store which the busy and boundless fancy of man has painted on it with an almost endless variety?' These impressions, he says, come from the two fountains of knowledge—from our senses and from reflection, i.e. from observation and perception of sensible objects and from our 'thinking, doubting, believing, reasoning, knowing, willing', the ferment of ideas which goes on wholly within the man himself. We cannot, says Locke, see with other men's eyes or come to knowledge by other men's understandings: 'so much as we ourselves comprehend of truth and reason, so much we possess of real and true knowledge'. He explains the obvious inequalities of mental ability in men by suggesting that the mind's retentive capacity varies in individuals.

Thus the appearance of Locke's waxen tablet disturbed several firmly held convictions. The Augustinian doctrine of original sin disappeared into the limbo of innate ideas, for clearly if there is no impression on the waxen tablet when we are born, we are not born in sin. This view, incidentally, tended to invalidate theological support for the moral value of Solomon's rod and raised again the question of punishment in the sphere of discipline in home and school. It also highlighted the issues of the age-long and still continuing debate about nature and nurture, and was to prompt Rousseau and his contemporary the Frenchman Helvetius to go a step further and declare that men were not only born equal but were equally educable—one sheet of white paper was as white as another. It therefore seemed to

[1] See E. B. Castle, *Moral Education in Christian Times*, pp. 125-207.

follow that when bad education was replaced by good education great benefits would accrue to the human race. Again, Locke's view that the organs of sense are our first teachers encouraged the belief that teaching should be grounded in the pupil's sense experience, not in books and words, a theme to be developed by Rousseau, Pestalozzi and Froebel and their followers to work a slow revolution in the education of children.

There is, in fact, in Locke's writings, either explicit or to be inferred, intimations of what we now regard as good educational practice. For example: the place of habit and reason in the formation of character; the function of play and spontaneous interest in the motivation of learning; the building of the curriculum with due regard to the principle of utility; the value of handicrafts and learning by doing; restraint in the use of punishment and the doubtful value of corporal punishment. We can even discern between the lines the foreshadowing of child study and a child-centred education—a term that would not have met with his approval.

These developments of his reflections on the education of children would have surprised Locke, for having suffered under the tyranny of Dr. Busby at Westminster, he had no respect for either schoolmasters or their methods, and recommended the Whig gentlemen for whom he wrote to place their sons under a private tutor. His great services to education in the eighteenth century were to encourage schoolmasters to think again about schooling and to initiate the debate that engaged the minds of rebels, prophets and philosophers for two centuries. This debate tended to polarize between the two concepts of authority and freedom in activity, which from his day to ours have competed for the teacher's allegiance. Disliking extremes, Locke asks the perennial question—how to steer a course between the opposing claims of liberty and compulsion: 'to avoid the danger that is on either hand is the great art; and he that has found a way, how to keep a child's spirit easy, active, free; and yet at the same time to restrain him from many things he has a mind to, and to draw him to things that are uneasy (difficult) to him; he, I say, that knows how to reconcile these seeming contradictions, has, in my opinion, got the true secret of education'.[2]

THE PROPHETS

It is generally true in the history of culture, that the dissatisfaction and boredom of one generation with what the previous generation deemed good, produces a reaction in a contrary direction. This has been true of education, nowhere more vividly illustrated than in Rousseau's advice to teachers: 'Do precisely the opposite of what is usually done and you will have hit on the right plan.' The movement which Rousseau let loose in the middle of the eighteenth century was a revolution against the social and intellectual climate of his time. In France absolute monarchy supported a privileged Church in thrall to Jesuit influence; it held in subjection a purposeless aristocracy without depriving them of their privileges; it denied responsibility to a resentful bourgeoisie and repressed the opinions of a critical intelligentsia. Voltaire for instance was several times imprisoned in the Bastille.

In 1726 Voltaire visited an England whose monarch's power was restrained by constitutional safeguards, and where the aristocracy were usefully employed in ruling a country under a constitution whose apologist was John Locke. In England and France the patterns of polite society were similar: polished people discussed polite subjects in elegant language, governed by the convention that good sense was more important than enthusiasm, that intelligent people are not emotionally moved by what cannot be proved, that polite behaviour has a higher social value than adventurous thinking, and that it is bad form to be sentimental about oneself or the sad condition of one's inferiors. Even garden design reflected the soulless formality of the prevailing mood, as Pope protested in his Epistle to Lord Burlington:

> Grove nods at Grove, each alley has a brother,
> And half the platform just reflects the other.

[2] *Thoughts*, 46.

Pope's protest is one of the signs of change, not only when he proclaims that 'the proper study of mankind is man' but when he says with deeper feeling that a man's need is 'to feel another's woe'.

These early signs of revolt against the age of reason and aloof refinement made little impression on the English scene, but in France Voltaire's experience in England was to bear fruit. He returned from his three years' exile deeply impressed by the freedom of writers in England and full of admiration for Locke's individualistic philosophy and the anti-clerical deism of Pope's *Essay on Man*. There was already in France a restless impatience with the inhibiting constraints of conventional social attitudes careless of the welfare of individual men. The first move against the Establishment was the preparation of the *Encyclopedia* in 1751, edited by Diderot and including Voltaire, Rousseau and Montesquieu among its contributors. This movement of the 'Enlightenment' sought to subject all things in church and state to the light of reason and to the test of scientific knowledge. Yet the work of the Encyclopedists was but a half-way house to the far more destructive romanticism of Rousseau, who soon abandoned his friends to their intellectual reformation by declaring the sovereignty of feeling over reason. This was the essence of the romantic idealism which Rousseau loosed upon a society whose upper classes had lost confidence in themselves, whose middle classes were seeking new opportunities with 'an expectant energy of mind' and whose poor were awaiting relief from their condition: 'man is born free; and everywhere he is in chains'. Like Luther, Rousseau had proclaimed the value of man as a man, 'too noble a being to serve simply as an instrument for others'.

One aspect of the romantic revival was a reaction against the artificial, the classical and the formal, expressed in an escape from the drawing room into the world of nature, where once, Rousseau declared, primitive man, unspoilt by the corruptions of society, lived his simple life and reared his children. This is the point of departure from which Rousseau begins his thinking about the education of children. The *Contrat Social* (1762) was his social gospel; *Emile*, published in the same year, was his programme for education. The first prepared France for its political revolution; the second changed for ever our ideas about the education of boys and girls. Here we shall be mainly concerned with those of his ideas that most affect the work of the teacher.

Forty years before Rousseau's *Emile* burst upon a receptive world, a Swiss professor named de Crousaz had hinted that some radical change was about to take place in the role of the teacher. In 1722 he wrote a satirical work entitled *Traité de l'Education des Enfants* in which he suggested that the secret of education was to place the pupil in a situation 'that will enable him to give himself lessons, the opportunities and materials alone to be supplied by the teacher'. This remark was prophetic, for it described one of the distinguishing features of what came to be called 'progressive' or child-centred education, whose ancestry goes back to Rousseau. In *Emile* Rousseau presented the classic model of 'education according to nature' and in vivid strokes paints his alluring picture of the 'free' child.

What Rousseau was striving to do was to provide free play for the pupil's judgement, for this was for him the most desirable end of education. But Rousseau recognizes the incompleteness of childhood, those limitations to a child's freedom that are inherent in his being a child. He knew, perhaps through his own bitter failures, that maturity arrives in stages, that growth is childhood's essential characteristic, and hence that the essence of the teacher's task is to co-operate with the developing resources of sense, observation and reason progressively emerging in the pupil. To this end he devises a method whereby the child is hedged about with restrictions that enable him to *feel* free.

The method involves control—'well regulated liberty'—which avoids the appearance of authority and 'preserves the forms of freedom'. Give your pupils liberty, then, as in a garden planted with situations carefully devised to give them many freedoms— to jump, to run, to make a noise, to observe and to use freely all the opportunities suggested in the challenging objects around them. The tutor will also devise situations from which the pupils will learn not to desire for themselves what they cannot achieve for themselves. Restrict a child's desires to the attainable and he will be happy because he *feels* free; excite his desires by giving him all he wants and he will be unfree because frustrated, miserably bound to his craving for the unattainable. And behind all these planned freedoms is the watchful eye and silent tread of the tutor.

Thus in Emile's tutor the teacher emerges as the new authoritarian. The medieval schoolmaster, the birch and the grind of grammar are gone; but the teacher remains behind the scenes pulling the strings, organizing the push and pull of the physical, mental and moral environment, even with 'incessant hypocrisy and lying', as Godwin unkindly describes it. Thus the restraining bridle is not the overt authority of parent or schoolmaster, but the impersonal authority of nature interpreted through the 'coups de théatre pédagogiques' of an infallible tutor. The essence of the situation is that the pupil is to *feel* free but in fact to be under control. This is not so horrid a circumstance as purists so often claim it to be; and is no more fraught with hypocrisy than the often justifiable deceptions practised daily by sensible parents and skilful teachers.

Rousseau defends his deception on the grounds that in practice children feel free even in circumscribed activity, and that this is what really matters if they are to form their own judgements. He is stating the ineluctable fact that the self-directed activity that gives a child a sense of freedom—elbow room—is inevitably conditioned by some form of subjection to authority. This is a very old and durable idea as every teacher knows. Moreover in varying degrees and in different ways these themes of freedom, authority and self-activity, which Rousseau treats so originally, apply also to the child-centred education he inspired. Pestalozzi, Froebel, Montessori, A. S. Neill, in fact if not in principle, all control the learning situation. Every teacher must do so. What we must most carefully note is that the objective of all these reformers was not to shape children to a socially prescribed mould or to bemuse their minds with books, but to cultivate each child's understanding of himself and his world by his own discriminating and self-imposed activity.

Rousseau's *Emile* remains, as Lord Morley has said, one of the most seminal books in the history of literature. It cleared away 'the accumulation of clogging prejudices and obscure inveterate usage which made education one of the dark formalistic arts . . . it admitted floods of light and air into tightly enclosed nurseries and school rooms'. How true this is. Our image of the teacher even today is conditioned by Rousseau's rebellious creed and still challenges the modern teacher's technical skill and understanding of children. Despite his wilful exaggerations and half-truths, he presents us with a picture of the artist teacher at work, forcing us to ask what in fact we are doing when we try to educate a child. He disturbs the complacency of our assumed adult wisdom and reveals it as the hypocritical search for adult convenience—'masters away with your tricks, be virtuous yourselves'. It is not precepts youth requires but the example of good men. Don't make a child's future the criterion of your teaching but what he needs *now* for this particular moment of his development towards stability. Love him in an unsentimental way; identify yourself with his present strivings; observe the phenomena of growth in their infinite variety; feed his curiosity; watch, refrain, encourage, guide without seeming to. Rule not through the agencies of fear and repression but through the gentler appeal of mature example.

Rousseau's disciples, most of them closer than he ever was to the real facts of the classroom, tested his essential message in the actual conditions of the school. Most attractive of them all was Johann Heinrich Pestalozzi (1746-1827) who is the real father of modern progressive practice. In the first place he presents the teacher with his principle of *Anschauung*, the principle of concreteness, or close-up observation, which, interpreted, means something like this: The more closely we face children with the need for exercising their judgement on familiar situations in domestic and school life, the more frequently we make elementary calls on their responsible behaviour, the more effectively shall we help them to develop a sense of right and wrong. And further, if the teacher skilfully reinforces every tendency in a child to act rightly he strengthens his pupil's capacity to act rightly on all occasions. Like all sensible parents Pestalozzi knew that the age of responsibility emerged nearer five years of age than at twenty-one. In the second place, and consistent with this principle, he replaces Rousseau's lynx-eyed tutor with the model of the loving parent in the good home straightly exacting obedience within the bonds of mutual affection and trust.

Pestalozzi regarded obedience not merely as a condition of a quiet classroom but as a cardinal need of children to which parents and teachers must respond. He is not content, as Rousseau was, to rely on 'the discipline of natural consequences'. Liberty is good and so is obedience, he tells his teachers: 'Be thoroughly convinced of the immense value of liberty . . . let your child be as free as possible . . . what he can do for himself, let him do it. . . . But when you see the necessity of accustoming him to obedience prepare yourself with the greatest care for this duty.' This accent on obedience is a definite rejection of Rousseau's principle, but is entirely consistent with his own insistence that 'the natural way of teaching is not coercive'. He approves of punishment as a reasonable restraint on misbehaviour, but not when the teacher or the system is to blame or when there prevails 'the indescribable tedium which oppresses the juvenile mind'.

It is the deep humanity of Pestalozzi's image of the good teacher that is so attractive. He asks us to realize, as sheer sensible pedagogics, that the effort indispensable to learning need not be induced by fear, the great destroyer of interest and confidence; to remember that a child is 'an indissoluble unit', hand, head and heart, that compulsion accepted in moments of insight is more profitable than any primrose path, and that authority wisely exercised reinforces the pupil's inborn capacity to contribute to his own growth. Nowhere in educational writings is the theme of authority more consistently and fruitfully associated with self-activity, or the vague and often sentimental theme of 'education according to nature' more firmly anchored to the facts of human nature with which every teacher is confronted. How firmly anchored we may gather from Pestalozzi's own account of the life he lived with his orphans in his school at Stanz: 'everything done for them in their need, all the teaching they received, came directly from me; my hand lay on their hand, my eye rested on their eye. My tears flowed with their tears, and my smile accompanied theirs. Their food was mine, and their drink was mine. . . . I slept in their midst; I was last to go to bed at evening, and the first to rise in the morning. I prayed with them, and taught them in bed before they went to sleep.'[3]

It is his firm attachment to the concrete situation of the home and to the observed facts of ordinary sentient human behaviour, that keeps Pestalozzi's feet on the ground. He may conduct his classes in the cow byre or by the riverside or in the kitchen, but he never yields completely to the logic of the purist's 'natural education'—that education according to the nature of the child implies the teacher's total abdication of control.

When, at the age of twenty-three, Friedrich Froebel (1782-1852) faced a class of forty boys in the Pestalozzian Institute at Frankfurt he felt, he records, 'as happy as a fish in water or a bird in the air'. He had found his vocation. Froebel was neither philosopher nor scientist although something of both, but he was deeply influenced by the idealistic philosophy of Hegel and Schelling and by his passionate interest in the natural world. These two influences and his own miserable childhood conditioned his whole attitude to his life's work. From the first he derived his vague pantheistic concepts of the unity of man with his universe, part of 'an all-pervading, energetic, living self-conscious Unity which is God'; and from the second his view of man and society as undergoing an evolutionary process wherein man plays his part in the achievement of God's purposes. With fanciful analogy and dangerous logic he elaborates the theme of child development as a natural growth, governed much less by the external agency of the teacher than by the self-forming capacities innate in the child himself. With Froebel the biological view of child development is born: 'God neither

[3] J. A. Green, *Educational Ideas of Pestalozzi*, quoted by H. C. Barnard in *A Short History of English Education*, p. 46.

ingrafts nor inoculates. He develops. . . .'[4]

And so parents and teachers must adopt the method of their Creator who 'energizes, guides, protects' but leaves each individual to grow according to his own pattern through childhood and boyhood to maturity. Each stage of development will determine the stage that succeeds it: 'man is in the child . . . the education of boyhood rests wholly on childhood'. Thus we come to the kindergarten, a lovely if not entirely satisfactory image of children's education that has brought happiness and sound method to thousands of classrooms throughout the world. Here the analogy is between child and plant whose intrinsic nature cannot be changed but whose healthy growth requires the protection and skill of the teacher, the gardener, for its fullest flowering. The gardener's task is to secure the right response between the inner responsive impulses of the child and the external influences that bear in upon him from the world of sense impressions and social experience in which he lives. From this experience, and from his own purposeful activities, the child builds his own personality and in this sense is 'self-forming'.

We must note here Froebel's emphasis on *purposeful* activity. In this he sees more clearly than did Pestalozzi that mere 'self-activity', busy-ness in the classroom, is not enough. This is where the guidance of the teacher becomes important. He has to provide situations and materials that induce children to be actively engaged, whether in play or otherwise, in activities directed towards a desired end. It was this need that led him to devise his 'gifts' and 'occupations' based on fantastic analogies and symbolism, which brought deserved ridicule on the system —for example, coloured balls to represent the colour sequence of the rainbow spectrum, 'the symbol of peace between "God and Man"'. Perhaps in no part of his practice in the kindergarten did Froebel go further astray. A more ordinary and less imaginative man, and one less firmly held by a vulnerable philosophy, might have seen the ridiculous artificiality and unnecessary complexity of some Froebelian materials. As we shall see with Herbart's pedagogic practice, the mechanics of it was more

[4] *The Education of Man*, Section 105.

transportable than the core of valuable theory. But modern Froebelians throughout the world, having long since abandoned the frills for the substance, now witness with sufficient power to the enduring Froebelian principles that have completely transformed our infant schools, changing both teacher and children from the press-button automata of Victorian classrooms to living and learning persons.

Unfortunately both worshippers and critics of Froebel have been side-tracked by the success of the kindergarten to almost complete neglect of his views on the education of older children. Here Froebel does not ask the teacher to relinquish his control of his pupils, as is too often supposed. The teacher may use restraint, including punishment, to urge into action the boy's innate capacity for self-control, to fortify, as he puts it, 'his power to persevere in the pursuit of good purposes'. His insistence on discipline in boyhood is quite specific, especially notable in his surprisingly modern views on physical education: 'In boyhood the will has not made constant control of the body; consequently the body should be trained to carry out automatically the intentions of the mind, as we see in a skilled musician . . . without this, real discipline, which is the very centre of education in boyhood, is impossible.' His prescriptions for systematic physical education include instruction on the structure and functioning of the body and its proper care; and surprisingly enough in an advocate of spontaneous play for little children, he recommends training in games for older boys if they are to benefit fully from their play: 'Boyhood is the time for discipline', for it is in adolescence that the young first become capable of realizing their own dignity and worth: 'the more clearly he recognizes the requirements of his own humanity, the more firmly should the educator insist on these [disciplinary] requirements. He should not even shrink from severity and infliction of punishment if the good of the pupil demand it.'[5]

This surely is not the advocacy of an entirely permissive education which Froebel's critics have so often accused him of upholding. Neither is this the old authoritarian education in a

[5] S. S. F. Fletcher, *Froebel's Chief Writings*, p. 95.

new guise. It is rather a refined use of authority aimed not at obscuring the evil propensity by punishing the overt act, but at revealing and trusting the good that is in the transgressor: 'the infallible remedy for all human wickedness is first to bring to light the original good tendency and then to nourish it, foster, train it'.[6]

A corollary to Froebel's attitude to discipline involves a concept of the educator's role which has always appealed to me as a teacher. This is his theme of *the third term* which when disencumbered of a mist of vague enchantments, can be reduced to a viable proposition of real value in teacher-pupil relationships. The argument proceeds thus:

To ensure the unfolding of our children's native gifts all education must be adapted to their nature. The educator's task is to secure the right response between these inborn capacities and the things, circumstances, people, frustrations that form the child's world. But the relationship between teacher and pupil is not to be one in which the teacher rules by arbitrary commands to which the child must submit, for both teacher and pupil are equally part of a divine order governed by 'an immutable law that excludes caprice'. Within this reign of law the teacher has both to guide and to be guided; he is to learn even in the process of teaching, including himself with his pupil within the law of the evolving rational universe. But what in fact is the teacher to do? For children are both good and bad, conforming to the 'law of opposites' which governs a world in which every virtue has its opposite—love and hatred, honesty and deceit, courage and cowardice—a thoroughly Hegelian piece of dialectic.

First, says Froebel, we must recognize the dual nature of education and the sensitive responses it demands from the teacher; who must 'give and take, unite and divide, be firm and yielding'. It is his job to encourage the right 'opposites' when wrong tendencies show themselves in the child's behaviour, not just to quell them. How do we do this? It is here that Froebel introduces his concept of the 'third term', the 'third something' which is inherent in any relationship between teacher and pupil,

[6] S. S. F. Fletcher, op. cit., p. 76.

to which the teacher and pupil are equally subject and to which each must equally submit.

What then is this 'third something' which supervenes over the conflicting situation between teacher and taught? It is the right and best which inheres in any educational situation; that element in the human encounter between the teacher and his pupil which offers a chance of creating a promising out of an unpromising situation. Seek for this solution in the smallest details of each daily encounter 'and observe what follows in each particular case from thy action, and to what knowledge it leads thee'. A perfect example of what Froebel means can be gathered from a careful reading of the story of Jesus dealing with the agonizing conflict between her judges and the woman taken in adultery.[7] He creates a promising situation out of a singularly unpromising one. Maybe Froebel exaggerates the discernment of children; and maybe he demands too much of the teacher. But he reminds us that there lies deep in most human encounters in home and school a challenge that cannot be met with any slick response. And in this image of the teacher as the trustee of the child's capacity for self-direction, he reveals him as the supremely sensitive practitioner, not in the mechanical manipulation of teaching aids but in the intuitive control of the two-way traffic between maturity and childhood.[8]

THE PHILOSOPHERS

We turn from the prophets to the philosophers, from what Nietzsche petulantly called Rousseau's 'slave pedagogy of things' to Immanual Kant's 'master pedagogy of the spirit', to the education that is concerned with training the righteous will to realize itself in action. Kant (1724-1804) lifts Rousseau's discipline of physical necessity into the realm of conscious morality which aims always 'to treat humanity, whether in thine own person or in that of another, in every case as an end, never as a means only'. Thus Rousseau's discipline of 'things' is replaced by a moral culture; in practice, and for children, to be derived from

[7] John 8 [1-11].   [8] *Education of Man*, Section 13.

'maxims' rules of conduct to be applied by the child himself to his own actions, 'the reasonableness of which the child is able to see for himself'. The 'maxim' is a kind of 'categorical imperative' for juveniles, *less* than 'the moral law within' valid for the mature person, *more* than mere external restraint. The maxim must appeal both to the reason and the will of the immature.[9] Thus Kant's teacher becomes the preceptor in a highly personal moral education and also the builder of his pupils' conscience, assisting them 'to substitute the fear of their own conscience for the fear of man and divine punishment'. At his lowest Kant's teacher is a little man with a book of 'maxims' in his pocket; at his highest a prophet who holds before his pupils a plumb-line —and he doesn't care whether they call it duty or conscience or God. 'Do not look at me;' the Kantian teacher suggests, 'look where I am looking.'

The Hegelian teacher is a more formidable figure. Against the background of an evolving and rational universe governed by mind, the absolute and ultimate reality, Georg Wilhelm Friedrich Hegel (1770-1831) presents us with an image of the teacher as a sort of midwife assisting at the rebirth of his pupils from natural man to spiritual man. This metamorphosis is achieved through education: 'pedagogy is the art of making man moral'. The rebirth is achieved by erecting a wall between our instinctive impulses and our spiritual perceptions. This is Hegel's doctrine of 'self-estrangement': we lose our life in order to find it. There are three stages in the process: the stage of childhood when children live in the vivid world of sensuous contact in self-activity; middle adolescence when older children become receptive to the world of ideas; and the years approaching maturity when the student, in possession of his spiritual self and conscious of his intellectual power, turns to the service of mankind.

Mothers and fathers play their part: it is from them that a child learns the habit of obedience; but it is at school that the pupil's moral perceptions are sharpened, for here he encounters ideals in the community that fit young men for public service.

[9] A translation of Kant's little book *On Pedagogy* is given in A. Churton, *Kant on Education*, 1899.

It is at this stage, says Hegel, that 'we must imbue the conscious mind with moral ends, strengthen it in its moral resolutions and lead it to reflection upon them.' This is the teacher's job. Hegel's school at Nuremburg (1806-1816) must have been par excellence the model for unmitigated philosophical idealism. Its curriculum was centred on the study of the values of classical times, on rights and duties, morality, law, as they affected the family, the state and mankind. We are reminded of Arnold's sixth forth—stern and scholarly, but morality the aim. Kant's 'moral law within' did not suffice for Hegel. The cult of individuality was out. The pupil must be made to realize the inadequacy of merely individual experience: 'We ought not,' he says, 'to stimulate individuality too highly, rather must we regard as empty words the assertion that teachers should cultivate it in their pupils.'[10]

The subjugation of individual caprice begins in school where the youthful vision is extended beyond self and home to the nation, for 'the state is the reality of the moral idea, the realized moral life', 'the Divine Idea as it exists on earth', the source in fact of such reflections of eternal truth as may be glimpsed by a human being. Thus, in the practice of the supreme art of making man moral, the teacher finds himself securing the obedience of his pupils to the communal will. For the school is an artifact of the community and exists to serve and to be subordinate to the state—and by the same token the teacher becomes a civil servant. The issue is clear cut: do citizens exist for the sake of the state; or the state for the good of its citizens? Hegel holds the former view; Locke and all the liberal philosophers since his day hold the latter view.

Kant, we should note, provided a philosophical framework for doing what St. Augustine and good teachers through the ages usually do. Hegel does this too, but goes much further, and in the wrong direction, by accepting Plato's least acceptable idea and identifying 'the Divine Idea as it exists on earth' with the state, and in practice with the German nation. But in education it is usually dangerous to carry an argument to its logical con-

[10] See M. MacKenzie, *Hegel's Educational Theory*, pp. 57-63, and 94.

clusion; for at the end of all philosophical talk there stands a boy or a girl.

Hegel neglected Kant's warning that 'the ultimate aim of princes is not the promotion of the good of mankind, but the well-being of their own state and the attainment of their own ends . . . that the management of schools is best left to the most intelligent experts'.[11] Hence Hegel's doctrine of the state becomes a horrific instrument in the hands of dictators, for as we well know, through the brainwashed teacher and under powerful social pressures the minds of a whole generation can be turned to evil in the service of the state. Perhaps the most depressing aspect of Hegelian idealism is that the great mind of its progenitor can itself be conditioned by a conception of the state which in the minds of racial fanatics can be translated into the romantic nonsense of blood and race. Nevertheless, Hegel's great themes remain, a reminder that mankind's moral experience, the rigorous exercise of intellect, the call to social duty and a sense of human destiny, may be as necessary to the rearing of the young as due attention paid to their future pay packets and industrial usefulness.

Johann Friedrich Herbart (1776-1841), a teacher and a philosopher, rejects Hegel's apotheosis of the state and returns to the individualism of Rousseau and Kant. He argues with Kant, whose chair of philosophy he occupied at Königsberg, that the only good thing in the universe is the 'good will', but he was not satisfied with Kant's definition of what the 'pure will' was or of its relevance to education. Reduced to its elements his argument runs thus: the aim of education is to make good men; a good man is one who wills rightly; our acts are determined by our desires; our desires by our interests and our interests by the education we receive. And by 'interest' Herbart refers to no momentary titillation of bored minds but to a persistent interest that stimulates prolonged effort, produces self-generated activity and a desire to extend the knowledge we possess. Moreover this interest must be many-sided, deep and permanent, enriching continuously the content of the mind, actively co-ordinating new

[11] W. Boyd, *The History of Western Education*, p. 318.

knowledge with past experience. What Herbart is here emphasizing is the character-forming power of the content of the mind. This is the core of his teaching: we cannot be good unless 'we know and think while we know' to use John Henry Newman's phrase. As John Adams has said, if all Herbartianism could be gathered up in one sentence, that sentence would be:

'The will takes root on the circle of thought.'[12]

Here is a formidable conception of the teacher's job. His field of professional operations is his student's mind; education in its total span from formal instruction to the presentation of man's noblest achievements can modify character by forming the 'good will'. The proposition is wildly optimistic of course. Nevertheless teachers of today have reason to take heart and to believe that even if but partially true Herbart's encouraging conviction is supported by the experience of their own best teaching with their own best pupils. Half a century ago the wise John Adams, who never backed a cause without good reason, said this:

'What is needed, in fact, in modern educational theory is a little more of this hopeful element. We are so hemmed in by evolutionary theories with their ramifications into the forces of heredity and environment, that we are unduly depressed, and tend to become hopeless regarding our work as educators. Nothing great can be hoped for in the case of men and women who go about their educational work full of conviction of how little education can really effect. Certain of our later writers seem to take a positive pleasure in emphasizing the limits of education as a moral force.'[13]

Two experiences of our own time support this view. First, who can doubt that the corrupted minds of Nazi youth were the product of conditioning 'the circle of thought' by the presentation of ideas and the emotional impact of propaganda? Secondly, the general trend of recent genetic and psychological research is steadily removing from the educational scene the dead hand of heredity and depressing judgements on the educability of

[12] *Evolution of Educational Theory*, p. 327.
[13] Op. cit., p. 326.

children. Thus the recent history of nations, our own observation of children, and especially, perhaps the findings of expert inquiry —the Crowther, Robbins, Newsom and Plowden reports, for instance—sustain the view that the teacher plays a fundamental role in society and that Herbart's key themes were not non-sensical.

Unfortunately other fundamental teachings of Herbart have remained buried beneath the mass of pedagogic lumber accumulated by his followers: for example that discipline is the art of human intercourse between teacher and pupils; that the power of discipline only reaches as far as the pupils' assent meets it; that all single acts of external discipline depend for their effect on the ethos of the school community in which they are exercised; that moral instruction in a moral society can be one means of reinforcing moral purpose. Is not this last what Lionel Elvin was saying in a discussion on education and secular humanism in 1964? 'What we have to do is to form in every young man and woman, so far as we can, an ethical sensitiveness and a critical discrimination that will enable them to form a sound judgement in action.'[14] This is the objective Herbart had in mind; and these are the real ingredients of Herbart's conception of the teacher's task. They reveal a role in which intellect, artistry, human sympathy and technical skill are beautifully allied and might seem to justify a very high social status for the teaching profession. Unfortunately the machinery of Herbart's classroom method, being more exportable than the art of making children good, became the working tools of the nineteenth century training colleges, and ensured the lowly status of practitioners content to plod faithfully up and down a stairway which had only Five Steps.[15]

---

[14] See *Religious Education 1944-1984*, ed. A. G. Weddespoon 1966.
[15] Note on the Herbartian Five Steps: Herbart formulated five stages in effective instruction, which undoubtedly brought sounder methods into the classroom:
1. *Preparation:* the aim of the lesson must be explained; and the teacher will make sure of the pupils' existing knowledge of a subject before proceeding to the learning of more (this of course involves question and answer).

AUTHORITY, FREEDOM OR BOTH

This chapter has been chiefly concerned with a description of changes in educational theory which have permanently affected the work of teachers. That some revolt against the rigid formalism of traditional teaching was called for few will deny. But, as G. H. Bantock wisely remarks, 'If all revolutions occur in answer to a need, that does not mean that all which thus occurs is necessarily good.'[16] Nor, on the other hand, need we assume that all the good results are necessarily founded on unassailable premises. The trend away from the teacher's traditional authoritarian role towards greater freedom and individual activity in schools has without doubt 'admitted floods of light and air into tightly enclosed nurseries and schoolrooms'. But we must nevertheless examine more closely the assumptions in which this fertile revolution had its roots.

Broadly speaking there are two propositions involved in this discussion whose validity we must examine, the first derived from Locke, the second from the 'nature' educators. Nowhere have they been more succinctly analysed than in C. D. Hardie's *Truth and Fallacy in Educational Theory* which every teacher should read and upon which the following argument is based.

The first proposition runs as follows:

1. Sense impression of nature is the only true foundation of human knowledge and, therefore, the *only* true foundation of human instruction.

The first half of this proposition seems to be true if we assume

2. *Presentation:* new knowledge must be presented in detail, not as a whole, so that each fact is clearly apprehended.
3. *Association:* new material is associated with what is already known— e.g. by discussion.
4. *Condensation:* A reflective stage when new and old knowledge are united into an orderly whole.
5. *Application:* What has been learned must now be tested to discover whether the new knowledge is true and that it works, e.g. in arithmetic or science. Old fashioned as the Five Steps are, and sadly as they were made to enslave the poor training college student, they nevertheless remain at least the bare skeleton of sound classroom method.

[16] *Freedom and Authority in Education*, p. 62.

that sense impressions are acquired by *description* as well as by actual observation of the object through our senses. For instance we can get a clear impression of a kangaroo in the zoo, and another impression based on the description of a kangaroo supported, say, by the expert authority of the director of the Zoological Gardens, who has seen a kangaroo—on the important condition that we understood every constituent detail of the description he provides. But, asks Hardie, can we acquire a clear idea of the hidden laws of physics, or the laws of language, and we might add, of the human conflicts and achievements of the past, *only* by sense impressions? The answer seems to be No. But it is needful that this other type of knowledge should be learned by children. It seems to follow, therefore, that sense impressions of nature cannot be the *only* true foundations of human instruction.

The importance for the teacher of this conclusion is clear: There is an area of learning which requires teachers to provide abundant opportunities for children, especially young children, to see, hear, touch the objects that surround them in the home and the natural world. For this is where knowledge begins. But it is not where knowledge ends. Hence to starve children of the experiences to be gained from the drama of human existence as portrayed in literature, history and art, in which the guidance of the teacher presents to them 'the vision of greatness', is to deprive them of essential elements in their emotional and intellectual growth. On the other hand, to confine their activities to the two-dimensional world of books is to exclude them from the three-dimensional world in which they live. This is what the exponents of 'education according to nature', with all their false analogies but with deep insight into the needs of children, have in effect been teaching. And even they, as we have seen, were not unaware of that other means of learning whereby the teacher with the authority of greater knowledge imparts what he knows in more formal teaching.

This brings us to our second proposition:

2. A child should be left free to develop according to the laws of its own nature.

or, to keep to Froebel's analogy, a child is like a plant and therefore a teacher should be no more than a gardener who tends its growth.

The assumption here is that the process of education is analogous to the natural processes of the botanical kingdom. It is assumed that what happens to a seed in its response to its physical environment of soil, rain and sun is at least similar to what takes place when the inner growing potential of a child responds to its very different environment. The analogy fails of course, and fails completely, when we recognize that a child's growth involves not only physical development but the unfolding of a whole complex of emotional and mental characteristics the plant does not possess.

Nevertheless we have seen that in one form or another the advocates of 'education according to nature' have each provided some form of control; disguised in the case of Rousseau, but explicit in Pestalozzi's theme of love and obedience and in Froebel's use of authority and punishment in the years after childhood. Kant and Herbart too, unrepentant individualists, both acknowledging a debt to Rousseau and both admitting the value of free activity in the early years, finally turn the teacher's attention towards cultivation of the good will and the informed mind. As we have seen in the case of Herbart, this training does not preclude all kinds of individual and social activity that encourage learning and enrich experience, but in his case the authority of the teacher is exercised more overtly and on more traditional lines. It remains, then, for the teacher to move between the two poles of authority and freedom as the learning and teaching circumstances demand. My wife once asked a new boy whether he would like jelly or fruit salad for his tea—'Both, please,' he replied. A good principle. In the education of children there is no need to belong exclusively to one extreme school or the other.

13 The school community as teacher

There is no clearly discernible origin of the teacher's role as a builder of the school's community life. We have seen it partially evident in Vittorino's school at Mantua, in Mulcaster's St. Paul's, in Pestalozzi's association of the good school with the good home and in Herbart's reference to the ethos of the school as a moral influence. It becomes more explicit in Sir Thomas Wyse's book *Education and Reform* (1836) in which he suggests that a master's authority counts for less than the total impact of the ethos of a school community on its members. This observation was a product of Wyse's extensive examination of new types of school in England and on the continent. He was impressed with the three schools founded by von Fellenberg at Hofwyl, near Berne, and with the experiment in self-government at the Hills' school at Hazlewood, both of which seemed to him incomparably superior to the English public schools of his time. In this chapter, then, we shall consider the idea of the school as a teaching community and note the very different ways in which it was expressed: in the work of von Fellenberg at Hofwyl, in the Hazelwood experiment, and in Rugby under Thomas Arnold and Uppingham under Thring. In the achievements of Miss Buss and Miss Beale we shall see the same theme for the first time developed in girls' education, and fresh interpretations of the old idea appearing in the 'new education' movement beginning at the close of the century.

VON FELLENBERG AT HOFWYL

Obedient to his mother's advice 'the great have friends enough;

be thou the friend of the poor', a sentiment reinforced by his admiration for Pestalozzi, Philip Emanuel von Fellenberg (1771-1844) purchased an estate at Hofwyl, near Berne, in 1799 and there founded the most significant group of schools in the Europe of his time. He first established an agricultural school for poor children to which he later added a technical institute for young farmers; he then completed the class structure of the community by adding a high school for the sons of wealthy families. In 1831 he established what became a renowned teachers' training centre which he placed under the imaginative supervision of his chief assistant Wehrli, a passionate and utterly dedicated disciple of Pestalozzi, who eventually became director of a larger training college at Kreuzlingen on Lake Constance. Although no rebel against the class structure of society, von Fellenberg was convinced that greater sympathy would exist between the classes if children, even though educated separately and on differing curricula, were not forced into isolation. Modern educational planners would have found fewer obstacles to adapting Hofwyl into a comprehensive school than they sometimes encounter in England in the 1970's.

In the early nineteenth century benevolent paternalism undoubtedly produced the best schools of the period. In most of Europe headmasters were seldom paternal and as little inclined to benevolence as they were to the reception of new ideas. Von Fellenberg had all these virtues to a high degree. He was capable of accepting the ideas of the 'new education', for example Rousseau's principle of a guarded education, without their extravagances. His temperamental affinity with 'Father' Pestalozzi ensured that his relations with his pupils were founded on obedience and trust; and his experience in his own school served to confirm his view that good school communities can be built only on unremitting care for children. Thus at Hofwyl a nice balance seems to have been preserved between orderly routine and scope for individual initiative. There was no attempt to mould approved models of boyhood, as in the English public school: 'No educator,' said von Fellenberg, 'should permit himself to misapprehend, or to pervert according to his own contracted views, that which the Creator has ordered.'[1]

Moral education at Hofwyl was grounded in Christian ethics, but it was on the penetration of Christian morality into the whole life of the school that von Fellenberg relied. So important did he regard slow and quiet absorption of a boy into the ethos of the community that he would seldom admit more than three boys at a time into the school. The boys lived under a mildly protective régime which was remarkably free from repression. Although discipline was mild it was unyielding and consistent. The pupils were under constant supervision at work and games but, as in the schools of Port Royal, its impact was softened by the friendliness of the masters, and, unlike Port Royal, boys were deliberately challenged with the type of temptation they were likely to meet in the outside world. Visitors to Hofwyl, for instance, were often amazed at the liberal supply of food and wine permitted on festive occasions. This occasional break in their frugal life was intended to cultivate sober habits by teaching them 'to partake in moderation even in the midst of prodigality'.[2]

Von Fellenberg's attitudes to punishment were derived from his Christian convictions: 'We seldom see the Divine hand extended *visibly* to punish the offender.'[3] Rousseau's discipline of natural consequences he accepted as part of a divine dispensation; he regarded the corrective effect of social disapproval as a natural consequence of living in a community governed by Christian standards, and the exclusion of a pupil from class or games as a logical result of laziness or the misuse of freedom. Even his best friends doubted whether this mild régime would have worked in tougher schools. Von Fellenberg agreed with them while pointing out that harsh discipline was merely a symptom of bad relationships between teachers and pupils: 'the arbitrary and violent punishments which appear to have no other source than the will of the master are the cause of serious injury to *character*, although they may be effectual in repressing

[1] *Letters from Hofwyl, by a Parent*, p. 237.
[2] Op. cit., p. 262.
[3] Op. cit., p. 264.

the *exterior defects* of the pupil'.[4] That his gentle ways were successful there was no doubt: after two years' sojourn at Hofwyl an eye-witness describes 'a degree of order and industry . . . which I have rarely seen in a public institution, and which I have never witnessed where force and violence were the instruments of government'.[5] 'Father' Fellenberg, as staff and pupils called him, would have attributed this success to his view of the schoolmaster's role: 'the educator should be like the Saviour, the child's best friend, not his tyrant'.[6]

Von Fellenberg's treatment of religious instruction was as unusual and as remarkable in his day as his disciplinary practice. Indeed he regarded these aspects of school life as two sides of the same coin. This was a time, we must remember, when religion in school was almost universally treated as a strict exercise in formal worship and catechetical instruction. There was no place for indoctrination at Hofwyl. 'We established our institutions,' Von Fellenberg said, 'upon the basis of genuine Christianity', not on the inculcation of doctrine but on the practice of Christian values by every member of the school community. For the school is the 'first world' of children, and here they must see with their own eyes what he called 'living examples of abstract truths'. In this Fellenberg was beautifully Pestalozzian.

Religious instruction was accomplished through living within a continuing social experience, whereby 'abstract truths' involving loving respect for persons were made real to the children not only in the history of the saints but in the people and events of their own day and in the intimate encounters of their own school life. He was convinced that in the community which children *know* they first begin to reflect on the values that bind people together, and to appreciate the relevance of Christian worship to the lives they are living. Hence in the simple non-sectarian evening assemblies for worship the material for meditation was gathered from the familiar events of life at Hofwyl itself. Today there seems little remarkable in this creedless approach to school religion; but in von Fellenberg's day it was

---

[4] Op. cit., p. 265.   [5] Op. cit., p. 267.   [6] Op. cit., p. 257.

near to heresy. In a stiff-necked society, in which church attendance and sermons were deemed to be the better part of moral education, he was bitterly criticized for thus forsaking the formal system of orthodox religious schooling, even though he made ample provision for sectarian teaching and worship for those boys whose parents required it.

My own admiration for von Fellenberg is largely due to his success in a sphere of the schoolmaster's job that has been more written about and less practised than any other branch of running a school. For I have seldom encountered in the annals of education a more realistic recognition of the truth that the glowing precepts of parsons and schoolmasters are not by the grace of God alone translated into the day to day confrontations of school life. Von Fellenberg seemed to achieve the desirable condition that his 'living samples of abstract truths' really did become evident in the ethos and daily life of his schools. In effect this means that he and his staff were living samples of the simple Christian virtues, sincerity, honesty, charity without sentimentality and with an undespairing respect for children. In this sense they were religious men, i.e. teachers who were steadily striving towards a coincidence between belief and practice, which is surely the essence of being religious. When we remember that von Fellenberg's Hofwyl was exactly contemporary with John Keate's royal Eton, whose headmaster believed that no boy ever told the truth, of whom the only kind word said was that he flogged the son of a duke and the son of a grocer with equal impartiality, where staff and boys, as in most other famous schools, confronted each other in hostile camps, we have some measure of his achievement.

The institutions of Hofwyl enjoyed a European fame, and in the young American republic von Fellenberg had his devotees. But it was not so much his educational principles that finally attracted the economically minded Anglo-Saxons of England and America as the success of his agricultural school, which among its utilitarian advantages possessed the special virtue of being able to pay its way. The splendid enterprise at Hofwyl died with its founder for lack of public support, a fate which sometimes befalls institutions that depend too much on the inspiration of one great man. But the story of Hofwyl remains as an example of the school community as teacher, and a good sample of the teacher's role as a builder of community.

THE HILLS AT HAZELWOOD

A less noble failure of a good idea was the Hazelwood experiment in school government, which might have been more successful than it was if its founders had been blessed with the human touch of von Fellenberg. The plan was a brave attempt to establish a school community based on self-government. Unfortunately the idea was over-elaborated and in its results was in some ways as unattractive as the régime of the public schools against which it was a protest.

Thomas Wright Hill and his sons Rowland and Matthew Davenport opened their school at Edgbaston, Birmingham, in 1819. Several unusual and interesting assumptions determined their enterprise: that in all education the pupil should be accepted into partnership by his teachers; that it is better to learn than to be taught; that a school is a place where socially valuable experience can be acquired by a wide distribution of personal responsibility among the pupils; and finally, that motives deemed honourable in society are valid motives for stimulating industry and good citizenship in the school community. These were remarkably advanced views for the time.

The system was thus explained by the two daughters of M. D. Hill:

'The purpose of the system was to impart the power of self-government and self-education. To accomplish this the pupil's mind must be enlisted heartily in the cause and coercion must gradually be withdrawn. Thus as far as possible all power was left in the hands of the boys. The school in fact constituted a Republic of which the Head-master was President. The teachers regulated the routine and hours of study, but all other laws for the government of the community were made by a committee, elected by ballot from among the pupils, by themselves; the master's assent alone to their enactments being necessary—an assent which he had never occasion to withhold. A "Jury Court" for the trial of both civil and criminal causes, from which the committee formed a Court of Appeal, and an effective staff of officers for the preservation of order, were appointed by the boys from their own numbers.'[7]

In several respects the system worked: bullying was rare and the rights even of the smallest boys were protected. The 'courts', it was claimed were an exercise in clear thinking which refined the boys' sense of justice, and from the teachers' point of view had the virtue of releasing the masters from the accusation of favouritism or severity. But beyond the courts, which were the most obvious implements of self-government, there was a code, which by 1827 had become a document of 112 pages, in which was elaborated as fantastically complex a system of rewards and punishments as ever perplexed a schoolboy. In unimaginative conformity with the current competitive society of middle class England, competition was encouraged as the mainspring of personal effort and the foundation of school relationships, whether it were achievement in the classroom, behaviour on the playground or manners at the breakfast table. By means of a school currency of dummy coins achievement was rewarded and malingerers fined. On the principle that 'it is impossible long to maintain any medium between great order and utter disorder', absolute silence was imposed in classrooms and refectory and a 'paid' official dignified by the rank of 'Silentiary' and hatted as a sign of office, stalked around in noiseless slippers imposing fines on any disturbers of this monastic peace. The clock and the bell governed each moment of the day. The Hills seemed to be obsessed with the dangers of standing and staring; they were 'constantly in search of means for ensuring the effective employment of every minute which is spent in the classroom'.[8]

The Hazelwood scheme is a splendid example of good ideas gone wrong. Its justification is its protest against the senseless

[7] R. & F. Davenport Hill: *Matthew Davenport Hill* (1878), p. 60.
[8] Op. cit., p. 13.

barbarities current in the public schools, and it was a sincere if misguided attempt to devise a more humane régime. The Hills were right in believing that the higher social values of adult society were relevant to the immature society in a school, but they were woefully blind to the fact that relentless competition was not one of them. They were right in emphasizing the importance of personal responsibility, but forgot that the most acceptable form of personal obligation can never be paid for in cash. Their desire to induce a sense of partnership between teachers and pupils was so new that only today has the word 'participation' any wide meaning in staff-student relationships. But at Hazelwood the régime imposed a weight of social coercion that inhibited the natural exuberance of lively boys. There was, indeed, little of that true respect for individuals that brings us into much greater sympathy with von Fellenberg's kindly paternalism. Our judgement on Hazelwood must, then, be that it was a brave but humourless attempt to create a school community that was also an educative community. But even its failure to achieve its entirely commendable aim is valuable as an object lesson. The last word on the matter is given by a former pupil:

'By juries and committees, by marks, and by appeals to a sense of honour, discipline was maintained. But this was done, I think, at too great a sacrifice; the thoughtlessness, the spring, the elation of childhood were taken from us; we were premature men: one of my younger schoolfellows told me that as an older boy, being appointed after I left a guardian over his juniors, the responsibility weighed on him so heavily that he meditated suicide; and yet there was not a tinge of morbidness in his temperament. The school was in truth a moral hotbed, which forced us into a precocious imitation of maturity. I have heard an Oxford friend say that Arnold's men had a little of the prig about them: I know too well that some of us had a great deal of the prig about us . . . but I have comforted myself by observing that in later life my school fellows (perhaps therefore I myself) outgrew this unamiable character.'[9]

[9] W. L. Sargant, *Essays by a Birmingham Manufacturer*, Vol. II. pp. 186-92.

Nevertheless the Hills' failure represented a sincere reaction against the authoritarian régime of the public schools of that time. This desire to bring children into responsible relationships within the school community has become a valuable element in modern education. The pioneers in the progressive school movement of more recent times have successfully introduced various forms of self-government into the school régime which have improved staff-pupil relationships and have now become an even more important factor in the education of the 'participation'-conscious boy and girl.

We now turn to the public schools to discover if they had a better way of building a school community.

THE PUBLIC SCHOOLS

The Hazelwood plan was not to be the model of the school as a community in Victorian England. In this country the idea had other and less auspicious origins than the experiments of radical reformers. Its roots grew in the intense but quite unconscious sense of community existing among the boys of the public schools, and its flowering was due to the reforming zeal of headmasters who were determined to rid school life of the barbarities which were offending liberal opinion at the turn of the century. Thus the idea of the school as a community was a joint product of schoolboy loyalties and of England's peculiar genius for producing great headmasters, among whom Thomas Arnold of Rugby and Edward Thring of Uppingham were outstanding. These two men provide us with contrasting examples of the teacher as headmaster.

In the early nineteenth century each public school was in effect two distinct communities, the masters and the boys, who waged incessant war on each other. The 'school' was the boys, who regarded themselves as repositories of rights and customs, often senseless and barbaric, to be defended against all innovating authority. Boy solidarity was complete, and bitterly did the more sensitive natures suffer from it: 'cruel the suffering and wrong; wild the profligacy' wrote Edward Thring of his experience in

Long Chamber at Eton in 1832. The weapons of the headmaster and staff were flogging and expulsion, used in a rearguard action against the armies of stubborn boyhood. The boys adhered to their own primitive standards: to bait a master, to inflict pain on another boy, lying in the cause of schoolboy solidarity, were not sins against the schoolboy code; to flinch beneath the rod, to hold independent opinions, were serious betrayals. These schoolboy conventions were symbols of an obstinate conservatism resistant to all authority. We can forgive Keate the flogging of his confirmation class, even his conviction that no boy ever told the truth, when we remember that he himself taught the sons of the British aristocracy in classes of 100 to 170 and that after 'reform' in 1833 there were 9 masters for 600 boys at Eton. As for religious teaching, Gladstone who attended Eton from 1821 to 1827 declared it to be 'almost dead'.

Nevertheless it was out of this unpromising situation that one of England's greatest contributions to education was made. The boys won the war: for the headmasters secured a continuing armistice by conceding special rights and privileges to the older boys and thus transformed the spearhead of revolt into an instrument of discipline. By developing a more orderly structure of boy government by prefects, not to be confused with 'self-government' as it sometimes is, honour was satisfied for both contestants. This was a slow process and prefecture was not invented by Arnold. It was an institution even then centuries old, but under the guidance of able headmasters from Butler of Shrewsbury to Thring of Uppingham and beyond, who used the prefect system as an instrument of indirect rule, the English public schools were gradually transformed into conservative but educative communities whose compulsive ethos became the major formative influence on their boys.

Thus the reform of the public schools from within was the work of headmasters supported by lesser but equally devoted men: big personalities, stern Christians, fine scholars, uncompromising moralists and authoritarians, they changed the image of the teacher from that of the fighting usher in the prolific line of Orbilius to that of builders of community. Not of a community bound by democratic rights and duties, but a pyramidal hierarchy, and a very solid pyramid it was:

> 'On neat graduations of ascending ranks
> Reigned order—there, by firmest law secured
> Right triumphed over might.'[10]

John Moultrie's was a wishful Etonian thought. Nevertheless he describes the objective of the community-building teachers of public schools in the nineteenth century. This was the day of the autocratic headmaster who ruled his staff and boys in the manner of an eastern potentate. The success or failure of his school depended on him, and only in a diminished degree is it true today that on him rest great responsibilities for the welfare and reputation of his school.

Reform was in the air before Arnold went to Rugby in 1828. Dr. Samuel Butler headmaster of Shrewsbury from 1798 to 1836 ruled through his prefects in ways that foreshadowed Arnold's use of his sixth form; he was deeply concerned for the welfare of the younger boys; he exalted scholarship above all other school concerns; and he taught boys how to study, a rare improvement in teaching for whose general application we are still waiting. But Arnold of Rugby and Thring of Uppingham tower above all other reforming headmasters—and for entirely different reasons, which present us with interesting contrasts in the art of building a school community.

Arnold's aim was to make 'Christian gentlemen' for he had no hope of making Christian boys. He was obsessed with the 'devil in the midst of them' and never rid himself of the oppressive vision of sin in the young. If he could have had his way with his Maker he would have abolished adolescence altogether. He ruled through his sixth form, a manner of remote control that gave the false impression (to the young, of course, a seemingly true impression) that he was not interested in the younger boys. This chosen élite he conditioned in a moral hothouse, imbuing them

---

[10] John Moultrie, *The Dream of Life*, 1843.

with his ideals and stiffening their moral crusade among the lower ranks with his authority. These older boys lived through him. This is not a rare phenomenon among schoolmasters and parents; but it is fraught with grave dangers. It is not healthy for youth to be nourished from the bloodstream of a big personality, for spiritual dependence inhibits the process of growing up. When the umbilical cord is severed disaster may follow. Arnold's own sons as well as his pupils suffered from this error in a great man. Harold Nicolson suggested that Arnold's dominance was 'that of the upas tree which casts a blight over those who linger too long beneath its branches', as Arnold's eldest son repined:

> We who till then in thy shade
> Rested, as under the boughs
> Of a mighty oak, have endured
> Sunshine and rain as we might,
> Bare, unshaded, alone,
> Lacking the shelter of thee.

Arthur Hugh Clough writes of his 'strange distorted youth'. Harold Nicolson believed it was not Thomas Arnold but Thomas Hughes through *Tom Brown's Schooldays* who created the public school spirit.[11]

What Arnold did was to impose on those who were responsible for the education of boys a high moral purpose founded on the formation of Christian character. He did little to reform the curriculum, nothing to abolish flogging or fagging, and contributed no new ideas to the management of the school's daily life. With passionate sincerity he proclaimed that goodness mattered, but he failed to realize that it takes more than a moral whirlwind to cleanse the secret places of schoolboy morals. This was why von Fellenberg before him and Thring after him were so much more successful, for they realized that there are more humdrum affairs to attend to if a school is to become a good community. When he died in 1842 the evils in Rugby against

[11] *Good Behaviour*, Ch. XIII.

which he had waged his Olympian war still remained. Even his message seemed to have died with him until his devoted follower A. P. Stanley two years later produced the *Life and Correspondence of Dr. Arnold*, the first of innumerable biographies written on this controversial figure. This, and Thomas Hughes' *Tom Brown's Schooldays*, created the Arnold legend. But, as Dr. T. M. Bamford has said in his admirable reassessment of the great man's achievements, 'it matters little if gods are false, provided that good things are done in their name'. At least part of Arnold's legacy of reform was like that of Magna Carta, whose influence on the English constitution may be attributed as much to what people thought it to be as to what it really was.

But one thing Arnold did for which some schoolmasters will be grateful: he did much to raise the status of the teacher, at least in the public schools. He stated his views in vigorous words:

'. . . as to what regards the position of a schoolmaster in society, you are well aware that it has not yet obtained that respect in England, as to be able to stand by itself in public opinion as a liberal profession; it owes the rank which it holds to its connexion with the profession of a clergyman, for that is acknowledged universally in England to be the profession of a gentleman. Mere teaching, like mere literature, places a man, I think, in rather an equivocal position; he holds no undoubted station in society by these alone; for neither education nor literature have ever enjoyed that consideration and general respect in England which they enjoy in France and in Germany. But a far higher consideration is this, that he who is to educate boys, if he is fully sensible of the importance of his business, must be unwilling to lose such great opportunities as the clerical character give him by enabling him to address them continually from the pulpit, and to administer the Communion to them as they become old enough to receive it.'

With the clerical emphasis we need not agree; perhaps this again indicates the restricted scope of his vision. But teachers today will appreciate his insistence on paying good wages to those who teach. During his tenure at Rugby staff salaries were doubled. A housemaser earned over £1,500 a year; Arnold's own income was over £4,000, 'equivalent to over 100 teachers in lower class schools'. This amazing disparity of income was one of the causes which has permanently operated as a divisive factor in the teaching profession from Arnold's day to the Public School Commission of 1968.[12]

It was not Arnold's Rugby but Thring's Uppingham that provides us with the best example of community building. The more I think of Arnold as a schoolmaster the less I respect him as a headmaster. By keeping his eye closer to the ground Thring got his boys much nearer to heaven. Edward Thring (1821-1887) took over a school of 25 boys in 1853. He based his management of Uppingham on a group of simple propositions devoid of all pious aspirations: that every boy should be *known*; that every boy is capable of something, be he clever or dull; that every boy should receive individual attention; that a school must conform to 'the grand principle of working with fit tools'. How can a boy be 'known', he asks, when he is one of a herd of boys in a large school and taught in large classes? (There were still 60 boys to a class at Rugby twenty years after Arnold's death.) So Thring restricted the size of his classes to 25, his boarding houses to 30, and his school to 320. He attributed the grosser evils of school life not to the inherent sinfulness of boys but to obvious and removable causes. Provide school life with 'a little moral drainage', for moral evil can be dealt with like 'a fog in an undrained field'. Briefly, provide conditions where good behaviour and good learning get a chance to flourish and sin will cease to be interesting.[13]

It was part of Thring's genius to encapsulate important principles in telling phrases, and to translate them into the working fabric of the school's daily life. He never ceased to insist on what he called 'truth in schools'. Boys and masters are not inclined to virtuous lives by preaching but by living in a situation

[12] See T. M. Bamford, *Thomas Arnold*, pp. 176-8 & 190.
[13] G. R. Parkin, *Edward Thring, Life, Diary and Letter*, 1900, p. 219.

that evokes truthful attitudes, 'for all true feeling is unconscious in proportion to its perfection'. In all school organization, in every act of co-operation, there must be 'no falseness in government, no falseness in the working plan'. The principle of 'truth in schools' demanded that 'whatever is professed shall be done'. It was as simple and as difficult as that. If a school professes to teach or to board boys, then every boy must be taught according to his individual capacity and every boy must be well fed and lodged and cared for. To do otherwise is an acted falsehood committed by those who manage the school, for 'that which is professed is not done'. Thus Thring, devout and prayerful though he was, laid the foundations of school morality not in the school chapel or in moral admonitions, but in the coincidence of what was done with what ought to be done. This is the only sure foundation for the building of community.

Thring's concept of 'truth in schools' had its corollary in his equally fertile principle of 'the almighty wall'. It was an odd circumstance that the schools, who obstinately persisted in maintaining the classical tradition in which the nation's rulers were educated, should have so completely neglected Plato's plea that youth should 'breathe in beauty from every quarter'. The sons of the wealthiest lived, worked and slept in crowded and squalid classrooms and dormitories. Thring was convinced that schooling in slums was not conducive to high thinking or good behaviour. The size and design of school buildings, their functional effectiveness, whether it be school chapel, classroom or workshop, must play their civilizing role—Good classrooms, he said, were 'an honour to lessons'. This was another facet of 'truth in schools': 'talking of truth and honour and trust is one thing, and having the structure true and honourable and trust-deserving is another'. It is doubtful whether ten per cent of Thring's contemporaries gave a thought to such frivolities despite Ruskin's preaching.[14]

Thus for Thring good building and equipment were more than fee-winning amenities: they were also a means to achieving a civilized society of adults and boys, each doing his job with

[14] Op. cit., pp. 218-21.

no consciousness of opposing interests between boys and staff either in work or play. Boredom he knew to be the great enemy, and lack of satisfying occupation the main cause of juvenile delinquency—as it still is and always will be. Every fresh interest he said, 'is a fresh barrier against evil, and every fresh subject is a net which catches someone and educates those who are neglected and left to rot'.[15] He was never tired of declaring that every boy can do something well. So new opportunities were provided. French and German appeared in the curriculum and those most backward in classical studies were permitted to 'take refuge' in science. In 1859 there appeared at Uppingham the first gymnasium in an English school; and also wood and metal workshops, school gardens and a swimming pool. Greatest achievement of all for a man quite unmusical—but typical of his wider vision—was the encouragement of music, fostered wonderfully by the music master Herr David. Thring lived to see a music staff of seven masters. This was a great advance in the aesthetic education of boys. These broadening conceptions of education were all part of the theme of 'the almighty wall' or 'the grand principle of working with fit tools'.

But they were also part of his design for disciplined community life in which reasonable people, old and young, could live and trust each other. He consistently based his relationships with boys on this assumption: 'Boys at school should be protected by all their surroundings. . . . The whole structure should act as an unseen friend. . . . No words, no personal influence, no religion even can do instead of the holy help of the wall, or overcome its evil, if evil. . . . The whole atmosphere should be an atmosphere of work and life, with time fully occupied, and an involuntary, quiet throwing of light on all the boy's life. Neglect and faulty structure breed impurity as in a hotbed.'[16] Boys, he said, should *feel* they are trusted, and trust should be unlimited. For, he said in another lovely phrase 'a boy need not be false'. Thring's aim was to make school life so interesting and satisfying that rowdiness and grossness ceased to yield their furtive delights: there is 'no cure for animalism unless high

[15] Op. cit., p. 45.   [16] Op. cit., p. 277.

tastes and occupations engross the mind'.[17]

Thring insisted that a headmaster cannot know his boys unless he teaches them. He once said that if a headmaster does not know his boys then the assistant master who does is the headmaster's headmaster. He was himself an able classroom teacher with strong views on the art of teaching:

'Pouring out knowledge is not teaching.
Hearing lessons is not teaching.
Lecturing well is not teaching.
No mere applying of knowledge is teaching.
Teaching is getting at heart and mind, so that the learner begins to value learning, and to believe learning is possible in his own case.'[18]

Can we today say much more?

A former pupil, the Rev. J. H. Skrine, wrote of him 'Among the secret springs of discipline was his tenderness . . . of that pure sound love-compelling quality which belongs to natures of which the grain is stern. . . . He had a power of finding where the spark of fire lay in the coarsest human clay . . . he had a masculine understanding of the plain simple temptations to which youthful flesh is heir. A boy felt that the warning or the counsel came from one who owned an animal nature as forceful and enjoying as his own. . . . A few score words, broad and plain, and gentle without a touch of sentiment, and the heavy-witted leaden-natured boy, had looked and seen himself in an enchanted mirror.'

Arnold may have been a greater man, but Thring was an incomparably better schoolmaster and headmaster. Arnold knew his sixth form; Thring knew all his boys. Arnold had little aesthetic feeling and spent too much time outside the school to realize the importance of 'the almighty wall'; both men trusted boys to tell the truth, but Arnold with gloomy doubts about the result and Thring confident that in a trustful society 'a boy need not be false'. Arnold attempted to purify his school through

---

[17] Op. cit., p. 279.
[18] *Theory and Practice of Teaching*, p. 239.

the moral fervour of his chosen leaders; Thring by creating a community situation where adults, men and women, and all boys, young and old, were in continuous and friendly contact. Thus Thring avoided what has always been the danger of dominant moralistic headmasters—the debilitation of the upas tree.

Nevertheless in these men we find two outstanding models of the teacher as authoritarian headmaster and also two contrasting attempts to create England's peculiar version of the school as a community. The pyramidal hierarchy of school society represented the shape of the national community; such free speech, self-government and administration of justice as was permitted was initiated from above. But one over-riding condition supervened over all considerations of personality, size of school, and details of school government: the distinguishing feature of all the public schools was in Arnold's time, and is today, its 'common life'. Welded into a living organism by its hierarchical principle, it became itself the mould of character and *mores*, and the beneficent mother to whom all loyalties are due. In diluted forms its influence has penetrated into the state system, especially into the grammar schools, and now is appearing in the comprehensive schools. And so today, when a new headmaster settles tentatively into his new chair at a new desk in a new school, he thinks a little about curriculum and timetable, but very much about how to make his school a community. And when this job is well done this is usually a good kind of school; but when the school becomes a closed community self-consciously concerned to preserve its own privileges, and therefore its prejudices, its value to the larger community becomes less obvious and the teacher's community-building role less admirable.

MISS BEALE AND MISS BUSS

To leave the impression that the building of the educative school community was the privilege of men only would present a false view of education in this period. It is indeed an easy transition from the community building of Thring to the same theme in the sphere of girls' education, for Thring himself was a powerful advocate of higher education for women. Our choice of personalities is made for us. Not even Arnold or Thring compel our admiration more than the two outstanding women teachers of the century—Miss Beale and Miss Buss. Against prejudice and on meagre resources these two women laid the foundations of girls' secondary education in twentieth century England.

Reform in the higher education of girls was part of the liberal and feminist movements of the 1850's which in England and America began to assert the right of women to receive an education less restrictive than that of the convent and more useful than that of the academy for young ladies. The best education for women was given in the cultured home under personal tutors and governesses. It was, in fact, from the need to train governesses for more academic responsibilities in the homes of the affluent middle class that girls' secondary education began. In 1843 the Governesses Benevolent Institution was founded with the object of improving the teaching capacity of this humble profession. But it was found that the standards of attainment of the potential trainees were so low that further instruction was necessary. For this purpose F. D. Maurice and Charles Kingsley, with the help of liberal-minded colleagues from King's College, London, founded Queen's College for Ladies in Harley Street in 1848. Among its first students were Frances Mary Buss and Dorothea Beale.

Frances Mary Buss (1827-1894) began teaching in her mother's private school in Kentish Town at the age of fourteen, supplementing her inadequate schooling by wide reading and later by attending evening classes at Queen's College. In 1850 the school was moved to Camden Street and assumed a more public character under the new name of the North London Collegiate School. This school proved to be both the spearpoint and the model for the development of girls' secondary day schools for the next hundred years. This outcome was not only due to the quality of her school but to the pressures she was able to bring on the Taunton Commission in 1865[19] by the sheer excellence of her

[19] i.e. The Schools Inquiry Commission which sat from 1864 to 1867 and reported in 1868.

own educational achievement and the power of a distinctive personality. The ultimate results of Miss Buss's influence on the Commission will be discussed later. Here we must pause to consider her immediate contribution to the education of girls.

An obituary notice described Miss Buss as 'a personality of singular charm, wholly without pedantry or self-consciousness, [who] persuaded Royal Commissioners, City Companies, Lord Mayors and Royal Princesses, physicians and even universities, that women might be thoroughly educated without any danger to themselves or the State'.[20] Like all successful headmistresses she had a devoted concern for the welfare of individual girls. She was motherly not with a sweet but with a firm reasonableness. Her discipline was rationally persuasive and seldom lacked a touch of humour in its application, especially when she was fighting her battle against the prim conventions of the ladies' academy—'a sudden dash of very cold water in the face' was her remedy for the girl showing an inclination to faint. Like Thring, of whom in many days she was the female counterpart, she believed in the benign influence of 'the almighty wall', with perhaps an over-emphasis on tidiness which from the days of Miss Buss has been among the lesser virtues of girls' schools.

Three principles governed her attitudes to girls' education: first the 'whole girl' should be educated and her individuality respected and catered for; secondly, to use her own words, 'there is no such thing as a woman's education apart from that of education generally . . . the real question is how is the child of either sex to be trained to the measure of the stature of the perfect human being'; thirdly, class distinction has no place in education. The curriculum she devised for her pupils was surprisingly modern. In an age when girls were trained to be good wives through the medium of insipid 'accomplishments' she added French, history and mathematics to the range of studies and her school became renowned for the proficiency of its science teaching. The girls' health was checked by regular medical inspection and improved in a gymnasium provided at her own expense.

[20] Quoted in R. L. Archer, *Secondary Education in the Nineteenth Century*, p. 93.

Such attitudes and practices may today seem unremarkable. In fact a minor revolution had taken place: a woman had changed the whole direction of girl's education; she had created a new kind of girls' school which under her guidance became itself an educative community, and, with her equally distinguished contemporary Dorothea Beale, she had indicated that a headmistress could be 'great' as headmasters could be great, no longer the object of amused tolerance, but weighty persons to whom respect was due.

Like Miss Buss, Dorothea Beale (1831-1906) was largely self-educated in a cultured middle class home where with unprompted zeal she read history, biography, science and mathematics and literary reviews. In 1848 she attended lectures at Queen's College and from 1849 to 1856 she herself taught classes there. For a year she was mistress at the Clergy Daughters' School at Casterton, Westmorland, but soon fled from its stark restrictions, which in an earlier period had been pilloried as Charlotte Brontë's Lowood in *Jane Eyre*.[21] Her life's work began in 1858 when she became headmistress of Cheltenham Ladies College, then in the fifth year of its existence and undergoing a somewhat dismal period of futility.

The struggle was long and arduous. Miss Beale's aim was not to prove that girls had intellectual capacities equal to those of boys by impressing on them an identical curriculum. Her plans were based squarely on what she thought girls needed, but she believed that girls required a curriculum equally demanding even if different in detail. History well taught could be an intellectual exercise; German could be a suitable equivalent to Latin. Although she was herself a good mathematician she dared not introduce Euclid until later: 'had I done so it might have been the death of the College'. But later she devised a method of teaching geometry well in advance of current boys' school practice. 'Accomplishments' designed to get husbands rather than to make good wives were pruned to make way for more serious activities. She was an inspiring teacher, devout and frugal in her personal life, shy but always accessible, knowing her girls inti-

[21] See E. Raikes, *Dorothea Beale of Cheltenham*, Ch. III.

mately, seeking only to serve them and the cause of women's education. A colleague wrote, 'The College, as Miss Beale made it, was an organism, the product of inner forces, needing constant renewal of vitality, not a vast machine.'[22]

In 1864 there were 130 pupils and a boarding house had been opened; by 1883 there were 500 girls and ten boarding houses. Before she died Miss Beale had built up an institution which comprised a senior department for girls taking higher certificate and university scholarships; a secondary section for pupils aged 12 to 16, and also a junior and kindergarten departments. When we add to this achievement St. Hilda's Hall founded to provide residence for Cheltenham girls at Oxford, there emerges a total system of girls' education 'without precedent in our educational history'.[23] Like Thring's Uppingham this was the creation of one great personality.

Great as were the achievements of Miss Buss and Miss Beale in the creation of their individual schools, it is doubtful whether these outstanding examples of what girls' education might be would alone have produced their reforming impact had it not been for the impressive evidence they presented to the Schools Inquiry Commission.[24] Three results followed. The Endowed Schools Act of 1869 contained a clause extending to girls 'the benefit of endowments' which was described as the Magna Carta of girls' education. Secondly the Taunton Commission recommended the establishment of a girls' high school, on the model of the North London Collegiate School, in all the principal towns of England. Thirdly, in 1872, the Girls Public Day School Trust was constituted with the result that thirty-six Girls' Public Day Schools were founded by 1891. Thus the endeavours of Miss Beale and Miss Buss laid the foundations of all girls' secondary education in this country.

These two remarkable women present us with a new image of the teacher. They elevated the status of headmistress in British education to a level equal to that of the headmaster; they proved

[22] E. Raikes, op. cit., p. 275.
[23] See H. C. Barnard, *A Short History of English Education*, pp. 188-9.
[24] See E. Raikes, op. cit., pp. 136-46.

the capacity of women to engage in school reform with the intelligence, leadership and administrative talent equal to that of men; and although their feminist fervour may have led them to model their schools too closely on boys' schools, they evolved over the years school communities whose educative impact on the pupils was deep and lasting and in some ways more civilizing than the ethos of boys' schools.

But girls' education was not to petrify in pale imitations of these two successful schools. An interesting example of more radical change can be seen in the enlightened work of Miss B. M. Baker at Badminton between 1911 and 1946. This provides a suitable transition from the reformed but formal schools we have been considering to 'the new school movement' treated in the next section. Miss Baker's Badminton introduced girls to wider interests in social and international problems by informed discussion of current affairs, visits to Shaw and Galsworthy plays in Bristol, and study of the League of Nations including visits to its sessions in Geneva. Typical of her strongly ethical emphasis in religion were the non-sectarian Sunday services in the Peace Memorial Hall, opened in 1928 to establish 'the defences of peace which must be constructed in the minds of men'.[25]

NEW INTERPRETATIONS OF THE COMMUNITY IDEA

Reactions against the public schools became evident in the 1890's. Had Thring said the last word? Could the ideal of the common life be more richly interpreted in terms of greater freedom for individual activity and initiative? Were the reformed girls' schools the final solution for girls' education? 'If it is in school that the foundations of the future are laid,' asked J. H. Badley, 'is it not a factor of success that those who will together do the building should from the outset learn to work together?'[26] These were the questions asked at the close of the century, with the result that the next fifty years saw many deviations from the old tradition in a movement generally known as 'the new educa-

[25] See W. A. C. Stewart, *The Educational Innovators*, Vol. II, pp. 48-50.
[26] *Bedales. A Pioneer School*, p. 65.

tion' or 'progressive education'. In England the pioneers were
Cecil Reddie and J. H. Badley. But whether in the inspired
moderation of T. F. Coade at Bryanston, or in the progressive
conservatism of the older Quaker Schools, or in Kenneth Barnes'
enlightened education at Wennington Hall, even in the schools of
the extreme left like Dartington Hall and A. S. Neill's Summerhill, the new theme was to combine individual freedom with
community living.

It was under the influence of Edward Carpenter the socialist
reformer and friend of Walt Whitman that Cecil Reddie (1858-
1932) conceived his idea of a boarding school run on new lines.
His experience of public school education was limited to his own
schooling at Fettes and to a year's science teaching at Clifton.
In 1889 Reddie, already a violent critic of the public school
system, founded the New School at Abbotsholme in the delightful
rural surroundings of Derbyshire's River Dove. His aim was no
less, he declared, than to train 'a higher type of human being'.
The school was to be a cultured home where boys were to co-
operate in the creation 'of the objects of their daily lives'. Modern
languages, science, music and the arts and crafts replaced the
old classical curriculum; labour in the hayfield and farm was a
partial substitute for organized games. An equally significant
departure from tradition was Reddie's non-sectarian attitude to
religion which was to become a characteristic of the 'new school'
movement: 'it is enough and best,' he declared, 'to turn their
minds towards those ideals which no one refuses to reverence
rather than to doctrines that divide humanity'.[27] And again,
morality is 'the outcome of the whole influence of the school, as
this is expressed in every act of school life'.[28] Some relics of
the public school he retained, however; notably among them
were prefecture, fagging and corporal punishment: 'The hier-
archic organization is essential in school life as well as in all
communities.'[29]

Unfortunately Reddie revealed fateful defects of character that
ultimately denied him success in his own school. He retained
the image of the headmaster potentate, with the added disability

[27] *Abbotsholme*, p. 78.   [28] Op. cit., p. 31.   [29] Op. cit., p. 83.

of an excessive egotism and a temperamental incapacity to tolerate opinions different from his own. These were not the ingredients of success in a new educational venture aiming to create 'a higher type of human being', by which Reddie meant, it seems, according to a later pronouncement, 'a directing class . . . trained to obey'. He had in a few years forsaken Carpenter's mild prescription for a socialist democracy which had once inspired him. This was partly due to Reddie's admiration for all things German. He had taken his doctorate at Göttingen; he had studied Herbartian pedagogy under Professor Rein at Jena and had acquired the authoritarian attitudes of German education and society so congenial to his own temperament. Colin Sharp, Reddie's magnanimous successor, penetrated most deeply beneath the surface of this complex character in the following sympathetic judgement:

'Reddie bristled with inconsistencies. A believer in love, friendship and co-operation as the mainsprings of life, yet impatient, intolerant, even ruthless towards those who opposed him . . . convinced of the importance of individuality and independence of thought, but an imperious autocrat who sought to crush all resistance to his will inside and outside the school. . . . Unsentimental to the point of indifference, yet capable of deep and lasting affection for boys, to whom he devoted his life.'[30]

As far as community building is concerned Reddie was both a pioneer and an object lesson. In 1927, at the age of sixty-eight, he was left with two pupils and no staff. He was asked by a committee of old boys to resign and accept Colin Sharp as his successor, a circumstance which at least indicated the faith of Reddie's own pupils in the future of his school. His is the fateful example of the reformer sincerely convinced that he has encompassed the whole realm of reform in a single act of creation. But the dialectic of educational progress never permits that to happen. In Reddie's hands no further growth of the school community was possible because he allowed no opportunity for the school's purposes to ripen over the years into something richer

[30] See W. A. C. Stewart, *The Educational Innovators*, Vol. II. p. 266.

than its crude beginnings.

But on the continent Reddie's influence was considerable. On visits to Abbotsholme Herman Lietz and Paul Geheeb saw the essence of Reddie's ideal more clearly than Reddie himself and transported it to Germany where they founded a group of country boarding schools—Landerziehungsheime—in some of which co-education was developed in co-operative communities far in advance of Abbotsholme practice.[31] Edward Demolin founded the École des Roches in France on similar principles. And we shall see later that Kurt Hahn acknowledged his debt to Abbotsholme along with that to Plato, Goethe and Eton. Whatever Reddie's defects of character, one fact dispels any readiness to indulge in easy criticism: he was the founding father of progressive schools in England.

John Haden Badley (1865-1967) succeeded where Reddie failed. He too was a great admirer and friend of Edward Carpenter, but unlike Reddie he retained throughout his life his early sympathies with the liberal social movements of his time. He was educated at Rugby and Trinity College, Cambridge and in 1889, after gaining a first in classics at Cambridge, he went to Abbotsholme as a foundation member of the staff. Badley admired Reddie greatly but found his autocratic behaviour to staff and boys entirely inconsistent with the community objectives of the school. Nevertheless throughout his life Badley never ceased to recognize that it was Reddie's vision and dynamic genius which set him on the progressive path in education. In 1893 Badley left Abbotsholme and founded Bedales School in Surrey—later to be moved to Petersfield. For what he regarded as an outrageous betrayal Reddie never forgave him. Reddie's 'passionate sense of proprietorship' extended even to his ideas: the master's flame had been stolen to burn in another hearthstone. What should have been to Reddie a natural growth from his own sowing became needlessly a thorn in the flesh.

Because of its undisturbed development Bedales displayed to the world a more comprehensive view of the new education than any school before 1930. The marks of the new school were the

[31] See W. A. C. Stewart, op. cit., pp. 64-78

modernized curriculum, mild forms of pupil participation in government, the freer personal relationships, the provision for music, arts and crafts aiming to sublimate the errant passions and develop personality, the open air life and freedom of dress, an ethically based non-sectarianism. Badley added a new dimension both to progressive education and to the theme of the educative community by starting co-education seven years after the opening of Bedales. The neglected female half of mankind was now to share equally in the task of community building. But the lessons of Badley's achievement are not learnt only from his pioneering work for co-education, which he deemed but one facet, although an obvious one, of progressive education. He was a scholarly man, a classic and historian equally touched with ancient as with modern wisdoms, always willing to go on learning from carefully assessed experience. A schoolmaster who knew both Abbotsholme and Bedales directs our attention to a peculiar quality of Badley's achievement in a tribute to Badley on his death at the age of 102:

'Bedales is now 74 years old, and has changed continuously. It is a marvellous example of the *evolving* school. There have been no revolutionary changes, no great dramas. Things have unfolded, the implicit has become more explicit . . . he created an *educational outline* which he knew would fill out and develop as the years passed by; that he would contribute further component parts—the decision to become co-educational, for example, or the establishing of the School Council in 1913—and that others, the staff in other words, would contribute also. . . . Most great headmasters have dominated; he did not.'[32]

In 1933 there appeared in England a prophet from Germany who presented to many admirers yet another version of the educative school community. Kurt Hahn came to England, a refugee from Nazi oppression, at the age of forty-seven. In 1920 he had founded the Schloss Schule Salem under the patronage of Prince Max of Baden and it was during this earlier experience that he worked out the principles which governed his contri-

[32] *John Haden Badley: 1865-1967*, p. 54, Bedales Society 1967.

butions to British education, first in the foundation of Gordonstoun and later in the Outward Bound movement. Implicit in all Hahn's attitudes to contemporary education was a conviction that the state and public school systems were no more than an inert apparatus imposed on children and incapable of resisting the devitalizing influences evident in modern civilization.

For Hahn the aim of education is 'the renewal of life' involving a conscious attempt within each school community 'to release the vital energy of youth'. Hahn's generalized abstractions always had a concrete bearing on practice in school. His central theme is thus summarized by Hermann Röhrs.[33]

'In the seemingly well-ordered everyday life of civilization there lurk dangers which are able to destroy the original integrity and beauty of the young mind. As reaction to morally unhealthy environment, there occur those crises of adolescence which are interpreted by conventional educationists as an inevitable stage of development. . . . Hahn has consistently opposed this dogma, particularly with regard to the theory of the unavoidable "degradations of the years of puberty". Entirely in accordance with the view held since Rousseau, that tasks motivated by social and moral concern help to alleviate the crisis of puberty, he deliberately devised the various factors of his "experience therapy" with its "poisonless passions" and "wholesome habits" as an antidote.'

The interesting aspect of Hahn's view of puberty, quite out of step with current psychology, was his conviction that the 'psychoanalyst's dogma' is false; that 'what they consider a normal development is in fact a grave and avoidable malady'. Röhrs explains the operation of Hahn's 'experience therapy' thus:

'This "experience therapy" is one of those basic concepts of Hahn's which lead us to the heart of his conception of education. In modern society, in view of the complicated requirements of life, young people are kept in the dependent position of learners

[33] In an article entitled 'The Realm of Education in the Thought of Kurt Hahn, in *Comparative Education*, Vol. 3, No. 1, Nov. 1966.

well into the age of adulthood; they need to test and prove themselves if they are to discover and realize themselves. Youth is
socially sick, because in the framework of modern society it is
not led by natural challenge to its powers to develop the basic
human capacities. In this situation a special therapy is required,
and it is provided in Hahn's scheme of education by an elastic
system of training devices: the breaks for athletics, the expedi-
tion, the project and the rescue service. For this a strong ethical
basis to the relationship between teacher and pupil is necessary
and one which sets sensible limits to freedom—such as Pestalozzi
called for in opposition to Rousseau's supposedly unlimited
freedom. Spiritually akin to him, Kurt Hahn asserts even more
emphatically that a personal renewal in the young can take place
only if "voluntariness is supported by compulsion".'

Compulsion involved a training plan of graded athletics in
the Greek style—running, throwing, jumping—and also team
games, strictly limited to two days a week. Hahn was convinced
that physical vitality had a direct bearing on the release of self-
achieved confidence which enables adolescents to 'defeat their
own defeatism'. This he said 'deserves the name of a discovery:
that the so-called deformity of puberty should not be regarded
as a decree of fate'. Like Dr. Arnold, Hahn was above all things
a moralist, but unlike Arnold he had faith in the compassion and
spiritual capacities of youth to yield their harvest in the right
soil. He views the progress from childhood to adolescence, says
Professor Stewart, 'almost as a morality play, which Hahn,
usually a brilliant, fastidious and dramatic phrase spinner in
English, occasionally takes close to melodrama'.[34] Hahn seldom
claimed originality for his ideas: in a broadcast in 1934 he said,
'We cribbed from Plato, from Dr. Arnold of Rugby, from Eton,
from Abbotsholme, from Herman Lietz. . . . We did not believe
in originality in education nor in experiments on human beings.'[35]
This outright recognition of his debt to the past should serve as
a reminder to teachers that educational practice, and in Hahn's
case of a very dynamic kind, is seldom a product of present
experience only.

[34] See W. A. C. Stewart, *The Educational Innovators*, Vol. II, p. 199.
[35] *The Listener*, 28th Nov. 1934.

Hahn may have used grandiloquent phrases to define his ultimate purposes but they were invariably translated into concrete practice. The compassion of youth, the love of adventure and the testing moments of danger which physical adventure involved, were harnessed in fields of endeavour for 'the neighbour' —the Gordonstoun fire service, the lifeboat rescue and coastguard services, the Outward Bound mountaineering rescue scheme, estate work, care for the aged, practical assistance in hospitals, were all applications of 'experience therapy' which ultimately spread beyond the bounds of Gordonstoun. Hahn's plans for inculcating a sense of responsibility were consistent with his principle that goodwill must be stimulated by compulsion. There is of course, much to be said for forcing a person into responsible behaviour, for responsibility must be felt before it is understood. Nevertheless it is doubtful whether Gordonstoun's hierarchical organization of responsible persons, each with appropriate insignia, was a necessary expression of the idea of responsibility. We are reminded of nineteenth century Eton's 'neat gradations of ascending ranks' (see p. 153). The redeeming features of Hahn's system, so closely comparable with public school prefecture, was its insistence that higher rank involved no privilege beyond increased personal obligation.

In the work of these three teacher-headmasters we see radical developments from the cruder expressions of community displayed in the nineteenth century public schools. Reddie's Abbotsholme was the blunt but effective spearpoint of change; Badley's Bedales immeasurably enlarged the concept of the teaching community by the inclusion of girls; and his receptiveness to the ideas of his colleagues made possible a continuing extension of the original idea. Badley created an evolving community. And that is his lesson for teachers, for the nature of their task requires them to have faith in the future of their own unfinished business. In Kurt Hahn the teacher emerges as a visionary in poignant contact with the ills of his age, but also as a man capable of translating his vision into the daily activities of the school community.

14 *Social experience as teacher*

While the English model of a school community was slowly changing its character there appeared in the United States the movement towards 'social guidance' led by the American philosopher John Dewey (1859-1952). Among the influences contributing to Dewey's educational philosophy were the Hegelian concept of the evolutionary nature of thought and of society and its reinforcement, as Dewey believed, by the theory of evolution developed in Darwin's *Origin of Species* published in the year of Dewey's birth. Among the implications of the Darwinian theory Dewey saw a prospect of human intelligence, properly guided, itself partaking in the beneficent evolution of human society. Even more important was the biologically derived psychology of Dewey's contemporary William James, whose memorable *Principles of Psychology* (1890) gave form to a physiological theory of mind whereby intelligence is regarded as a kind of behaviour, a *process* of action and reaction between man and his environment. Mind is no longer conceived as an autonomous entity; body and mind are inseparably linked in human personality. Dewey's theory and practice of education are partly derived from this biological concept of intelligence.[1]

But Dewey's educational philosophy was also a response to a crisis in American civilization. During the 1890's successive waves of European immigrants and increasing industrialization were transforming the old rural communities into rootless urban agglomerations of mixed descent. Dewey was convinced that the

[1] See F. W. Garforth, *John Dewey, Selected Educational Writings*, pp. 5-17.

assimilation of these diverse cultural traditions into an integrated American culture was a primary task of the schools. How, he asked, should education respond to the impact of an industrial and social revolution, the disruption of family life, the removal of children from the intimate life of the village to the artificial life of multi-lingual cities? He sought the answer in a typically American and pragmatic way—by founding his Laboratory School at the University of Chicago in 1896 and testing the hypothesis that the solution lay in education founded on social experience.

Dewey was almost as critical of 'progressive' education as he was of the formal schooling of Europe and America. Neither 'the authoritative inculcation of fact', he declared, 'nor the sentimental idealization of childish immaturity' satisfy the proper conditions for learning. Sympathetic as he was with the child-centred Froebelian view, he denied the existence of what he called the 'sheer self-activity' of the Froebelians, because all activity and all thinking derived from activity, takes place in a medium, i.e. in a social situation. While, then, he accepted the Froebelian emphasis on 'child-centredness' this did not hold a central place in his educational philosophy: 'true education', Dewey insisted, in his *Pedagogic Creed*, 'comes through the stimulation of the child's powers by the demands of the social situations in which the child finds himself'. Hence teachers should be less concerned with methods of teaching than with programmes that stimulate a child to learn through his own first-hand social experience.

This view is consistent with Dewey's instrumentalist philosophy, which in its essentials is a pragmatic interpretation of the Pestalozzian doctrine that 'life educates'. Pragmatism in its simplest meaning may be defined as the attitude that judges the truth of a hypothesis by its consequences: does it work? Dewey was convinced that the education of his day did not work. Why? Because educators have assumed education to be a preparation for future living rather than the experience of living now. You cannot prepare a child for the future because you do not know what the future will be like. Such an education assumes a static society whereas society in the twentieth century is not static. Similarly, morality changes: there are no eternal values or unchanging moral principles. We can only know what we ought to do by discovering what we ought to do now. Hence education is not the pursuit of ideal ends presented to children in the form of moral injunctions or by appeal to abstract virtues. Concepts of morality will develop only in so far as children are actually trying out in a social setting the conduct that works and the conduct that does not. Again, learning is a social activity, 'a continual reconstruction of experience', a series of transactions between individuals and their human and physical environment, each step evoking the use of intelligence, each discovery impelling to further discovery. In this way knowledge is acquired, intelligence develops and personality grows. Hence, the essence of educational method is to put the child in a problem solving situation.

Such a situation Dewey devised in 'occupations', or what we now call the project, where the operative factor is the child-in-the-group, not the teacher or the curriculum or the text-book, which are 'outside' the pupil, i.e. not a part of his own felt experience. With the idea of the project readers of this book will be familiar. Here it will suffice to mention the important conditions upon which Dewey insists if this plan of group inquiry is to be successful. The project must stimulate interest—not merely ephemeral excitement or an idle curiosity, but interest which lays hold of emotions and desires that evoke thought; it must be intrinsically valuable, not merely pleasure-giving, it must awaken curiosity and create a demand for new information—'there is nothing educative in an activity that does not lead the mind out into new fields'. Finally it should involve a long period of time so that a succession of logically progressive activities can be created.

We may well ask where the necessary element of individual freedom and initiative enters into this co-operative activity. Dewey answers that freedom 'is the part played by thinking—which is personal—in learning': that individual is free who in his relationship with others in group activity shows intellectual initiative, independence of observation, capacity for invention and adaptation. When, Dewey claims, each individual child contributes freely to a group occupation the school has achieved conditions of freedom combined with social guidance.[2]

We may also ask how Dewey faces the problem of discipline in a school community where the usual forms of authoritarian compulsion are absent. His answer is consistent with his theme of education as 'process' or 'transaction': Discipline, he says, 'is a product, an outcome, an achievement, not something applied from without. All genuine education *terminates* in discipline, but it *proceeds* by engaging the mind in activities worth while for their own sake', and by co-operating in and contributing to the common life of the school. Thus a child becomes his own disciplinarian by freely exercising his own restraints as he finds this necessary to achieve his own ends. A striking passage on moral education in *Democracy and Education* is worth quoting:

'Moral education in school is practically hopeless when we set up the development of character as the supreme end, and at the same time treat the acquiring of knowledge and the development of understanding, which of necessity occupy the chief part of schooltime, as having nothing to do with character. On such a basis, moral education is inevitably reduced to some kind of catechetical instruction or lessons about morals. Lessons "about morals" signify as a matter of course lessons in what other people think about virtues and duties.' He then proceeds to the positive aspect of his argument: 'what is learned and employed in any occupation having an aim and involving co-operation with others is moral knowledge. . . . For it builds up a social interest and confers the intelligence needed to make that interest effective in practice. Just because the studies of the curriculum represent standard factors in social life, they are organs of initiation into social values. As mere school studies, their acquisition has only technical worth. Acquired under conditions where their social significance is realized, they feed moral interest and develop moral insight.'[3]

[2] See *How We Think*, passim.
[3] pp. 411-14.

In this brief sketch of Dewey's radical emphasis on the school as a community we see the teacher in two dimensions. First, there is Dewey himself: the academic teacher of philosophy who teaches that philosophy and education are two sides of the same coin, that without a philosophical foundation education lacks purpose and guidance; and on the other hand, that the school is the laboratory in which the validity of any philosophy is tested, and thereby redeemed from the sterilities of academic debate.

Secondly there is Dewey's concept of the role of the teacher in a school community which is engaged in the task of revitalizing the Great Society. Dewey's teacher steps down from his dais, dispels the aura of authority, ceases to direct from above and merges with his pupils in the adventure of learning. He has to be something of a sociologist and at least an amateur psychologist. His job is to 'psychologize the environment', as Dewey puts it, to simplify and arrange the material, to 'take it and develop it within the range of the child's life'. He organizes the sources of information relevant to the activities of the co-operating group. In this way the teacher *creates* the pupil's environment by presenting the problems to be solved and thus 'by indirection to direct'. Bertrand Russell has wickedly suggested that this is a method whereby: 'If I am given a pack of cards in disorder, and asked to inquire into their sequence, I shall first arrange them in order and then say this was the order resulting from my inquiry.'[4]

This may be a fair criticism, but it does not invalidate the method involved in the project; for all education of the young involves some simplification and re-arrangement of the sources of knowledge to bring them 'within the range of the child's life'. Indeed, in requiring this of the teacher, Dewey accords him a high respect as a skilled professional who uses the school community and its neighbourhood as the medium in which mental and moral development takes place. In my view, which is the schoolmaster's view, few theories of education challenge the teacher's skill more than this of Dewey, and few practices are

[4] *History of Western Philosophy*, p. 851.

more fruitful in encouraging personal initiative and the emergence of valuable social attitudes. Unfortunately, in failing to understand that the aim of the project is an exacting exercise of the pupil's intelligence, many of Dewey's followers have betrayed their master by mistaking superficial busy-ness in the classroom for purposeful mental activity.

Nevertheless, Dewey's general theme of co-operative activity and the association of the school with its neighbourhood, has exerted an immense influence on educational practice throughout the schools of the new world and the old. The project method, in various adaptations where it is combined with more formal instruction, is now a commonplace of school practice. Dewey did not invent these methods: we have even seen them in embryo in Vives' injunctions to his teachers, and they were sometimes practised in American schools of his time. But Dewey gave form and philosophic purpose to fumbling endeavours. Nevertheless, with some reason his critics refer to the inadequacy of social guidance alone as the foundation of a full education.

We may well ask whether it is true that mind and personality are formed only by the changing stresses of our social environment? Are there not ancient values and ideals approved by the wisdom of mankind that may escape the observation of the particular group with which the child is working? Are aesthetic values discernible only in a communal setting? Is there not a place for authority wisely deployed? Are there not fields of knowledge which require more formal instruction than the chancy ways of juvenile exploration? Is there not 'something uniquely mine', as Pestalozzi puts it, that will exercise its own insights; some autonomous element in personality that flourishes best in solitude? These are questions we have to ask. Some of them may be explained away by the fact that Dewey had little to say about education after fifteen.

But none of these doubts need weaken our conviction that a child's growth in mental and moral perception takes place chiefly, although not entirely, when he is actively engaged in the experience of living in community, man's natural milieu. And for this the home, classroom, school and neighbourhood provide him with the initial experience on which his growth depends. It can at least be truly said that 'wherever at the present time children have been released from the tyranny of book and board, wherever they are allowed responsibility and initiative in learning and are encouraged to exercise intelligence in discovery, there is some debt owing to Dewey'.[5]

We must note also that Dewey's concern for the survival of democratic societies impelled him to associate every school with the larger community it was intended to serve, and this in a definite and concrete way. He insisted that the school was the primary institution for making men realize that individuals could not grow into social and self-respecting persons without identifying themselves with the group in which they lived; not only in the school group but also in the neighbourhood and the national communities. It is this extension of the idea of the educative community beyond the school into the strivings of men in field, workshop and into the institutions of social democracy that Dewey makes his major contribution to any conception of the community as teacher.

[5] F. W. Garforth, op. cit., p. 40.

PART V

The British teacher today

Up to this point the teacher has been presented in several dimensions: as a formative influence in western civilization, as a teacher of teachers and as a teacher of children. It is with teachers in school that these final chapters are concerned. As the problems of the British teacher are broadly representative of those in most advanced communities the discussion is confined to British education. From a static society we have moved into a socially mobile world in which everyone is to be educated. This democratization of education coincides with a period of rapid social and technological change. Hence the teachers of this generation are working in a situation markedly different from the circumstances in which they themselves were educated. They are called upon to play a more central role in society, not only as transmitters of new skills but in the initiation of young people into constructive social attitudes and personal maturity. In this setting these final chapters discuss the adequacy of the teacher's present education and training for his new and complex responsibilities, and the factors involved in his claims to membership of a self-regulating profession. These issues are presented against the historical background of the growth of the teaching profession in the nineteenth century, its divisions and snobberies which have left their mark on the profession today. The final chapter seeks to relate the experiences of the recent past to the conditions of contemporary schooling by means of a group of propositions, testable hypotheses, involving value judgements and their relevance to school practice, whose validity the modern teacher can test in the working conditions of his school.

15 The beginnings of a profession

With variations due to differences in national temperament and social history, the story of the humble schoolmaster of the eighteenth and nineteenth centuries is very similar throughout western Europe and America. His social value was frequently recognized in patronizing terms but was seldom recompensed by any willingness of taxpayers to pay him proportionately to his usefulness. In 1833 Guizot, whose good intentions for French education are not in question, candidly admitted in his important statement on primary education that 'the resources at the disposal of public authority will never succeed in rendering the humble profession of village teacher as attractive as it is useful. . . . It is necessary that a profound sense of the moral importance of his work sustain and animate him.' In this spirit the administrators of the century were committed to raising the standard and qualifications of teachers without raising their pay. In mid-century the annual wage of a French teacher was £24; in England it was £51 for men and £26 for women.[1] Today, fortunately, rulers at least admit that no profession can have a corner in saints; but the view that teachers should be badly paid because they are likely to go to heaven has for long conditioned the thinking of those who pay.

Few modern nations have less reason for pride in the growth of its elementary schools system as England, and none was wealthier when the programme might have begun. But population was growing and teachers were in short supply because in 1800 no provision existed to educate and train them, either at the secondary level or in higher education. Only slowly was it

[1] See A. D. C. Peterson, *A Century of Education*, pp. 225-8.

recognized, and chiefly by men of the calibre of James Kay-Shuttleworth and Matthew Arnold, that national educational systems are cyclic in pattern—primary school, secondary school, college—and that the cycle begins and ends with teachers.

THE SOCIAL SCENE

In 1820 Henry Brougham declared that 'England must justly be looked on as the worst-educated country in Europe'. This distinction was not regarded with any dismay by the ruling classes or by powerful voices in the Anglican Establishment. Whitbread's Bill of 1807 which proposed the financing of parish schools out of rates was rejected in the Lords on the objection of the Archbishop of Canterbury that it infringed the rights of the clergy. In the Commons the same Bill was denounced by a future President of the Royal Society (Mr. Giddy) on the grounds that: 'However specious in theory the project might be of giving education to the labouring classes of the poor, it would be prejudicial to their morals and happiness; it would teach them to despise their lot in life, instead of making them good servants in agriculture and other laborious employments; instead of teaching them subordination it would render them fractious and refractory.'[2] These sentiments represented a large section of English upper and middle class opinion in the early years of the nineteenth century. Fearful of dangerous thoughts spreading across the channel from revolutionary France they remained suspicious of the reforming ideals of the Swiss and French reformers. It was philanthropy rather than philosophy that first watered the meagre seed plot of English elementary education.

That philanthropy was needed there could be no doubt. Describing working conditions in the cotton mills of industrial Lancashire, Trevelyan tells us: 'mothers and children worked for twelve or fifteen hours a day under insanitary conditions, without either the amenities of life which had sweetened and relieved the tedium of family work in the cottage, or the con-

[2] See G. M. Trevelyan, *British History in the Nineteenth Century*, p. 162.

ditions which make factory life attractive to many women today. The discipline of the early factories was like the discipline of a prison. Small children were often cruelly treated to keep them awake during the long hours which shortened their lives or undermined their health. The men were in little better case. Often out of employment, they were forced to sell their wives and children into the slavery of the mills, while they themselves degenerated into squalid idleness.'[3] In the mining areas a large proportion of the population worked underground, 'women were used there as beasts of burden, and children worked in the dark, sometimes for fourteen hours'. These were George Crabbe's 'murmuring poor, who will not fast in peace', victims of a doctrine which held that national prosperity was dependent on buying the saleable commodity of labour in the cheapest market.

The dame schools and common day schools of the eighteenth and early nineteenth centuries emerged as a convenience for mothers whose children were too young to earn wages. In *The Borough* (1810) Crabbe gives us his familiar picture of the 'deaf, poor, patient widow' plying her needle while 'sitting in' for the working mother:

> Infants of humble, busy wives, who pay
> Some trifling price for freedom through the day.
> At this good matron's hut the children meet,
> Who thus becomes the mistress of the street.

The term 'common school' referred to an odd assortment of private venture schools suspended in precarious balance between the dame schools for the poor and the superior refinement of the academies for young ladies and gentlemen. The less genteel of these were usually staffed by the indigent and ignorant, derelict servants or bankrupt tradesmen who for a small fee attempted to teach reading and writing to children but little less proficient than themselves. It was to improve these conditions that the Society for the Propagation of Christian Knowledge, founded as

---

[3] G. M. Trevelyan, op. cit., p. 156.

early as 1698 under the religious impulse of Puritanism, had initiated the charity schools movement for the Christian education of the poor. By the middle of the eighteenth century over 2,000 schools accommodating 40,000 children had been established. This was the beginning of popular education for England's children. In these schools all was for humility and godliness: the catechism ensured the charity child's submission to God; his sober garments were designed to remind him of his benefactor's charity; even the hymns he was taught to sing witnessed to the bounty of his social superiors:

> Obscured by mean and humble birth
> In ignorance we lay,
> Till Christian Bounty called us forth
> And led us into day.
>
> Oh, look for ever kindly down
> On those who help the poor,
> Oh, let success their labours crown
> And plenty keep their store.[4]

This firm association of the pauper's gratitude with the comfort of those who dispensed this uncompromising charity was long a-dying: we hear of the Dorset parson's wife in Queen Victoria's day, sincerely concerned for the welfare of the children in the local charity school, who devised a social catechism in supplementation of the village parson's catechetical instruction. It included the following gem:

Q. What is my duty towards my betters?
A. To preserve them in the enjoyment of their possessions and to restrain the covetousness of the ungodly poor.[5]

Apart from religious instruction, the core of the curriculum,

[4] Quoted from M. G. Jones, *The Charity School Movement in the 18th Century*, p. 75.
[5] From a private source.

there was a grounding in the three R's and much manual labour, in a schoolday often extending to fifteen hours. Even so there were those who violently opposed this meagre instruction on the grounds that to raise children above their station by thus imparting the elements of literacy would deprive the nation of recruits for manual occupations. But on the whole the charity schools marked an advance in the education of the poor, although their historian describes the teachers as 'the humblest of their kind and too insignificant for praise or blame'.[6] Almost as poor as their pupils, it was laid upon them 'to train the poor to poverty, an honest, upright, grateful, industrious poverty'.[7]

It is easy to look back with facile cynicism on these social attitudes, but we must distinguish between the brutal exploitation of child labour of current economic doctrine and the sincere desire of the better-off to take their religion seriously: 'the eighteenth century,' wrote M. G. Jones, 'was marked by a very real sense of duty and responsibility for the children whose physical and spiritual interests were lamentably neglected . . . it would be a misreading of the age of benevolence to see in the prominence enjoyed by the principle of subordination a harsh and unsympathetic attitude of the superior to the lower classes. Far from it. The eighteenth century was the age of well-defined social distinctions and it used a language in accordance with its social structure.'[8] Nevertheless, while praising Evangelicalism for bringing 'rectitude, unselfishness and humanity into high places' Trevelyan reminds us of its one great defect: 'Finely alive to the wrongs of negroes and the corruption of slave drivers, it was as callous as the "high-and-dry", or the employers and landlords themselves, to the sufferings of the English poor under the changes wrought by the industrial revolution. Hannah More and her friends sincerely believed that the inequalities of fortune in this world did not matter, because they would be redressed in the next. They even persuaded themselves, and endeavoured to persuade the starving labourers, that it was a spiritual advan-

---

[6] See M. G. Jones, op. cit., pp. 102-3.
[7] C. Birchenough, *History of Elementary Education*, p. 23.
[8] M. G. Jones, op. cit., p. 4.

tage for them to be abjectly poor, provided they were submissive to their superiors.'[9]

Such oddities of pious and comforting logic dispensed greater warmth to its inventors than to the bodies and souls of the abjectly poor to whom it was applied. Nevertheless charity did its work. The industrial schools appearing towards the end of the eighteenth century, where young children were taught to spin, knit, plait straw and cobble shoes, were neither popular with industrialists because they reduced the supply of child labour, nor with parents who were thus deprived of the pitifully small wages of their children. On the other hand, the Sunday School movement associated with the names of Robert Raikes of Gloucester, Sarah Trimmer and Hannah More, was popular with both, because learning to read on Sundays was no impediment to factory work on weekdays. In the early years of the nineteenth century, 300,000 children were learning to read in the Sunday schools. But there were still hundreds of thousands who remained illiterate and the population in the towns was rapidly increasing.

In the course of the eighteenth century the population of England and Wales had increased from $5\frac{1}{2}$ million to 9 million, this being partly due after 1780 to developments in medical science, applied in the great teaching hospitals and dispensaries —St. Thomas', St. Bartholomew's, Guys, Westminster, St. George's, the London and Middlesex Hospitals were all founded before 1750—and also to the healthy change of popular taste from gin to tea.[10] There were, therefore, thousands more children to be educated; and teachers were scarce. How scarce and how badly paid may be gathered from the report of an investigator on the educational conditions existing in South Wales as late as 1848: 'he had found teachers working part-time as overseers of roads, parish clerks, cow keepers, rate collectors, dress makers, preachers, turnpike men, publicans. . . . Nearly all had taken to teaching after other works, and among their previous occupations he lists—attorney's clerk, artillery man, blacksmith,

[9] Trevelyan, op. cit., p. 54.
[10] See G. M. Trevelyan, *English Social History*, pp. 341-5.

barber, carpenter, collier, domestic servant, farmer, fisherman, milliner, millwright, huckster, limeburner, malster, shoemaker, tailor, tiler, weaver. . . .'[11]

Thus challenged to greater efforts middle-class philanthropists supported the monitorial system of teaching invented by Andrew Bell and Joseph Lancaster whereby 'one master alone can educate one thousand boys' and 'seven children could be educated for a guinea a year'. The system of training boys to teach boys—'the grand principle of the division of labour applied to intellectual purposes'—met with astonishing success. It was cheap, the children did at least learn something, and, although dependent on a mechanization of instruction unsurpassed before or since, and on a system of discipline morally repressive but never brutal, it removed the barbarities of the birch at least from the schools of Bell and Lancaster. It was chiefly the sons of the upper classes in the famous public schools who suffered this physical indignity.

The system also met with resounding approval on the continent and was by far the most widely used method of instruction in Western Europe for twenty years after Waterloo.[12] Bell was a devout Anglican clergyman, Lancaster was a Quaker. Bell's supporters having taken over the parochial charity schools in 1811, founded the National Society for Promoting the Education of the Poor in the Principles of the Established Church; Lancaster's Royal Lancastrian Association in 1814 became the British and Foreign Schools Society and represented the nonsectarian element in English education. Thus the stage was set for the religious controversies that have bedevilled English education until the twentieth century. But the essential fact remains that in 1838 there were 600,000 children out of a total of two million receiving schooling of some sort, and it is to Bell and Lancaster that we owe the establishment of the elementary school for the nation's children and the beginning of the training

[11] J. Lawson, *Aspects of Education No. 3* 'The Professional Education of Teachers', 1965. *Journal of the Institute of Education, University of Hull.*

[12] See H. M. Pollard, *Pioneers of Popular Education 1760-1850*, pp. 101-10.

of teachers. But before turning to the training of the elementary teacher we must consider aspects of social thinking which assisted the trend towards the state provision of elementary education.

We have already noted the opposition to popular education on the grounds that it would deprive the factories of cheap labour and seduce the minds of the working classes with revolutionary thoughts. In *The Wealth of Nations* (1776) Adam Smith set forth the opposite view, that the state derives no inconsiderable advantage from an instructed people: 'the more they are instructed the less liable they are to the delusions of enthusiasm and superstition, which, among ignorant nations, frequently occasion the most dreadful disorders. An instructed and intelligent people are always more decent and orderly than a stupid one.' For these reasons he advocated state provision of compulsory elementary education. Twenty years later in his famous *Essay on Population* (1798) T. R. Malthus examined the disturbing phenomena that pauperism was becoming a permanent feature of industrial society because, according to his pseudo-scientific formula, population increased in geometrical progression while the means of subsistence increased only in arithmetical progression. Increased national wealth was not therefore an answer to the increasing poverty of the masses. This was a severe check to the unthinking optimism of those among the middle classes who had fondly believed that, if their charity kept pace with their increasing wealth, poverty could be adequately dealt with. But population growth and its attendant pauperism, Malthus declared, could be arrested only by individual restraint encouraged by the improved education of those expected to exercise it. Here is the much-quoted passage:

'We have lavished immense sums on the poor, which we have every reason to think have constantly tended to aggravate their misery. But in their education and in the circulation of those important political truths that most nearly concern them, which are perhaps the only means in our power of really raising their condition, and of making them happier men and more peaceful subjects, we have been miserably deficient. It is surely a great national disgrace, that the education of the lowest classes of people in England should be left entirely to a few Sunday Schools, supported by a subscription from individuals, who can give to the course of instruction in them any kind of bias which they please.'[13]

Thus at last the forces of social philanthropy and political economy became associated in uncomfortable partnership to provide a more comprehensive education for the lower orders of society. Already the more intelligent and literate of an increasingly self-conscious working class had been inoculated with the virus of radicalism by Tom Paine's *The Rights of Man* (1791), and in the next half-century other powerful voices were raised on the same behalf, especially to proclaim the fundamental educability of men. In his famous article 'On Education' in the *Encyclopedia Britannica* of 1825 James Mill, a disciple of Helvetius, declared: 'this much, at any rate, is ascertained, that all the difference which exists, or can ever be made to exist, between one *class* of men, and another, is wholly owing to education'. Robert Owen asserted in *New View of Society* (1813) that 'any character from the best to the worst, from the most ignorant to the most enlightened, may be given to any community'. Here is the dim foreshadowing of the idea of equal educational opportunity, although its realization has been long delayed. In Parliament Samuel Whitbread, Henry Brougham, John Arthur Roebuck and Sir Thomas Wyse worked for the cause of popular education through legislative action. The first government grant in aid of education was made in 1833—£20,000 to build 'school houses'. This trivial but significant grant marked the first step in state aid for the schools. But how were the teachers to be educated and trained to teach the children?

THE TRAIL OF CHEAPNESS

Today every teacher, whether of infants or sixth-formers, com-

---

[13] *Essay on Population*, Bk. IV, ch. 9.

pletes his schooling in a fully equipped secondary school and passes on to a college of education or university for three or four years higher education. The education teachers receive is broadly cultural and may be academically exacting, varying it is true in depth and quality but nevertheless infinitely superior to that provided a century ago. Teachers today represent an almost complete cross-section of the national community. Public money expended on their training is lavish compared with nineteenth century standards and the amount of this expenditure is seldom a matter of public controversy. In the nineteenth century none of these conditions prevailed. The elementary school teacher was recruited from the social class whose children he was to teach, or from the abler members of the lower middle class who were one stage removed from the 'deserving poor'. They were regarded as useful instruments for ensuring a modicum of literacy in the nation and therefore requiring just so much learning as would keep them ahead of their pupils.

The respect accorded to them, even by those who realized their value, may be gathered from Brougham's speech in the Commons in 1820: he looked upon the schoolmaster as one 'employed in an honourable and useful capacity—so honourable that none was more highly esteemed, if the individual were faithful in the discharge of his duty—so useful that no man effected more good in his generation than a good parish schoolmaster'. And yet schoolmasters, he was sure, would not be offended when he observed 'that they moved in an inferior situation of life', and that £20 to £30 per annum was adequate remuneration for their services. The schoolmaster continued for long to live under this general assumption of his social inferiority: 'Point to an individual as a physician, a clergyman, or a lawyer,' wrote Henry Dunn, Secretary of the British and Foreign Schools Society, 'and though his cranium be as devoid of eminence as the surface of a plate of glass, yet you give him a passport to the name of gentleman and the best society; but let any one be named a schoolmaster and a feeling of insignificance and disrepute, and the idea that he is a fit companion for the vulgar, will be the consequence.' Again, in 1847 Kay-Shuttleworth, Secretary to the Committee of Council on Education, declared that 'there is little or nothing in the profession of an elementary schoolmaster to tempt a man having a respectable acquaintance with the elements of even humble learning to exchange the certainty of a respectable livelihood . . . for the mean drudgery of instructing the rude children of the poor. . . . For what is the condition of the master of such a school? He has often an income very little greater than an agricultural labourer and very rarely equal to that of a skilled mechanic'.[14]

This sad situation was due to the low social status of the families from which the teachers came, no matter how respectable they were: to the meagre demands of the teacher's work on his knowledge and personal culture; to the correspondingly poor quality of the instruction he received to qualify for his job; and not only to the parsimony of those who paid for his training but to the fact that it came from public funds. The time had not yet come when every boy and girl worthy of assistance, whatever his parentage, could legally claim it from a welfare state.

We must now briefly sketch the progress of the training of teachers in the nineteenth century. The monitorial system had proved utterly inadequate for the production of a corps of teachers capable of educating a nation. Reform began with the appointment of Dr. J. P. Kay (1804-1877), later to be known as Sir James Kay-Shuttleworth, to a Committee of the Privy Council established in 1839 for 'the consideration of all matters affecting the education of the people'. This remarkable and humane administrator, the first of his kind in England, had already visited pioneer schools at home and abroad; in Scotland he was impressed by David Stow's Normal Seminary in Glasgow and with John Wood's school in Edinburgh; on the continent he visited Holland where normal schools had existed since 1816; he admired the work of Werhli, Von Fellenberg's assistant in the industrial school at Hofwyl, who was then training teachers at Constance. These experiences convinced him that only by producing better teachers would better education be possible, a consummation

[14] See C. Birchenough, *History of Elementary Education in England & Wales*, 1914, pp. 357-66.

not to be expected from the monitorial system. He confessed that the clue he was seeking for must be associated with the honourable name of William Rush, an orphan boy of thirteen whom he found taking competent charge of a class during the illness of the master. Hence arose Kay-Shuttleworth's institution of the pupil-teacher system whereby promising boys were apprenticed to their masters from the age of 13 to 18. They earned stipends ranging from £10 to £20.

Training colleges had already been established at Borough Road and Battersea in 1840; St. Marks, Chelsea, and a college for women at Whitelands appeared in 1841. By 1860 there were thirty-four colleges in England and Wales providing training for over 2,000 teachers. The system of apprenticeship was keyed in to the colleges by the award of Queen's Scholarships to promising pupil-teachers, whom Matthew Arnold described as 'the sinews of English primary education'. In 1846 the government instituted the Teachers Certificate based on an annual examination conducted by inspectors. The instruction given in the colleges varied greatly, from sincere attempts to provide at least a touch of liberal culture for students of the most limited cultural background, to strictly utilitarian instruction in the subjects of the elementary curriculum and in methods narrowly conforming to Herbart's Five Steps. In 1852 Matthew Arnold described the teaching in the schools as too often 'pedantic, too mechanical and too much lost in routine', because 'meagre, dry and empty' of any richness that might have been acquired in the teacher's personal education. All self-critical teachers know the lack of confidence that comes from a knowledge of their own ignorance. This is a weakness that can be overcome. But there is also the pathetic dogmatism that is the dead sea fruit of unrecognized ignorance, a mark of the truly uneducated person; and this was in the beginning and until recent times a result of inadequate education in the training colleges. So often their product was the person who did not know enough to know how little he knew. Indeed, except in rare instances, these students were not receiving a general education comparable to that given in the secondary schools of their time. Robert Bridges assesses the consequences:

How should not childish effort, thus thwarted and teased,
recoil dishearten'd bruized and stupefy'd beneath
the rough-shod inculcation of inculcated minds,
case-harden'd by their own thoughtless reiterations?[15]

But when we add to these deficiencies in personal education
the dismal burden imposed by the Revised Code of 1862, which
petrified such initiative as a teacher possessed with the system of
'payment by results', we are able to realize how poor was the
chance of his rising above the station society deemed proper for
him. At this juncture the enlightened mind of Kay-Shuttleworth
was no longer guiding the fortunes of public education. In his
stead the principles of the market place were applied by Mr.
Robert Lowe, Vice-President of the Education Department, in a
system whereby school grants depended on inspectorial examination of each pupil in the 'three R's'. Mr. Lowe explained the
principle: 'If it is not cheap it shall be efficient; if it is not
efficient, it shall be cheap.' The Revised Code debased every one
concerned with the elementary school: the school managers
watched the teachers with anxious eye; the teachers feared the
inspectors, knowing that their report might make or break
them. Not surprisingly, each inspection too often became a game
of subterfuge in which the children were pawns and the stakes
the teacher's wages. The teachers' suspicion of the inspector
became a tradition which did not die with the system in 1897. His
function as a purveyor of rote learning did not enhance respect
for the teacher's status either in the eyes of his employers or in
society at large. Moreover, the impact on the teachers' colleges
was disastrous: the curriculum was narrowed to an elementary
school syllabus magnified and made more difficult. It was many
years before this curriculum was broadened or before the
miserably paid college staff could claim to possess the literary
culture and academic attainments suitable for the education
of teachers. Nor were the gloomy buildings and restricted accommodation, the absence of social amenity and confinement within
a closed community, conducive to intellectual excitement. In

[15] *Testament of Beauty*, IV. 708-11.

1914 the average pay of a primary male teacher was £130 and for a woman less than £100.

Most of these depressing conditions, referred to by the McNair Report of 1944 as 'the trail of cheapness', were removed in the post-war years. Intending primary teachers now receive a full secondary education before proceeding to a three or four year course at a college of education, whose standard of entry is becoming only less exacting than that for universities. The institution of the degree of Bachelor of Education opens up possibilities of graduate status for the whole profession. Teachers' organizations, notably the National Union of Teachers, have immensely increased the teacher's collective bargaining power. Large sums of public money have transformed the colleges into finely equipped educational institutions; the academic qualifications of their staff and the breadth of the curriculum ensure not only a better professional training but a much broader education than primary teachers have ever before enjoyed.

The story of the secondary school teacher is very different. Up to the end of the nineteenth century his 'training' was hardly considered: he had a university degree which since the Middle Ages gave him a licence to teach, as it does to this day. He taught in the grammar schools or in the public schools and received a salary varying from about £100 in the smaller schools to the princely stipend of £800 enjoyed by Arnold's assistants, which in the larger schools might be augmented by the profits of a boarding house. But whether well or meagrely rewarded his background was that of the professional middle class which supplied church and state with curates, bishops, soldiers, lawyers and doctors. By virtue of his M.A. he could claim to be a gentleman, whose family connections and education had removed him sufficiently far from the life of his inferiors. Even when the Day Training Colleges, founded in 1890 and the forerunners of the University Departments of Education, began in 1895 to train secondary teachers, the fact that graduate students were often subsidized by the state did not reduce the social division between graduate and non-graduate. Thus the training institutions themselves ended in emphasizing the cleavage between elementary and secondary teachers. Furthermore the teachers' associations have tended to follow the alignment imposed by the history of the two branches of the profession.

The Teachers Registration Council founded in 1907 with high hopes of a united and self-governing profession, and in 1930 dignified by the title of Royal Society of Teachers, failed to gain the effective support of either the Ministry of Education or of the appointing authorities, or indeed of the majority of teachers. The R.S.T. died quietly in 1949, a casualty witnessing to the social and academic divisions in the profession.

Thus there have been two streams of social conditioning—three if we place the clerical public schoolmaster in a separate category—which partly account for the divisions among those who teach at the end of the twentieth century. Is it possible that teachers whose qualifications and work vary so widely can ever be welded into a self-governing profession comparable to the 'brotherhoods' of law, medicine, engineering, architecture and the rest? One aspect of the situation that may in the future tend to unify the profession is the closer association of graduates and non-graduates in the secondary sector of education. Whether it be in grammar, comprehensive or secondary modern schools, graduates and non-graduates work together as members of a single staff team as they have never done before. Even in the primary schools graduates who find themselves attracted to the education of younger children are finding satisfaction in an area of schooling once entirely in the hands of non-graduates. On the one hand colleges of education are training students for specialist work once exclusively performed by graduates in secondary schools; on the other, university departments of education increasingly provide professional training for primary teachers. And the close association of colleges of education with the universities in the Institutes of Education bring together university and college teachers, graduates and non-graduates, not only in the pursuit of common aims but in closer social contact.

Much more important than all these tendencies towards unity is the fact that for the first time in the history of the teaching profession a high proportion of teachers who have commenced their teaching career since 1945, whether educated in training college or university, come from the same social groups: they are the same sort of people. With the democratization of higher education disunity in the profession has become less a result of ancient snobberies than of wide differences of qualification for a wide range of differing responsibilities. Thus the gap between the graduate and non-graduate is decreasing. But we have to ask whether the status gap between the teaching and the established professions is also closing.

PROFESSION AND STATUS

A report presented in 1967 to the National Association of Schoolmasters by *The Economist Research Unit* said: 'It appears to us that the status of the school teacher in the minds of society as a whole and in those people considering teaching as a career, is still declining.' This judgement seems to include both graduate and non-graduate members of the profession, and, if true, is a sad outcome of a century's striving for improvement in the education and status of teachers. Most depressing is the suggestion that teaching as a career is less attractive than in the 1930's. Undoubtedly the academic quality of graduate teachers, especially in mathematics and science, has tended to decline during the post-war years. This suggests that teaching fails to offer graduates the attraction of other occupations in the new technological world. Teachers believe that their public image would be improved and their economic status enhanced if they were members of a united and self-governing profession. We have then to ask how far existing conditions could contribute to this end.

First there is the problem of unity in a profession whose members possess widely differing qualifications and whose work in schools varies from infant to sixth form teaching. We have already noted the relative absence of either academic or professional bonds between the elementary teacher and the man or woman emerging from the charmed circle of university graduation. This isolating influence still exists although, as we have seen, to a diminished degree. Nevertheless the movement towards unity faces obstacles embedded in the past but operating strongly in the present, not least the inevitable circumstance that the range of academic attainment among those who teach is wider than in any of the established professions. Writing in 1965 J. Lawson observed: 'it may still be more convenient than meaningful to talk about a teaching profession. Whilst the humblest curate may feel that he follows the same vocation as the Archbishop of Canterbury, and the youngest barrister that he is the same sort of person as the Lord Chief Justice, the primary school teacher can have little sense of shared purpose or community of interests with the Headmaster of Eton, the Master of Trinity or the Dean of Christ Church.'[16]

It is true, of course, that in the major public schools for a century there have been headmasters and staff acceptable as Fellows and Heads of Oxbridge colleges and as Vice-Chancellors of Universities. In sharp contrast most teachers in our primary schools have had no more than two years' college education. In the grammar schools are graduates of varied attainment, many of them at least comparable in academic ability to members of the established professions; others with poor degrees which nevertheless give them the licence to teach. In the colleges of education the proportion of graduate lecturers is lower than that in the grammar schools. This vast range of attainment cannot easily be discounted by the argument that a 'teacher is a teacher' whether of an infant class or of a sixth form. Moreover the qualifications held are not only different in standard but different in kind, for the various branches of teaching demand various types of training and involve, as they should, different qualities of personality and expertise that are not amenable to measurement and regulation.

What is lacking for teachers is an *enclave* to which they can claim to belong. Our curate and archbishop are within the enclave of the Church; the newly fledged barrister and the Lord Chief Justice

---

[16]*Aspects of Education* No. 3, 'The Professional Education of Teachers', Hull University, 1965, p. 14.

are within the enclave of the Law; the newly qualified G.P. has similar firm associations with the Presidents of the Royal Colleges of Physicians and Surgeons and holds degrees of those institutions; university teachers have their enclave in the university. But to what clearly defined group do the kindergarten mistress, the sixth-form master, and the lecturer in the college of education or in a technical college belong? We can only say they all teach. In the broadest sense teaching is a profession because teachers accept their own professional standards of conduct as inherent in their conception of themselves as servants of the community. Teaching is not a trade or a craft in the strict trade union sense; nor is it a profession as law and medicine are professions because teachers do not constitute a self-governing group. With good reason, the major teachers' organizations aspire to professional status in this stricter sense of membership of a self-governing corporation, convinced that only in this way can their social and economic status be raised. The underlying assumption here is that social esteem is measured in terms not only of membership of a recognized professional body but also in terms of remuneration. That these assumptions are at least partly true no one can doubt; that they are wholly true or ought to be true is open to question.

Is social esteem always dependent on income? Not in the case of parsons or missionaries, who are highly esteemed, sometimes because they give devoted service for low wages; or of turf accountants and speculators in property who are low in public esteem despite their wealth. Is public esteem the same thing as social status? Not if we agree that an absentee member of the hereditary house of peers ranks higher in the public image than a teacher. Again, does a big income invariably confer high social status? Sometimes it does; but not in the case of pop singers, professional footballers and proprietors of one-armed bandit saloons. All seems to depend on whose esteem we desire. What matters for teachers is that they secure the esteem of people whose opinion they respect, and are paid at least as much as men and women with similar qualifications who play as important a role in society.

In an interesting paper on 'Professional Implications in Status and Training'[17] on which the following paragraphs are based, Dr. T. M. Bamford notes that in the five social classes used by the 1951 Census for the classification of occupations, teachers are placed in Class II. Class I includes occupations generally regarded as 'professional'—administrative civil servants, managers in various highly paid posts, company directors, judges, magistrates, barristers, doctors, clergymen, professional engineers, architects, authors, editors, publishers, commissioned officers in H.M. Forces, and so on. Teachers appear in the second class along with farmers, the executive civil service, auctioneers, midwives and superintendents of police. Dr. Bamford notes the very high qualifications and rare qualities of mind that some of Class I possess and also notes that they represent less than 600,000 persons in a total male census of over 17 million people.

Teachers belong to a group (Class II) of over $2\frac{1}{2}$ million which includes the executive civil servants. Dr. Bamford compares the respective salary conditions of civil servants and teachers and notes a fundamental difference in pay structure between them: whereas in 1963 25 per cent of civil servants have chances of promotion to salary levels above £2,000 only 1·5 per cent of teachers, including headmasters, reached that level. He concludes that 'teachers' salaries need to be increased by at least £1,500 a year at the 25 per cent mark if their claim to professional (Class I) status is to be taken seriously'.

Nevertheless the mark of the established professions is not their remuneration but their exclusiveness. The charmed circle is defended by several devices: not only by control of entry and of qualifications for admission, but also by the duration, academic standards and cost of the training involved in acquiring specialist knowledge. The knowledge they acquire is usually of a kind not easily attainable by the majority of citizens, which is in constant demand and which possesses an element of mystery to the clients who demand its use on their behalf. The most obvious instances are medicine, the Church and the law; but the architect, the engineer, the surveyor and all the higher

[17] *Aspects of Education* No. 3, 1965. Hull University

ranks in a technological civilization carry the same prestige in their public image. All these are carefully regulated and self-governing professions. If control of entry, self-regulation, and prestige-giving salaries are the main components of the professional image, then nowhere in the world have teachers achieved this end.

More intractable is the fact that civilized communities require many teachers. If the children of Britain had their rights there should be 500,000 teachers in the 1970's—twenty times the number of doctors. It has been estimated that half of those receiving higher education will be required as teachers. If, however, one of the characteristics of a profession is the possession by its members of rare skills not attainable by most people, it is difficult for teachers to make this claim when half a million people are involved, i.e. the total of all professions grouped in Class I. And if they were all to receive increments of £1,000, say, which would be a minimum to propel them into the professional salaried group, the cost to the exchequer would be the formidable sum of £500 million.[18] Nor should it be assumed that a totally graduate teaching corps would automatically bring professional status in the strict sense, for by the year A.D. 2000 graduation will be a requirement for a vast area of the nation's occupations. And now that an egalitarian society pays for the university education of aspirants to all professions and not only to that of teaching, we are bound to conclude that teachers must look far beyond mere graduate status for the improvement of their social image.

On what basis, then, can the teacher's hopes be founded? First, on a quality of professional training equivalent in duration and discipline to that of, say, medicine, architecture and engineering. In 1967 Sir Ronald Gould, then General Secretary of the National Union of Teachers, bluntly told teachers to keep the professional characteristics they had and to acquire those they had not, knowing well that the future demands on teachers in the spheres of scholarship, general culture, clinical and sociological knowledge and techniques of instruction, would increase with the changed structuring of society. The teacher's status will also

---

[18] See Bamford, op. cit., p. 89.

depend less on his membership of a strong trade union than on his proved capacity to meet the needs of millions of children and adolescents, about whose mental and moral capacities we know too little and who will be entering a world greatly different from that in which their teachers were educated.

16 New roles for the teacher

THE TECHNOLOGICAL REVOLUTION

Among the most important social changes of this century has been the functioning of education as a social accelerator—like the chemical additive that speeds up the garden compost into something sometimes rich and strange. Under the solvent of democratized education a once static and class-stratified society is now experiencing a mobility never known before. The career open to talent has at last arrived. Knowledge, taste, manners, opinion, artistic and scientific achievement are no longer passed on through the 'mediating sieve' of an educated élite—the modern versions of Erasmus, Montaigne, the eighteenth century gentleman, Matthew Arnold—but directly, through the impact of the mass media, especially through the open and visible forum of T.V. For the brighter spirits there is the layman's university of the paper-backs. During this period of change the spiritual certainties of the Edwardian parent, and also his carefully guarded respectability, were threatened by his children's Georgian disillusionments and finally destroyed by the irreverence and shattering frankness of his Elizabethan grandchildren. None of these things has happened without loss. We cannot be entirely happy with the substitution of permissiveness and anxiety for moral certainty and confidence.

With the general impact of the technological revolution on our ways of living we are equally familiar, but it is doubtful whether we have estimated the effect of the additional strains of continuing technological change on our educational services.

In future almost every person will have to be retrained at least twice in his lifetime because skills learned at school or on the factory floor will repeatedly become obsolete. Such retraining will involve not only instruction in new processes, most of them tending to replace human labour with electronic machines, but also initiation into the basic principles on which the new machines work. We must hope, too, that the young generation will be educated into a new social consciousness, into a moral and social responsibility capable of controlling the robot tendencies of a society whose major activities are concerned with the production of gadgets.

That the future will demand more technically proficient people, as well as more robots, presents us with problems. But more disturbing for those concerned, as teachers are, for the happiness and emotional stability of persons, is the dismal and even terrifying prospect of almost unlimited leisure. For this we are not preparing. No one can pretend that men and women are ready for a life in the twenty-first century punctuated by intensive production of capital and consumer goods under a régime of three days' work and three days' free time, and maybe ending in thirty years of retirement. Sitting in loneliness amidst a flashing computer system, one man can already feed electricity to a whole town. The computer manages our wages and our taxes, and at some point every article from the books we read to our breakfast bacon is computerized. There is something basically anti-human in all this. The human spirit can have no warm intercourse with stainless steel buttons.

We don't know how much regular occupation, the routine use of hands and brain, team work on a job and the companionship this brings, the tensions undergone in the joint solving of problems on the work floor, the joy in work when it is over—we don't know how far these satisfactions, unconsciously felt but nevertheless real, contribute to men's herd needs and therefore to their mental health. But we suspect that a day's fishing, or a holiday at Butlins, or a deck-chair at Southend, are satisfying only because they give temporary release, not because they are desirable as permanent occupations. In our present unpreparedness for almost unlimited leisure the next century faces us with boredom. Boredom is both debilitating and dangerous. The normal response to boredom is desire for excitement, and many there are who are cashing in on an increasing demand. £2,000 million are annually exchanged in the gambling rackets; violence is the escape of the aggressive type; alcohol and drugs the resort of the introverted. Uninhibited sexual experiment follows the doctrine that 'sex is the healthiest and most important human sport'. In the metamorphosis of Computerized Man into Leisure Man can Homo Sapiens survive?

The most vulnerable to the dangers of increased leisure are the old and the young. Few retired people have learned how to use 'time on my hands'; the young have too few outlets for constructive activity either individual or social, and too many regard spare time merely as an opportunity for passive entertainment. Educational background seems to determine to a large degree whether free-time activities are of the self-created or passive kind. The less literate and the less skilled are seldom capable of devising occupations that hold their continuing interest. It is probable that the home-making wife and mother will experience fewer personal frustrations than her husband and older children. Her problem will be the domestic one of a council house cluttered up with aimless and restless males.

THE SIGNIFICANCE OF ADOLESCENCE

Research during the last half century has convinced us of the importance of early childhood for the emotional development of children throughout the years preceding adolescence. This emphasis on the childhood phase has deflected our attention from the equally significant needs of adolescence and has resulted in a far too casual treatment of an age-group making the crucial passage from childhood to adulthood. Until recently the education of adolescents has plodded along the routine paths of secondary schooling largely but not entirely, it is true, devoted to the accumulation of factual knowledge. In this restricted enterprise the secondary schools have performed moderately well with 15 per cent or so of the nation's children. But the democratization of education in Britain since 1945 has transformed the circumstances of secondary schooling, and calls for a radical reassessment of a wide range of assumptions on which the education of adolescents was formerly based.

More adolescents than ever before, from all income groups, remain at school till 16 or over. Possibly owing to improved nutrition, both boys and girls attain physical maturity earlier than they did in their grandfather's day:

'the present day 14-year-old *is*, in physique and probably in brain maturity also, the 15-year-old of a generation ago, and he must be treated accordingly. It is true he has had a year less education, and a year less experience of the world, but assimilation of experience is not measured by the calendar. If his social behaviour seems less rather than more mature (in the sense here of adult-like) that must be laid at the door of the social and educational pressures bearing or failing to bear upon him.'[1]

The essential fact here is that a far higher proportion of both boys and girls reach sexual maturity before leaving school. This is one of the more interesting consequences for education of our post-war affluence. For a large part of the population entry upon adult activities is now delayed by longer schooling, and must be so delayed if adolescents are to be prepared for the technological revolution that assails them, and for the bewildering range of vocational and moral choices with which the affluent society now surrounds them. The dangers are many and obvious.

In his assessment of the most recent research on adolescence,[2] written with his customary conciseness and wisdom, Dr. W. D. Wall emphasizes the need for teachers, parents and administrators to regard adolescence as a psycho-social-cultural phenomenon and its problems less as emanations of glandular changes than as a product of maladjustment in social relationships. The most evident characteristic of adolescence in our society is the

[1] J. M. Tanner, *Education and Physical Growth*, 1961, p. 123.
[2] *Adolescents in School and Society*, 1968, published by the National Foundation for Educational Research.

aggressive drive towards independence from parents and parental figures. This we all know. But the social conditions in which the adolescent grows up have radically changed. Parental control, so irksome and yet so security-giving even when rejected, has yielded place to indecisive parental permissiveness. The parent is seldom holding the tiller. His place seems to have been taken by an entirely new phenomenon, which some people call an 'adolescent culture', whose main characteristics are anti-previous-generation, anti-adult-discipline and anti-establishment. It is remarkably free from class alignments but distinctively a youth-product and a voice of protest. On its lunatic fringe it seems to be a decadent response to frustration, its music wild and raucous. But in its more serious literary and musical expressions—in some 'pop' songs, for instance—it is deeply moving, not merely an inarticulate expression of frustration but a thrusting and well directed protest against inhumanity, social injustice and stupidity in high places. At no point in my lifetime do I remember more concern for the underdog, more sympathy and practical helpfulness among young people. Their thinking is as muddled as that of their elders, but much more explosive.

Another new circumstance, of course, is the increased spending power of adolescents, which receives a ready response from the advertising media and market research. Whether it comes from wages or the indulgent parental pocket, the new juvenile affluence invites a bewildering array of choices in goods and behaviour. And behind all is the Bomb, ticking away no one knows where, or when and who will press the button. More sensitive than their elders to premonitions of things to come, and more articulate in formulating their own ideals, young people address parents, teachers and vice-chancellors with irresponsible frankness. It is difficult to discover what they want to construct, or indeed, to destroy, apart from barriers to their own freedom. 'Participation' is the word; a good word, which sums up the constructive element in the aggressive response of the modern young when they are not taken seriously.

These are some of the reasons which enable Dr. Wall to conclude that the basic problem of adolescence is *anxiety*. Dr.

Wall suggests that the adolescent road to maturity lies through the achievement of 'four selves':[3]

1. *A social self:* expressed in emancipation from dependence; orientation to others; a sense of belonging to society and a recognition of duties as well as of privileges.
2. *A sexual self:* capable of a range of feeling from friendly indifference to deep involvement with a member of the opposite sex, adequate adjustment in marriage and the ability to found a family.
3. *A working or vocational self:* this is a complex of self-knowledge in relation to vocational achievement; of self-respect derived from economic independence and a sense of being needed; and of being a person, more than a unit of 'man hours'.
4. *A philosophic or religious self:* founded on a simple set of values and standards capable of interpreting life, of directing decisions and determining behaviour.

Commenting on these adolescent 'growth tasks' Dr. Wall writes:

'Even the most summary comparison of these goals with the images which our society presents to the young, lays bare a multitude of points of strain and uncertainty and draws attention to the glaring fact that most of the older resources of guidance and support in choice, either no longer exist or are inadequate to the needs of many groups of boys and girls. If we compare the goals in detail with the manner of the education provided for teenagers the discrepancy seems even wider. Even for highly intelligent adolescents from stable and cultivated homes, it is doubtful whether a verbal-intellectual education does more than provide an incidental respite, and incidental food for thought on the problems which vex them.'[4]

To suggest with some authoritative backing the means by which education might be more deliberately directed towards the preparation of young people for their 'growth tasks', I must still

[3] Op. cit., p. 13.   [4] Op. cit., p. 13.

lean heavily on Dr. Wall's 'generalizations derivable from research'. For this I have his permission to adapt a series of propositions he presents for the consideration of teachers:[5]

1. Because adolescence in our culture is a psycho-social phenomenon, behaviour and social attitudes are modifiable if the appropriate means are found.
2. While the childhood years preceding adolescence are immensely important there are changes in personality and cognition which seem to be peculiarly a product of adolescent experience.
3. Being a highly sensitive emotional period, adolescence probably permits massive changes in the ways in which personality, attitudes and concepts of self express themselves in behaviour.
4. While it is doubtful whether full recuperation from the effects of earlier environmental deprivations is possible in the teens, the direct influence of home environment seems to decline and the influence of other environments to increase.
5. It is unlikely that the formal curriculum can satisfy the needs of adolescents in terms of the 'four selves'—social, sexual, vocational and religious (see above). This suggests that extracurricular activities, school method, attitudes to discipline, the frank discussion of fundamental social, economic and contemporary moral issues, should be part of the teenage programme.
6. Capacity to think objectively is not an automatic result of teenage development; it is dependent on education and experience and upon the level of general ability. Many adolescents, like many adults, are only partially able to think objectively on matters touching themselves personally. Hence adolescents should be taught to reason objectively on problems involving emotional undertones.
7. Adolescents, especially those whose interests are not academic, often question the relevance of studies seemingly unrelated to their vocational aims. This raises the question of the relevance of the curriculum to the aspirations of the adolescent's 'working self' and the relationship between a general and vocational education.

[5] See op. cit., pp. 67-70.

THE CENTRAL ROLE OF THE SCHOOL

In his book *Towards a Theory of Instruction* (1966) Jerome S. Bruner insists that as our technology grows increasingly complex in both machinery and human organization 'the role of the school becomes more central in society, not simply as an agent of socialization but as a transmitter of skills'. We are entering, he says, upon 'a period of technological maturity in which education will require constant redefinition'.

Bruner's views on the development of skills and the reconstruction of curricula form an interesting supplement to Dr. Wall's references to the education of adolescents. Like Dr. Wall, he presents them in the form of a group of propositions of 'testable hypotheses' that help us towards a reassessment of priorities in curriculum and method. These propositions are not a summary of startling discoveries—with many of them the well-informed teacher will be familiar. Their importance lies in the emphasis placed upon them by a lucid exponent of co-ordinated educational research. The following is a summary of those 'testable hypotheses' particularly relevant to the relationship between the learning of skills and the reform of the curriculum:

1. Unless certain basic skills are mastered—e.g. speech and language as a means of communication and as a vehicle of thought—more elaborate skills become increasingly and even permanently out of reach.[6]
2. The idea of readiness for learning is now acknowledged to be a mischievous half truth, because 'one *teaches* readiness, or provides opportunities for its nurture, one does not simply *wait* for it'. In these terms readiness for learning consists of mastery of those simpler skills that enable us to attain higher skills, e.g. 'if you wish to teach calculus in the eighth grade, then we must begin it in the first grade by the teaching the kinds of ideas and skills necessary for its mastery later'. There is an appropriate version of any skill or knowledge that may be imparted at whatever age one wishes to begin teaching it, however preparatory the version may be.

[6] pp. 28-9.

3. Intellectual mastery is rewarding; especially when the learner himself realizes that learning one thing permits him to go on to something that seemed beyond his reach. These 'self-reward sequences', the rewards of understanding, are a 'more robust lure to effort than we have yet realized'.[7]

4. The principal emphasis in instruction should be upon skills —skills in handling, in seeing and imaging and in symbolic operations (e.g. the operations in mathematics which are dependent on symbols) Bruner remarks: 'I do not think we have begun to scratch the surface of training in visualization—whether related to the arts, to science or simply to the pleasures of viewing our environment.'[8]

5. While the importance of factual knowledge must be recognized, curriculum building should be more deliberately directed than it is at present to the opportunities the curriculum provides for learning skills that lead to the mastery of more difficult skills.[9]

   What is implied here is not the ousting of factual material —e.g. in literature, history or science—but the organization of it, and the pedagogical use of it, in a way that develops skills in learning, in logical thinking for instance, *in the process of assimilating the material*. In other words, the shift need not be away from facts to skills—a contradiction in terms—but away from an entirely subject-based curriculum to a subject-cum-skill based curriculum.

6. If we are to respond to accelerating change we must reduce the time lag, so notable in our educational systems, in communicating new knowledge to the teachers who are to use it in schools.

   Bruner refers to a survey of high-school mathematics which revealed that no mathematics newer than one hundred years old was being taught. We are much more alive to this weakness today; but there remains a challenge for the teacher to keep up-to-date, and a responsibility laid on those working at the frontiers of knowledge to communicate with the teachers in school.

For Bruner's analysis of the methodology implied by these propositions the reader must turn to his book. What I am con-

[7] p. 30.   [8] p. 34.   [9] p. 35.

cerned to note at this point is their bearing on the teacher's function in society and on the professional difficulties of his task. When we interlock Bruner's concept of the school as 'an agent in socialization and a transmitter of basic skills' with W. D. Wall's broader appreciation of the school as a medium for fostering the accomplishment of the adolescent 'growth tasks', we are able to form a more comprehensive prospect of what the school's role ought to be. We see the adolescent struggling to maturity in an arena far wider and more challenging than his home and school, and in a historical context far different from that of the first half of this century. These changed circumstances suggest that his education calls for the teacher's special attention.

The object of this excursion into the needs of adolescence has been to emphasize the increasing difficulty of the teacher's tasks, and to ask whether existing programmes of professional training are equipping him to face them. The teacher's own 'growth tasks' become formidable. 'One wonders,' reflects Dr. Wall, 'how many teachers have been led by their training to perceive that the curriculum, method and social climate of the school are of immense importance in the guidance of adolescents, and how many are as well equipped to discuss the human relationships that are basic to friendship and love, or to find one's way among compelling interpretations of life, as they are to teach mathematics and geography.'[10] We can answer with little confidence.

If for lack of adequate preparation teachers fall down on their job, it is not likely that they will be accorded the higher social esteem they desire and which, in view of their potential role in society, they ought to receive. The way is not through a strengthening of the tenuous bonds between teachers' associations and the classical trade union movement—the N.U.T. backed by the T.U.C. More is required than a continuing struggle for higher pay and better working conditions, desirable as these are. The aspirations for a higher professional status will be realized only when the profession of teaching is recognized to be as important, as difficult, as demanding of specialist knowledge for the teaching

[10] Op. cit., p. 14.

of skills, for the preservation of mental and moral health, and for the formation of constructive social attitudes, as is the profession of medicine in protecting us from disease and death. Few teachers are within a thousand miles of realizing the immense scope and exciting possibilities of their job; and present training has little chance of making this truth evident to the students who so superficially prepare for a task whose dimensions they are seldom called upon to measure. Politicians, taxpayers and citizens in general expect teachers to do their job without tools.

EDUCATING THE TEACHER

Education is concerned with knowledge, with skills, with persons, with relationships between persons, and with values. The teacher is simultaneously involved with these different facets of education all his working life and every day. Hence, it is in the person of the teacher rather than in the curriculum or organization of the school, that all these aspects of education are harmonized. It is individual teachers who bring children 'inside the citadel of civilization so that they will understand and love what they see when they get there'.[11] This is what the great teachers have always tried to do. They may have had different views about what makes a civilized man, but they had no doubt that what was involved was quality of mind and manners not quantity of wealth or power. This view has not been shared by lesser men, by payment-by-results Robert Lowe or history-is-bunk Henry Ford, and those teachers of the modern age who can see no further than the textbook.

A great divide separates the teachers of even thirty years ago from those of today: in the past no one ever thought it was necessary to civilize everyone; it was enough to civilize those who could afford to be educated. Today we strive to civilize everybody and the task of the teacher takes on quite new dimensions. Thinking back to the earlier pages of this chapter where the nature of these changes was discussed, and to the 'testable

[11] R. S. Peters, 'Education as Initiation', in *Philosophical Analysis and Education*, ed. R. D. Archambault, p. 107.

hypotheses' of Bruner and Wall regarding the moral, intellectual and vocational needs of young people, we see more clearly both the central importance of the teaching profession and the meagreness of the teacher's equipment for good professional performance.

It has been generally assumed that a teacher moderately well grounded in the subjects he has to teach, with a smattering of 'educational psychology', trained in method and blessed with a touch of common sense, is adequately equipped to guide his pupils into the 'citadel of civilization'. But when we examine in depth the needs of childhood and adolescence in the new social setting, such a view surely implies a derisively superficial estimate of the teacher's work. If he is to be more than a purveyor of utilities at a cut price, then a teacher must become *an* authority in his own sphere of operations, rather than a person *in* authority for the performance of a limited range of useful tasks. The new teacher has to think himself into a quite new dimension.

The point of departure for the teacher's reassessment of himself is Dr. Wall's declaration that 'adolescent phenomena in behaviour, value structures, attitudes, *are modifiable if the appropriate means be found*'.[12] The teacher's training should be of a kind to enable him to discover and apply 'the appropriate means'. Hence the new dimension into which the teacher might enter extends beyond that of instructor in the classroom to a highly skilled guide through the stages of childhood and adolescence. The results of neglect in these formative years should be enough to convince us that the adolescent's achievement of his 'four selves' will not be automatic. To put children in school and hope for the best is a mere 'wait and grow' education. But that is the most the crowded secondary schools are likely to give them unless we increase the teacher's competence and also, of course, the number of teachers. Is it, then, unreasonable to require for him a professional preparation that will render him as capable of dealing with problems of childhood and adolescence as is a doctor of treating measles or a broken collar bone?

[12] Author's italics.

When the school-leaving age is raised to 16 in the early seventies an additional 300,000 adolescents will be staying on at school. These will be young people of average and less than average ability. The education of this particular age-group has become a problem for teachers and planners throughout the world, whether in advanced or developing countries. In this group are the potential producers who form the solid base of the community pyramid. In it also are the potential disturbers of the peace, the least motivated and consequently the most aimless of our young people, the rebels in the classroom and in the streets, the clients of the adolescent drug trade. Teachers in our tougher schools are very much aware of the portentous nature of this problem; no doubt also are a few who breathe the rarer atmosphere of Whitehall. Research institutions are working at useful pilot schemes of curriculum reform. But it is not so evident that teachers, planners and taxpayers realize that together they face the greatest educational challenge of the century, namely, the education of the most difficult and largest group in the adolescent population. Is the teaching profession, as at present educated, really competent to deal with so challenging a situation?

Consider, for instance, the staffing in a high proportion of the non-grammar secondary schools, the most difficult area of the whole teaching situation. These schools are the haven of the least competent of all our teachers, namely, the untrained graduate with a poor degree. He feels superior to his non-graduate colleagues because he has a degree, whereas he is in fact often inferior in teaching ability. His education has consisted of a narrow academic schooling followed by university experience in the bottom third of university ability. His motivation for teaching is negligible, not even sufficient to impel him towards the professional training deemed necessary for a teaching career About half the graduates trying to educate this explosive adolescent generation are of this kind.

It is not so much the pattern of the teacher's professional education that is at fault as its depth. We don't want teachers to be professional psychologists. Nevertheless we want them to be informed about those departments of psychology that help them to diagnose their problems as practitioners. The relationship of the psychologist to the teacher is like that of the pure to the applied scientist—of the physicist to the engineer, of the biochemist to the doctor. The teachers' training should be sufficient to keep him in continuing contact with research and to interpret and apply such new knowledge as he finds relevant and useful. At present few working teachers are capable of doing this without a deeper clinical understanding of learning and behaviour problems. When we cast a glance at the prospects for teenage education in the near future such professional knowledge appears as necessary to the teacher as are physiology and anatomy to the medical practitioner. The essential applications of psychology lie in the fields of child development, learning processes and their relation to curriculum building, motivation, emotional maladjustment, and a thorough examination of all the controversial issues tangled up with concepts of discipline, rewards and punishments, personal responsibility and community building.

There is another gap in the teacher's training. The Newsom Report *Half Our Future* (1963) suggests that teachers' training should include:

. . . some straightforward courses in recent social history; a study of the family and its changing function and structure in present day society; and guidance in understanding the current literature of sociology and psychology and the implications of research results. Some students may need to examine their own social preconceptions. It cannot be assumed, for example, that teachers with the same social and economic background as the pupils they teach will automatically have more insight into their pupils' difficulties; in so far as the teachers' own educational progress may have been untypical of others in their circumstances, they may even have less sympathy with environmental difficulties.[13]

Many colleges provide such courses, yet it is difficult to believe that with the time available they are able to give instruction at the depth and with the adequate case study required to give

[13] Para. 293.

them practical value. This is the point at which the training of the teacher and the social worker might be deliberately planned to overlap. From this more realistic training combined with a study of recent social history teachers might be expected to develop a *social intelligence*, defined as informed awareness of social and economic trends and their consequences for young people in a period of technological change. Teachers in difficult schools are well aware of the *results* of deprivation when confronted with young barbarians in the classroom, but they are insufficiently aware of their causes and consequently unlikely to tackle them as skilled practitioners in a profession that by its nature has its remedial duties.

The challenge is not to be met by the expenditure of more money on school accommodation, although the doctrine of Thring's Almighty Wall still holds good. Barbarism runs rampant in many custom-built school palaces. The Newsom Report aptly remarks that 'there is sufficient variation between individual schools to make it clear that a school in a bad building can get and keep a stable staff, and that the best architects cannot guarantee one'.[14] Why? Because a teacher's loyalty to a school is founded on his conviction that the school in which he serves is doing a good job; that it is winning. It is not stimulating to find oneself stemming a tide of boredom and insubordination; it can be inspiring to find a professionally directed attack based on skilled approaches, a relevant curriculum and appropriately tuned attitudes to discipline, bearing fruit in slum children in a slum building. Teachers, like their pupils and most human beings, tend to respond to the rewards of success.

If we refer to the propositions of Dr. Wall on page 210 we find there the ingredients of a programme that will enable teachers to discover their job to be worth while. Here is a picture of the excitements and opportunities involved in a teacher's professional undertaking, the knowledge and attitudes he requires to accomplish it, and his need to preserve a freshness of mind that sees all difficulties not as frustrations but as challenges to professional competence. And here is the heart of the matter:

[14] Para. 655.

the sense of defeat that discourages so many teachers is largely due to the meagreness of their training; its brevity, its lack of depth and its remoteness from the actual school situation.

Herbert Read once said that 'the education of the pupil is the self-education of the teacher'. What children and adolescents need is what teachers need, in the sense that the experiences and needs of their pupils are the materials on which the teachers have to exercise their skill and perception. Teachers have to know what these needs are in the total social setting of each period of change. Psychology, sociology, the subject-cum-skill-cum-vocationally relevant curriculum, his sense of values, are among the tools which help him to sort out his approaches to his professional task. The study of psychology and sociology does not preclude the entry of value judgements in the teacher's assessments of the facts these studies reveal. The relevance of these studies to education lies in the fact that value judgements are most valid when they are founded on knowing as much, as at any moment we can know, of people as individuals and of the collective experience of men in communities. To know *why* children from bad homes are undisciplined (psychology) and why bad homes exist (sociology) evokes the judgement that schools should counteract the effects of bad homes. To come to know and to feel these things is the self-education of the teacher in so far as it results from his studies in psychology and sociology. To regard the study of these sciences merely as a means of sharpening the teacher's *expertise* is to neglect their importance as value-forming influences.

We have suggested that education is concerned with knowledge, skills, persons, relations between persons and with values. These are the elements that seem to satisfy the traditional requirements that education should be a process of initiation into ways of life and modes of thought that the community deems necessary to its continued existence. Ministers of education and local authorities have no quarrel with the teacher's roles as purveyors of knowledge and know-how, as agents in 'socializing' the deprived children who have been 'desocialized' by slum conditions, as speech and language therapists for children rendered inarticulate in 'monosyllabic homes', and generally as men and women who strive to civilize their school communities. Public opinion also approves of the teacher in the role of conservator of national traditions and culture and as exemplars of acceptable moral values. But, asks R. S. Peters, will these tasks assist teachers to be regarded 'not only as custodians of a community's culture, but also as those who pass on forms of thought and awareness by means of which these values can be adapted and challenged as conditions change . . . or are they to be thought of only as experts on the means of transmitting such a culture and on training citizens in useful occupations for the state. . . . Is the teacher to be an agent of change and challenge as well as of cultural conservation?'[15]

It was perhaps enough that in the past the teacher should have been the conservator and transmitter of cultural values; but today so limited a view of his role is hardly tenable. If he is to wait until acceptable modes of thought have been approved by the Establishment, he will remain where he has usually been, a generation behind the needs of his pupils and for that reason in perpetual conflict with them. Professor Peters gives us a straight answer: 'The job of the educator is not simply to build on existing wants but to present what is worth wanting in such a way that it creates new wants and stimulates new interests.'[16] Here is an exciting image of the teacher—sure of what he knows and of what his pupil must know, but occasionally nibbling at the fringe of the unknown and raising his pupils' sights to what may be found there. We can see this kind of thing happening in the nursery school, school workshop, the lessons in literature or science, or in sixth form discussion when the teacher is in touch with the rife ideas of his age.

The discovery of what is worth wanting today is assisted by a study of the dialectic between perceptive minds in the past and the social and educational conditions of their time. In this way the student catches a glimpse of what is worth wanting and of

[15] See *Ethics and Education*, pp. 257-61.
[16] See his essay 'Education as Initiation', in *Philosophical Analysis and Education*, ed. R. D. Archambault, 1965, p. 109.

what is worth conserving. This is why for half a century training courses for teachers have rightly included courses on the history of educational ideas usually based on the contributions of 'the Great Educators' to educational thought and practice. Looking back to my own training fifty years ago, I realize that this was the only part of that experience which has fertilized any teaching I have done. I have no memory of 'method', but vivid recollections of my tutor and of the transactions between him and me that started me thinking about education. I was taught to think about values and their relevance to my vocation. It might be argued that it would have been more profitable to have begun my thinking about education in an East End primary school. But in my case I had been educated at an almost grim primary school, and I began to realize what had happened to me there when I saw it in the perspective of what might have happened if my teachers had felt themselves to be the spiritual legatees of a long line of teachers who had been concerned with more than 'existing wants'.

This sense of history is the soundest basis for any philosophical study of educational theory. It is so important for the teacher to feel that he has roots and that the wisdoms distilled from past experience have a message for him when he confronts the opportunities and conflicts among children in school. Can he realize, for instance, that the Hebrew prophets still call him to be 'a restorer of paths to dwell in'? Can he feel with Socrates that he is engaged in a joint enterprise with his pupils in the discovery of truth, and that he and they are equally subject to the disciplines of the search? Is he seeking with Plato to lead the young, astray in their world of tinkling gadgets, to their lost vision of the Good? Does Augustine's view of teaching as 'a dwelling in each other' have any meaning for him? Is his adult authority exercised with Montaigne's 'sweet severe mildness'; and does he have Saint-Cyran's love and pity for those who appear most defective and backward? More immediately relevant to the trials of his classroom, does the teacher believe with John Dewey that in a reconstruction of his pupils' environment he can begin to civilize his school? And if he believes this to be possible, has he derived from the controversies between philosophers, rebels and schoolmasters during the last two centuries, and from his own experience, a working pattern of the relationships between authority and freedom, discipline and responsibility?

To combine these historical, philosophical, psychological and sociological aspects of education in the teacher's professional preparation would involve a longer period of training than that he now receives, but not longer than he requires. The logistics of the operation present problems of time and money if the teacher's preparation is to be as thorough as that of the doctor. But is it beyond our resources to contrive a system of six or seven years' combined academic and in-service training during which the Bachelor of Education, or his equivalent graduates to the status of Master of Education, not by means of academic theses on esoteric topics remotely relevant to his actual teaching career but by successful clinical experience in the actual school situation? These real masters of their craft might with more reason aspire to higher status and perhaps acquire higher social esteem. We want more members of the profession capable of adventurous thinking and battling on the frontier situations of education—the Plowden priority areas, the socially deprived backward children, the city 'blackboard jungles', those areas of adolescent education where the vocational and the general, the formal and the informal, have not yet begun to contribute to the adolescent's 'four selves'.

17 *The conditions of education*

One of the less admirable characteristics of teachers throughout the ages has been their enduring capacity to resist the impact of a new idea. To cling confidently to inherited and unexamined opinions, to acquire virtue by teaching as we were taught, to treat the liberating ideas of pioneers as a commonroom joke, these are so often the only fruits of what is oddly called 'experience'. And yet teachers owe more to the rebel prophets than they do to the custodians of their rights. Even today when the professional status and remuneration of teachers is so powerfully and so rightly projected on to the public consciousness, society accords greater respect to the teacher as pioneer and prophet—to the centenarian J. H. Badley of Bedales and to the octogenarian A. S. Neill of Summerhill—than to the teacher as trade unionist.

Teachers belong to one of the most conservative professions in the world. This is a sad reflection on men and women directly involved in the education of the young. Fortunately many teachers redeem their profession by realizing that experience pays no dividends unless we learn by it. It is of course one of the functions of a profession to conserve the rights of its members, and the teaching associations have never performed this duty more faithfully than they do today. But a true professionalism involves more than conservatism. It involves also two types of reasoned response: first, readiness to examine objectively new demands arising out of new circumstances (the raising of the school-leaving age provides a good example); secondly, to be as willing to adopt a new way as to retain an old one, on the reasonable assumption that what is new is not necessarily right and what is old not necessarily wrong.

In the great library of Cambridge University there reposes one of the five codexes of our Bible, the *Codex Bezae*, which contains a verse—Luke 6⁶—not found in the other four versions. It reads as follows:

And on the same day Jesus saw a man working on the sabbath and said unto him, Man if thou knowest what thou art doing, blessed art thou; but if thou knowest not thou are accursed and a transgressor of the law.

This is a wonderful text for the teacher. Whether he achieves professional status or not, whether he teaches at Winchester College or Gas Works Primary or at Summerhill—blessed is the teacher who knows what he is doing.

And so, after fifty years of teaching I have in the end, somewhat to my own surprise, come to the conclusion that there may be no such thing as long-term aims in education; and that, if there are, they are nothing like as important as the attitudes that determine what we do with children from day to day. Put in another way, if we want to know whether we actually have aims, let us examine what it is we do now. If a teacher wishes to know what his aims are—and he should occasionally try to do this— he should honestly examine his attitudes towards his pupils and the quality of his day-to-day transactions with them.

I have, then, no intention of concluding this book on The Teacher with a statement on the aims of education or with a neat inventory of the qualities of a good teacher. Good teachers emerge in a multitude of guises. What seems to be more necessary is to suggest the convictions the teacher should have if he is to face squarely the sort of challenges presented by any school situation in which he works. For there are, I believe, a group of imperatives that every teacher should consider as relevant to his job. These imperatives involve value judgements which bear directly on his daily activities in school, but require him to subscribe to no particular religious or philosophical creed; only to the belief that the purpose of education is to help children to grow up. They can be most briefly presented as propositions—testable hypotheses—a kind of teacher's *Sic et Non*, whose truth cannot be proved by Abelard's logical analysis but only by thinking, working and observing in school. There are two ways available in our search for the truth: we can either assume to be untrue everything that has not yet been proved to be true; or we can take a risk and assume to be possibly true what has not yet been proved to be untrue.

Here are the propositions:

THE SCHOOL COMMUNITY

1. If one aim of a school is to civilize boys and girls then teachers must cultivate civility not servility. *Civility* is the demeanour of the self-respecting person towards a person he respects. *Servility* is the demeanour of a person lacking in self-respect towards one whom he fears. To choose the first expresses the desire to be civilized; to choose the second is to choose barbarism, which is the will to live in strife and to exercise power over others.[1]

2. The organization of a school is in fact an organization of values, the outcome of the value judgements of the staff when translated into the school's corporate life.

3. The ethos or 'climate' of a school depends on the nature of personal relationships informing its organization. These relationships should be founded on respect for persons—between head and staff, between colleagues, between teachers and pupils and between the pupils. Thus the primary condition for building a good school community is that everybody in it respects everybody in it. This condition will not prevail unless it is first evident among the adult members of the community.

4. The staff of a school must operate as a team with a common purpose and agreed principles of action. The first duty of the head is to create this team. Within the team there should be plenty of scope for individual expression of personality and of opinion.

[1] See R. G. Collingwood, *The New Leviathan*, pp. 306-9.

AUTHORITY

1. Authority in school should be known to exist as a source of security, of stability, of encouragement and stimulation, and felt by the pupils to be ultimately 'on our side'.

2. The exercise of authority loses its value and fails in its purpose when it causes resentment and fear.

3. The teacher's traditional authority over children in school is less likely to evoke respect among adolescents than it once did. This is one of the psycho-social aspects of our time and is not necessarily to be regretted but rather regarded as an opportunity.

4. The opportunity exists when the teacher relinquishes his traditional status-authority for a task-orientated authority.[2] In the new situation the teacher redeploys his authority in a co-operating form of leadership, in which his authority is displayed and exerted through the proved superiority of his contribution to any task, intellectual, vocational or social, that has to be done. His authority will be ensured by the respect of those he leads because his knowledge and skill are greater and better co-ordinated, and his thinking at a higher level than that of his pupils. His commands are likely to be respected and obeyed because they arise from the transactions necessary to the performance of the task.

5. The school ethos and organization should not be authoritarian in tone. Such a condition will not prevail unless the redeployment of authority takes the form of a wide distribution of responsibility from the head through the staff to the pupils.

When responsibility is confined to too few persons too many are deprived of the experience of *feeling* responsible; too many are waiting for orders, too few are using their initiative, and too few feel themselves to be engaged in worthwhile tasks. The vitality and enterprise of both teachers and pupils are sapped and inhibited when all feel themselves to be under orders.

6. To create these conditions the professional competence and

[2] See R. S. Peters, *Ethics and Education*, pp. 263-5.

personal qualities of the staff will be tested to the utmost. Teachers have first to dispel the age-long convention among boys and girls that the teacher's role as status-figure legitimately invites overt deference but hidden and sometimes open defiance.

FREEDOM, DISCIPLINE AND RESPONSIBILITY

1. There is no such thing as freedom unrelated to a purpose. The word freedom only conveys meaning when it is used in association with an objective: freedom from, freedom for, freedom to be, freedom to do.

2. Personal freedom is freedom from frustration, the condition that enables persons to use their abilities to the full. Children are free when they are assured of adult support, when they are striving successfully and overcoming obstacles, finding satisfaction in newly acquired skills and when they feel themselves to be accepted by the home and school communities.

3. Freedom is a product of discipline.

4. Discipline is of two kinds: external discipline and self-discipline.

5. The self-disciplined person is one who thinks and acts freely within the boundary of known and felt limitations. These limitations may be imposed by physical circumstances; by a knowledge of our capacities; by recognition of the rights of others; by the moral codes accepted by the community; and by the rules required to attain a desired skill, e.g. to paint a picture or to do a sum in arithmetic. Thus obedience to the rules gives us freedom to excel.

6. Self-discipline is an end-product of external discipline, which is the sum of experience—prohibitions, punishments, encouragements, guidance, suggestion and example—which ultimately develop the self-restraints that result in self-discipline and the freedom to perform within our own capacity.

7. Thus the aim of external discipline should always be to cultivate self-discipline, i.e. to arrive at the situation during the years of growing up where children gradually find their own discipline and learn to obey themselves.

8. A child's progress towards civility and self-discipline will be accelerated when he is given the experience of responsibility. A child has to *feel* responsible before he can know what responsibility is.

9. Half the teachers in the world have not begun to realize what miracles the experience of responsibility can work in the young.

THE DISCIPLINE OF WORK

1. One of the most productive disciplines, especially for the bright adolescent, is the discipline of work.

2. The cultivation of the pupil's intellect through his own self-discipline should be a major purpose of schooling in adolescence.

3. Intellect is the product of intelligence applied to experience and knowledge.

4. In the period of secondary schooling the foundations of the productive use of the pupil's intelligence are laid. It is during this stage that learning habits are formed. If bad learning habits are not corrected by the age of 18 or 21 they will probably persist throughout life.

5. The most common and the most dangerous of learning habits is to retain knowledge in other people's words and thought forms. Such knowledge is not assimilated because it is a product of learning without thinking and memorizing without understanding. Pressure of examinations puts a premium on this type of learning. It is the teacher's task to initiate the pupil into the assimilative method of learning whereby the pupil learns 'to know and to think while he knows'. Such intellectual discipline can become a formative influence in his growth towards intellectual maturity. It also dispels the illusion that knowledge is finite and helps the pupil to realize that the more he knows the more he knows there is to know.

6. It is wrong to assume that Rousseau and Dewey intended to liberate teachers and children from the need to think accurately and to work hard. Their aim was to enable teachers to organize

knowledge more effectively and to increase the pupil's power to form judgements upon the knowledge he acquires.

Hence, the view that all learning should be 'fun' is true only in the sense that productive, long-sustained drives of intelligent work are fun, that striving towards clear linguistic expression is fun, that submission to the exacting disciplines of a particular subject is fun, and that discovery of new facts by strenuous exploration is fun.

7. The boredom of bright children resulting from too easy tasks is as wasteful as the frustration of dull children when set too difficult tasks.

8. It is not the only function of education to assist children to live in community or to prepare them for 'real life situations'. It is also a function of education to liquidate ignorance, because it is impossible to learn how to think without facts to think about. Hence it is a mistake to assume that pupils engaged in uninformed 'free discussion' are involved in a valid intellectual exercise. Pooled ignorance cannot be a source of sound judgement.

REWARDS, PUNISHMENTS, INCENTIVES

1. Discipline is not to be confused with punishment which may be, but is not necessarily, an aid to discipline.

2. The effectiveness of punishment is governed by the nature of the personal relationship between the person administering the punishment and the person punished.

3. Punishment may produce estrangement. When a child regards parental punishment as evidence of the absence of parental affection, punishment at school may be felt as evidence of the teacher's hostility. If a child's hostility to teachers is not dissipated in the early years the pupil is likely to persist in defiant attitudes throughout adolescence.

4. The test of the effectiveness of punishment or reward is that they ensure good behaviour over long periods.

5. Corporal punishment is not an effective means of ensuring good behaviour over long periods.

6. Certainty of mild punishment is more salutary than the uncertainty aroused by threats of severe punishment.

7. Indiscriminate and frequent punishments inhibit co-operative and similarly positive relationships between teacher and pupil.

8. Sarcasm is a dangerous disciplinary instrument because it destroys a child's defences and diminishes his self-respect.

9. Praise, encouragement, curiosity, interest and good teaching are more conducive to effective learning and good behaviour than punishment. Powerful lures to further effort are the intrinsic rewards of increased understanding of the material, of new skills discovered, and the experience of successful accomplishment of tasks.

PROFESSIONAL

1. There can be no single image of 'the teacher'. The differing images he presents depend on the eye of the beholder. What matters is that his image is good among the reference groups whose respect and approval he desires. But, in whatever capacity he may serve, his image will depend on the degree to which he conceives himself to be an artist-scientist in an applied humanity.

2. Public esteem cannot be gained by demanding it, nor by increased remuneration, nor by membership of a trade union, nor by not supervising school dinners, nor by subservience to chief education officers or city councillors, but only by quality of service rendered to children.

3. Social status may be enhanced by higher remuneration, quality and duration of training and the degree to which teachers are a self-governing profession.

4. A good teacher is not only a communicator of knowledge but a model of competence. He imparts attitudes to his subject and attitudes to learning, thus becoming in himself a symbol of the educating process, a person who is learning as well as teaching.[3]

5. Teachers should accept Graham Wallas' criticism that 'the

[3] See J. S. Bruner, *Towards a Theory of Learning.* pp. 120-4.

teacher observes and marks the more obvious results of thought processes but not the processes themselves'. Teachers should be as interested in the means by which their pupils get results as in the results themselves.

6. What a teacher believes, he teaches. This he cannot help doing, because what he believes, he is; and what he is will be deeply incorporated in his every attitude, act and plan.

7. To enable his pupils to want what is worth wanting a teacher must himself want what is worth wanting.

If the teacher wants to know 'what he is doing' he will find the answers in the inner citadel ruled by his mind and heart. There is a striking passage in von Hügel's *Essays & Addresses on the Philosophy of Religion* which exactly describes the process of discovering the realities of any work we are engaged in. He is referring to Darwin's patient researches into the world of sub-human life:

'he was always learning, loving, watching, he was always "out of himself", doubling himself up, as it were, so as to penetrate these realities so much lower than himself. He had never done and finished; what he learnt today had to be re-learnt . . . yet always with the same sense that what he had learnt was not his own mind and its fancies and theories, but realities and their real qualities and habits. His life thus moved out into other lives. And what he discovered was not clear but vivid; not simple but rich; not readily, irresistibly transferable to other minds, but only acquirable by them through a slow purification and a humble, loving observation and docility like his own.'

Von Hügel then asks us to apply this patient method to our own search for reality:

'We get to know such realities slowly, laboriously, intermittently, partially; we get to know them, not inevitably nor altogether apart from our dispositions, but only if we are sufficiently humble to welcome them, and sufficiently generous to pay the price continuously. . . . And we get to know that we know these realities by finding our knowledge approving itself to us as fruitful . . . and all this in a thoroughly living and practical, in a concrete, not abstract, not foretellable, in a quite inexhaustible way.'[4]

There it is then—a day, a week, a year, a generation in the teacher's life. And some day he will retire with all his wisdom stored and some of it still unused; his desire for status and esteem quite gone, and only a hope remaining that he still deserves the respect which is every good man's due; but still believing with the wise Professor Campagnac that education is to make a man master of himself and of his own world; to make him aware of his neighbours and their worlds; and to teach him and them together to make of all their several worlds a new, a social world, a society which embraces, reconciles and transcends them, and to live in that new world.

[4] Algar Thorold: *Readings from Friedrich v. Hügel*, pp. 290-2.

Select bibliography

Unless otherwise stated the place of publication is London. The occasional comments are intended for the guidance of students.

PART I. THE ANCIENT WORLD

BARROW, R. H., *The Romans*, 1949. An admirable introduction.

BONNARD, A., *Greek Civilization*, 1957.

BOWRA, C. M., *The Greek Experience*, 1957. A vivid and scholarly portrayal of Greek culture.

BREASTED, J. H., *The Dawn of Conscience*, New York, 1935. For Egyptian and Hebrew wisdom literature.

CASTLE, E. B., *Ancient Education and Today*, 1961. A much fuller treatment of chapters 2, 3 and 4.

COWELL, F. R., *Cicero and the Roman Republic*, 1948.

DICKINSON, G. L., *The Greek View of Life*, 23rd edition, 1957.

EPSTEIN, I., *Judaism*, 1959. Indispensable for Hebrew background.

FOWLER, W. W., *The City State of the Greeks and Romans*, 1893.

FREEMAN, K. J., *Schools of Hellas*. Full of vivid detail.

GARDINER, E. N., *Athletics of the Ancient World*, 1930. The standard work.

GWYNN, A., *Roman Education from Cicero to Quintilian*, 1926. Essential for Roman education.

GUTHRIE, W. K. C., *The Greek Philosophers*, 1950.

HASTINGS, J., *A Dictionary of the Bible*, Edinburgh, 1909.

JAEGER, W., *Paideia, the Ideals of Greek Culture* (3 vols.), 1946. A work of profound scholarship.

KITTO, H. D. F., *The Greeks*, 1951.

LODGE, R. C., *Plato's Theory of Education*, 1947.

MANSON, T. W., *A Companion to the Bible*, Edinburgh, 1939.

MARROU, H. I., *A History of Education in Antiquity*, 1956. A work of outstanding scholarship and interest.

MORRIS, N., *The Jewish School*, 1937. The only reliable book on the subject. Unfortunately out of print.

NETTLESHIP, R. L., *The Theory of Education in Plato's Republic*, 1935.

WOODY, T., *Life and Education in Early Societies*, New York, 1949.

ZIMMERN, A., *The Greek Commonwealth*, 1911. A brilliant study of the Greek city state.

Texts: The Old Testament: Deuteronomy, Prophets, Psalms, Proverbs.

Translations: F. M. Cornford's Plato's *Republic*; E. Barker's Aristotle's *Politics*; other translations in the Penguin Classics and Loeb Classics.

PART II. THE GROWTH OF THE WESTERN TRADITION

St. Augustine, *Confessions*, trans. F. J. Sheed, 1944.

BURLEIGH, J. H. S., *Augustine: Earlier Writings*, 1953.

COPLESTON, F. C., *Aquinas*, 1955.

COULTON, G. G., *Medieval Panorama*, 1938. Vivid and scholarly. *Social Life in Britain*, 1918.

DRANE, A. T., *Christian Schools and Scholars*, 1881.

DUCKETT, E. S., *Alcuin, Friend of Charlemagne*, 1951.

LEFF, G., *Medieval Thought*, 1958.

GILSON, E., *A History of Christian Philosophy in the Middle Ages*, 1955. A standard work of comprehensive scholarship.

HAARHOFF, J., *Schools of Gaul*, 1920 (recently reprinted).

HASKINS, C. H., *The Renaissance of the Twelfth Century*, 1957. For Abelard and the revival of science.

HEER, F., *The Medieval World*, 1962. A vivid panorama of medieval life and thought.

The Intellectual History of Europe, 1966. For Augustine, Abelard, Aquinas and Roger Bacon.

HUIZINGA, J., *Men and Ideas*, 1960. Stimulating on Abelard.

JOLY, R. P., *The Human Personality in a Philosophy of Educa-*

tion, 1965. A useful monograph on neo-Thomist education.

JUDGES, A. V. (ed.), *Education and the Philosophic Mind*, 1957. Useful essays on Plato and Aquinas.

LAISTNER, M. L. W., *Christianity and Pagan Culture*, Ithaca, N.Y., 1951. For the Christian Fathers.

LAWSON, J., *Medieval Education and the Reformation*, 1967. An admirable brief treatment.

MCCALLISTER, W. J., *The Growth of Freedom in Education*, 1931.

PEERS, E. A., *Ramon Lull, a Biography*, 1929.

RICHARDSON, C. C. (ed.), *The Early Christian Fathers*, 1953.

PART III. THE BROADENING OF THE TEACHER'S ROLE

ADAMSON, J. W., *Pioneers of Modern Education*, 1905.

ASCHAM, R., *English Writings*, ed. A. Wright, 1904.

BARNARD, H. C., *The Little Schools of Port Royal*, 1913. *The Port Royalists on Education*, 1918.

BOYD, W., *The History of Western Education*, 1950. The best general history.

BURCKHARDT, J., *The Civilization of the Renaissance in Italy*, 1944 edition, first published 1860. A classic study.

CASTIGLIONE, B., *The Courtier*, ed. F. Watson, 1907.

ELYOT, SIR T., *The Boke named the Governour*, ed. F. Watson, 1907.

FITZPATRICK, E. A. (ed.), *St. Ignatius and the Ratio Studiorum*, 1933.

HODGSON, G., *The Teacher's Montaigne*, 1915.

HUIZINGA, J., *Men and Ideas*, 1960. For essay on Erasmus.

MONTAIGNE, *Essays*.

MULCASTER, R., *Positions*, ed. R. H. Quick, 1888.

WATSON, F., *Vives: On Education*, 1913. *The English Grammar Schools to 1660*, 1908, reprinted 1968.

WOODWARD, W. H., *Vittorino da Feltre: and other Humanist Educators*, 1905. *Desiderius Erasmus*, 1904.

Studies in Education during the age of the Renaissance, 1906.

PART IV. THE FOUNDATIONS OF MODERN TEACHING

ADAMS, J., *The Evolution of Educational Theory*, 1922.

ADAMSON, J. W., *English Education, 1760-1902*, 1930.

ARCHER, R. L., *Secondary Education in the Nineteenth Century*, 1921.

Rousseau on Education, 1912.

BADLEY, J. H., *Bedales: A Pioneer School*, 1923.

Memories and Reflections, 1955.

BAMFORD, T. W., *Thomas Arnold*, 1960. A critical reassessment.

The Rise of the Public Schools, 1967. An informed reappraisal.

BANTOCK, G. H., *Freedom and Authority in Education*, 1952. A conservative treatment.

BOYD, W., *The History of Western Education*, 1950.

Emile for Today, 1956. Useful selections and comments.

CASTLE, E. B., *Moral Education in Christian Times*, 1958. A history of school discipline.

CHURTON, A., *Kant on Education*, 1899.

DEWEY, J., *My Pedagogic Creed*, Chicago, 1897.

The School and Society, Chicago, 1900.

Democracy and Education, New York, 1916.

FLETCHER, S. S. F. and WELTON, J., *Froebel's Chief Writings*, 1912.

FROEBEL, F., *The Education of Man*, tr. W. N. Hailman, 1887.

GREEN, F. C., *Jean Jacques Rousseau*, 1955.

GREEN, J. A., *Life and Work of Pestalozzi*, 1913.

HARDIE, C. D., *Truth and Fallacy in Educational Theory*, 1942. Indispensable for students.

HERBART, J. F., *The Science of Education*, trans. H. M. and E. Felkin, 1892.

HILL, R. and F. D., *Matthew Davenport Hill*, 1878.

HOYLAND, G., *The Man Who Made a School*, 1946. An interesting character study of Thring.

LYTE, H. C. M., *A History of Eton College*, 1875.

MACK, E. C., *Public Schools and British Opinion: 1780-1860*, 1938. A critical estimate of their character and influence.

MACKENZIE, R. J., *Hegel's Educational Theory & Practice*, 1905.

NEILL, A. S., *Summerhill: A Radical Approach to Education*, 1962. A useful summary of Neill's extreme left position. But his other books should also be read, e.g., *Hearts not Heads in School*, 1945, *Talking of Summerhill*, 1967.

PARKIN, G. R., *Edward Thring, Life, Diary & Letters*, 1900. The standard biography.

POLLARD, H. M., *Pioneers of Popular Education 1750-1860*, 1956.

RAIKES, E., *Dorothea Beale of Cheltenham*, 1908.

REDDIE, C., *Abbotsholme*, 1900. A collection of descriptive pieces on Abbotsholme and of Reddie's views on education.

RIDLEY, A. E., *Frances Mary Buss*, 1895.

SADLER, J. E., *J. A. Comenius & the Concept of Universal Education*, 1966. A valuable reassessment.

STANLEY, A. P., *The Life & Correspondence of Thomas Arnold*, 1844.

SILBER, K., *Pestalozzi: The Man & His Work*, 1960.

STEWART, W. A. C., and McCANN, W. P., *The Educational Innovators*, 2 Vols., 1967 and 1968. Invaluable for progressive education; interesting and comprehensive.

THRING, E., *Theory and Practice of Teaching*, 1883.

WHITRIDGE, A., *Dr. Arnold of Rugby*, 1928.

PART V. THE BRITISH TEACHER TODAY

ARCHAMBAULT, R. D. (ed.), *Philosophical Analysis & Education*, 1965. An investigation into the role of philosophical concepts in education.

Aspects of Education, No. III, 'The Professional Education of Teachers', University of Hull, 1965. Excellent papers on professional status of teachers.

BANTOCK, G. H., *Education in an Industrial Society*, 1963.

BIRCHENOUGH, C., *History of Elementary Education*, 1938. For primary teachers' education in the nineteenth century.

BRUNER, J. G., *The Process of Education*, Harvard University,

238   *Select bibliography*

1960.

Towards a Theory of Instruction, Harvard University, 1966. Both Bruner's books are valuable studies on theory and method of learning.

CASTLE, E. B., *A Parents' Guide to Education*, 1968. A popular discussion of current problems.

CONNELL, W. F., *The Educational Thought and Influence of Matthew Arnold*, 1950.

FLOUD, J. E., *Social Class and Educational Opportunity*, 1956.

HIGHFIELD, M. E. and PINSENT, A., *A Survey of Rewards and Punishments in Schools*, 1952. A detailed investigation into facts and opinion.

JONES, M. G., *The Charity School Movement in the Eighteenth Century*, 1938.

LOWNDES, G. A. N., *The Silent Social Revolution*, New edition, 1969, Indispensable for chapters 15 and 16.

PARTRIDGE, J., *Middle School*, 1966. A lively personal account of discipline in a modern secondary school.

PETERS, R., *Authority, Responsibility and Education*, 1959.
Ethics and Education, 1966. A critical study of value judgements in education.

PETERSON, A. D. C., *A Hundred Years of Education*, 1952.

RICHARDSON, E., *The Environment of Learning*, 1967.

SMITH, F., *The Life of Sir James Kay-Shuttleworth*, 1923.

STENHOUSE, L. (ed.), *Discipline in Schools*, 1967. Admirable for disciplinary problems in school.

TANNER, T. M., *Education and Physical Growth*, 1961.

WALL, W. D., *The Adolescent Child*, 1947.
Adolescents in School & Society, 1968. A constructive summary of recent research. Essential reading.

Reports:
Teachers & Youth Leaders (McNair Report), 1944.
15 to 18 (Crowther Report), 1959.
Half Our Future (Newsom Report), 1963.
Children & Their Primary Schools (Plowden Report), 1966.

Index

Abelard, 45, 59-66, 225
Activity, 33, 126-8, 130-4, 137, 174, 175-8
Adams, J., 68, 138
Adamson, J. W., 117
Adolescence, 40, 50, 132, 135, 153, 170-1, 206-10, 215, 216, 226, 228
Aelfric, 56
Aeschylus, 23
Aims, 224, 232
Albert, of York, 56
Alberti, 75
Alcuin, 56
Amenemope, 5
Amos, 8
Anselm, 57, 59
Aquinas, 33, 45, 58, 66-9
Arabic scholars, 45, 58, 60, 69
Archer, R. L., 162
Areté, 20, 21, 75
Aristophanes, 22, 23
Aristotle, 32-4, 47, 51, 58, 59, 97, 116
Ars Magna (Lull), 70
Arnold, M., 154, 184, 194, 204
Arnold, T., 143, 151, 153-6, 171
Ascham, R., 90
Athens, 21, 22, 23, 26, 30
Augustine of Hippo, 33, 45, 50-2, 76, 109, 116, 221
Authority, 32, 67, 113, 121-42, 143, 160, 221, 226

Babylon, 5, 9, 10
Bacon, F., 71, 113, 115-16
Bacon, R., 45, 58, 69-70
Badley, J. H., 165, 166, 168-9, 223
Baker, B. M., 165
Bamford, T. M., 155, 156, 201
Bantock, G. H., 140

Barnard, H. C., 110, 111, 164
Barnes, K., 166
Basil of Caesarea, 49
Beale, D., 143, 160-5
Bell, A., 189
Ben Sirach, 11-13
Bentwich, J., 18
Bernard of Clairvaux, 59-65
Beth-hamidrash, 16
Beth-hasepher, 14, 15, 16
Bible, 7-16, 45, 54, 58, 102
Birchenough, C., 187, 193
Boethius, 58
Boke called the Governour (Elyot), 96
Bonaventura, 69
Bonnard, A., 23
Bowra, C. M., 18
Boyd, W., 104, 106, 137
Brain-breaker's Breaker, 90
Breasted, J. H., 6
Bridges, R., 195
Brinsley, J., 90
British and Foreign Schools Society, 189, 192
Brontë, C., 163
Brougham, H., 184, 191, 192
Bruner, J. S., 211-13, 215
Burleigh, J. H. G., 51
Busby, R., 90, 123
Buss, F. M., 143, 160-4
Butler, S., 152

Calvin, 94, 103-4, 115
Campagnac, E. T., 232
Carpenter, E., 166, 168
Castle, E. B., 5, 20, 91, 122
Castiglione, B., 95, 121
Catechism, 58, 102, 186
Cato, 35, 36, 76
Character, 17, 31, 67, 138